AQA History

A2

Unit 3

The Making of Modern Britain, 1951–2007

D0893074

Chris Rowe
Series editor
Sally Waller

Published in 2009 by:
Nelson Thornes Ltd
Delta Place
27 Bath Road
CHELTENHAM
GL53 7TH
United Kingdom

13 14 15 16 / 10 9 8 7 6

A catalogue record for this book is available from the British Library

978 1 4085 0315 7

Illustrations by: David Russell Illustration

Page make-up by Thomson Digital

Printed and bound in Spain by GraphyCems

Contents

Introduction

Nelson Thornes

Nelson Thornes has worked hard to ensure this book offers you the best support for your A level course and helps you to prepare for your exams.

How to use this book

This book covers the specification for your course.

The features in this book include:

Timeline

Key events are outlined at the beginning of the book. The events are colour-coded so you can clearly see the categories of change.

Learning objectives

At the beginning of each section you will find a list of learning objectives that contain targets linked to the requirements of the specification.

Key chronology

A short list of dates usually with a focus on a specific event or legislation.

Key profile

The profile of a key person you should be aware of to fully understand the period in question.

Key terms

A term that you will need to be able to define and understand.

Did you know?

Interesting information to bring the subject under discussion to life.

Exploring the detail

Information to put further context around the subject under discussion.

A closer look

An in-depth look at a theme, person or event to deepen your understanding. Activities around the extra information may be included.

Sources

Sources reinforce topics or themes and may provide fact or opinion. They may be quotations from historical works, contemporaries of the period or photographs.

Cross-reference

Links to related content within the book which may offer more detail on the subject in question.

Activity

Various types of activity to provide you with different challenges and opportunities to demonstrate the content and skills you are learning. Some can be worked on individually, some as part of group work and some are designed to specifically 'stretch and challenge'.

■ Question

Questions to prompt further discussion on the topic under consideration and to aid revision.

■ Summary questions

Summary questions at the end of each chapter to test your knowledge and allow you to demonstrate your understanding.

Study tip

Hints to help you with your study and to prepare for your exam.

Practice questions

Questions at the end of each section in the style that you can expect in your exam.

Learning outcomes

Learning outcomes at the end of each section remind you what you should know having completed the chapters in that section.

Introduction to the History series

When Bruce Bogtrotter in Roald Dahl's Matilda was challenged to eat a huge chocolate cake, he just opened his mouth and ploughed in, taking bite after bite and lump after lump until the cake was gone and he was feeling decidedly sick. The picture is not dissimilar to that of some A level history students. They are attracted to history because of its inherent appeal but, when faced with a bulging file and a forthcoming examination, their enjoyment evaporates. They try desperately to cram their brains with an assortment of random facts and subsequently prove unable to control the outpouring of their ill-digested material in the examination.

The books in this series are designed to help students and teachers avoid this feeling of overload and examination panic by breaking down the AQA history specification in such a way that it is easily absorbed. Above all, they are designed to retain and promote students' enthusiasm for history by avoiding a dreary rehash of dates and events. Each book is divided into sections, closely matched to those given in the specification, and the content is further broken down into chapters that present the historical material in a lively and attractive form, offering guidance on the key terms, events and issues, and blending thought-provoking activities and questions in a way designed to advance students' understanding. By encouraging students to think for themselves and to share their ideas with others, as well as helping them to develop the knowledge and skills they will need to pass their examination, this book should ensure that students' learning remains a pleasure rather than an endurance test.

To make the most of what this book provides, students will need to develop efficient study skills from the start and it is worth spending some time considering what these involve:

- Good organisation of material in a subject-specific file. Organised notes help develop an organised brain and sensible filing ensures time is not wasted hunting for misplaced material. This book uses cross-references to indicate where material in one chapter has relevance to material in another. Students are advised to adopt the same technique.

- A sensible approach to note-making. Students are often too ready to copy large chunks of material from printed books or to download sheaves of printouts from the internet. This series is designed to encourage students to think about the notes they collect and to undertake research with a particular purpose in mind. The activities encourage students to pick out information that is relevant to the issue being addressed and to avoid making notes on material that is not properly understood.

- Taking time to think, which is by far the most important component of study. By encouraging students to think before they write or speak, be it for a written answer, presentation or class debate, students should learn to form opinions and make judgements based on the accumulation of evidence. These are the skills that students will need to demonstrate in the final examination. The beauty of history is that there is rarely a right or wrong answer so, with sufficient evidence, one student's view will count for as much as the next.

Unit 3

The topics chosen for study in Unit 3 are all concerned with the changing relationship between state and people over a period of around 50 years. These topics enable students to build on the skills acquired at AS level, combining breadth, by looking at change and continuity over a period of time, with depth, in analysing specific events and developments. The chosen topics offer plentiful opportunities for an understanding of historical processes enabling students to realise that history moves forward through the interaction of many different factors, some of which may change in importance over a period of time. Significant individuals, societies, events, developments and issues are explored in a historical context and developments affecting different groups within the societies studied from a range of historical perspectives. Study at Unit 3 will therefore develop full synoptic awareness and enable students to understand the way a professional historian goes about the task of developing a full historical understanding.

Unit 3 is tested by a 1 hour 30 minute paper containing three essay questions from which students need to select two. Details relating to the style of questions, with additional hints, are given in the accompanying table and throughout this book. Students should familiarise themselves with both the question demands and the marking criteria which follow before attempting any of the practice questions at the end of each section of this book.

Answers will be marked according to a scheme based on 'levels of response'. This means that an essay will be assessed according to which level best matches the

Unit 3 (Three essay questions in total)	Question Types	Marks	Question stems	Hints for students
Two essay questions	Standard essay questions addressing a part of the Specification content and seeking a judgement based on debate and evaluation	45	These are not prescriptive but likely stems include: To what extent… How far… A quotation followed by, 'How valid is this assessment/view?'	All answers should convey an argument. Plan before beginning to write and make the argument clear at the outset. The essay should show an awareness of how factors interlink and students should make some judgement between them (synoptic links). All comments should be supported by secure and precise evidence.
One essay question	Standard essay question covering the whole period of the unit or a large part of that period and seeking a judgement based on debate and evaluation	45	As above	Evidence will need to be carefully selected from across the full period to support the argument. It might prove useful to emphasise the situation at the beginning and end of the period, identify key turning points and assess factors promoting change and continuity.

historical skills it displays, taking both knowledge and understanding into account. All students should keep a copy of the marking criteria in their files and need to use them wisely.

Marking criteria

Level 1 Answers will display a limited understanding of the demands of the question. They may either contain some descriptive material which is only loosely linked to the focus of the question or they may address only a part of the question. Alternatively, they may contain some explicit comment but will make few, if any, synoptic links and will have limited accurate and relevant historical support. There will be little, if any, awareness of differing historical interpretations. The response will be limited in development and skills of written communication will be weak. *(0–6 marks)*

Level 2 Answers will show some understanding of the demands of the question. They will either be primarily descriptive with few explicit links to the question or they may contain explicit comment but show limited relevant factual support. They will display limited understanding of differing historical interpretations. Historical debate may be described rather than used to illustrate an argument and any synoptic links will be undeveloped. Answers will be coherent but weakly expressed and/or poorly structured. *(7–15 marks)*

Level 3 Answers will show a good understanding of the demands of the question. They will provide some assessment, backed by relevant and appropriately selected evidence, which may, however, lack depth. There will be some synoptic links made between the ideas, arguments and information included although these may not be highly developed. There will be some understanding of varying historical interpretations. Answers will be clearly expressed and show reasonable organisation in the presentation of material. *(16–25 marks)*

Level 4 Answers will show a very good understanding of the demands of the question. There will be synoptic links made between the ideas, arguments and information included showing an overall historical understanding. There will be good understanding and use of differing historical interpretations and debate and the answer will show judgement through sustained argument backed by a carefully selected range of precise evidence. Answers will be well-organised and display good skills of written communication. *(26–37 marks)*

Level 5 Answers will show a full understanding of the demands of the question. The ideas, arguments and information included will be wide-ranging, carefully chosen and closely interwoven to produce a sustained and convincing answer with a high level of synopticity. Conceptual depth, independent judgement and a mature historical understanding, informed by a well-developed understanding of historical interpretations and debate, will be displayed. Answers will be well-structured and fluently written. *(38–45 marks)*

Introduction to this book

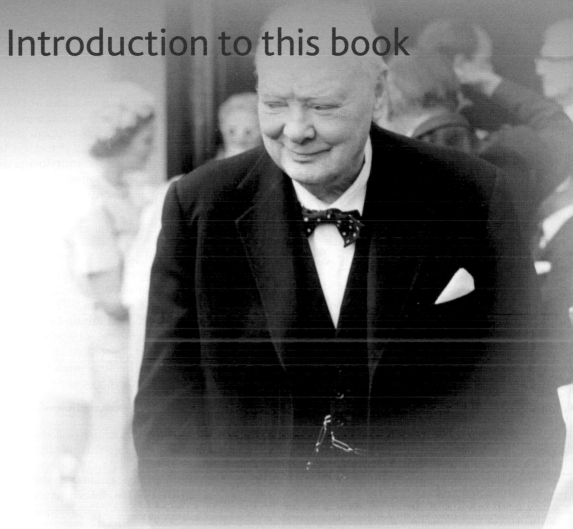

Fig. 1 *The Grand Old Man: Winston Churchill, Prime Minister, 1951–55*

▣ Britain in 1951

Politics

1951 is an important landmark in British history because it marked the end of Clement Attlee's post-war Labour government and the return to power of the Conservatives under Winston Churchill. There were other 'turning point years' later, notably 1979, with the start of the 'Thatcher revolution'; and 1997, with its landslide victory for Tony Blair and New Labour. Historians examine the state of Britain in 1951, trying to evaluate the Attlee legacy in the light of what followed: more than twenty years of rising prosperity and of 'consensus politics', a period when both the main parties followed similar centrist politics. Naturally, their verdicts are not always the same – historical judgements are always provisional, never final.

In the stock market of historical reputations, some prime ministers slide downwards after their departure from office; others rise. In his own time, Attlee was not much admired and nobody would ever have used the word charismatic to describe him. He had the image of a bank manager or civil servant, unassuming and modest. In the public eye he was completely overshadowed by the flamboyant, larger-than-life personality of Churchill. Since 1951, however, Attlee's reputation has gone up and up. He has frequently been described (at least by those who do not prefer to give the accolade to Margaret Thatcher) as Britain's greatest post-war prime minister.

▣ Cross-reference

The post-war consensus is discussed in Chapter 1.

Clement Attlee

Attlee (1883–1967) became Labour leader in 1935 and led the party for 20 years. He played a key role as deputy prime minister in Churchill's wartime coalition government from 1940 to 1945. He was then prime minister from 1945 to 1951 leading Labour's first-ever majority government and introducing the welfare state. He retired after the general election of 1955. Although he was often underrated during his lifetime, Attlee's reputation rose steadily afterwards.

Winston Churchill

Churchill (1874–1965) had already had a long and controversial career by 1951. On many occasions, between 1906 and 1940, he was a cabinet minister in both Liberal and Conservative governments. He became prime minister at the age of 65 in the war crisis of May 1940 and led Britain to victory by 1945. After the war, he continued to play the role of world statesman even though the Conservatives were in opposition. He was prime minister again from 1951 to 1955; his final mark on British politics was his impressive state funeral in 1965.

The chief reason for Attlee's reputation is the sense that he led a government that achieved its goals – not only by putting into action the aims set out in Labour's 1945 election manifesto, but by leaving behind a continuing legacy, above all the National Health Service and the welfare state. From 1951 to the mid-1970s, British society and politics remained in the mould set by Attlee's post-war governments, even though the Conservatives dominated the political scene for most of that time.

For many people, this political dominance was only to be expected; the Conservatives were the 'natural party of government'. The Liberals had ceased to be a major party in the 1920s; Labour had never seemed capable of achieving a governing majority before 1945. It seemed to many people that the Second World War and the Attlee governments that followed it were temporary interruptions to the natural order of things. For 35 of the 46 years from 1951 to 1997, Britain was under a Conservative government. Before Tony Blair, the Labour Party and its supporters showed the mentality of a party of opposition, even when they were in power.

In 1951, and for a long time afterwards, the two major parties had a near-total dominance of British politics. Third-party politics had been marginalised almost completely by 1951. The Liberals had been reduced to an insignificant rump of six MPs. There was little parliamentary support for nationalists. The Ulster Unionists were inseparable from the Conservative Party. The Scottish National Party and Plaid Cymru had negligible impact. The Green Party did not yet exist. Political extremism was weak. Right-wing extremism had been discredited by the defeat of fascism in the war; communists were completely overshadowed by the strength of Labour.

The political gulf between the major parties was also narrower than ever before. The Labour Party had proved itself to be both moderate and patriotic. The fears of 1945, that Labour would follow extreme socialism, had been disproved. The key policymakers in the Conservative government were '**One Nation Tories**', keen to build on ideas of national cooperation to maintain an essential post-war consensus.

■ Key terms

One Nation Tories: the reformist policy agenda of Conservative ministers like Harold Macmillan and R.A. Butler had many similarities with the policies of Labour thinkers like Anthony Crosland and Hugh Gaitskell. In 1954, The *Spectator* coined the word 'Butskellism' as a label for these similarities. Not until the mid-1970s would a real ideological gulf between the parties open wide.

■ Cross-reference

Harold Macmillan is profiled on page 12, R.A. Butler on page 12, Anthony Crosland on page 34 and Hugh Gaitskell on page 14.

The economy

The economic situation of Britain in 1951 was contradictory. In one sense, the country faced huge difficulties. The war had badly damaged the infrastructure. Britain was saddled with massive debts. Pre-war markets had been lost. The old staple industries had been in decline long before the war. From 1945, Britain had needed massive financial aid from the United States in order to begin economic recovery. Key industries such as coal, steel and the railways had just been nationalised by the Attlee government, partly in the hope of bringing faster modernisation. Rationing was only just coming to an end and many consumer goods were scarce and expensive.

On the other hand, Britain was still one of the leading economic powers in the world. British companies were at the forefront of key sectors such as oil, chemicals, tobacco, shipping and financial markets. British firms were major manufacturers and exporters of cars, electrical goods, armaments and industrial machinery of all kinds. There was considerable optimism about Britain's economic prospects in 1951, especially in view of the fact that European competitors, like Germany, had suffered even worse devastation than Britain.

In the event, the British economy after 1951 remained a curious mixture of growth and decline. Living standards rose almost continuously. People became better dressed, owned more cars, filled their homes with more consumer goods and had more opportunities for leisure and entertainment. By 2007, the word 'poverty' meant something significantly different from the way the term was used in 1951.

This did not prevent Britain sliding slowly down the league tables of the world economy. Britain's economic growth was to prove slower and more patchy than that of the United States, Japan and the emerging markets of the **EEC**. British governments, both Labour and Conservative, repeatedly attempted to launch ambitious programmes for economic modernisation, to increase investment, to improve **productivity** and **competitiveness**; but their hopes were never fully realised.

Society

British society in 1951 looked very different from the Britain of 2007. Television sets, in the relatively few homes that possessed one, showed flickering black and white images on what would now be thought tiny screens. Feature films at the cinema were mostly shot in black and white, as were most of the holiday postcards and the snapshots in family photograph albums. Public buildings, whatever the colour of the original brick or stone, were covered in the same deep, soot-black blanket of air pollution.

Britain did not just look different – in many respects it *was* different. There were no motorways. Private cars were few and far between. Double-decker trams were a familiar sight in most towns and cities. Shopping by car was a rarity; supermarkets had never been heard of. People still grumbled about rationing and the shortages of consumer goods. In residential streets local children played football or cricket, according to the season, with only occasional interruptions from passing traffic. Railways still reached into every corner of Britain, with most trains hauled by steam locomotives. Mass air travel remained a futuristic prospect.

Most towns and cities were dominated by the obvious signs of heavy industry, looming factories, smoking chimneys, men pouring out of the factory gates in their thousands at the end of their shift. Most men worked on Saturday mornings as well as Monday to Friday. Most women in employment were single – for the majority of women, marriage meant stopping work. Sundays were a separate day – churches were full, few

Fig. 2 *The author and his older brother at primary school in 1950*

places of entertainment were open, Sunday shopping was unheard of.

Leisure and entertainment still resembled the 1930s. Holidays were generally two weeks in the year, spent always within Britain at holiday camps or traditional seaside resorts. Few people had passports. Air travel or any trips abroad were for the privileged few. Mass entertainment meant listening to the radio or going to the local cinema. There was no such thing, yet, as youth culture or 'teenagers'.

Despite the sense of national unity fostered by the war years, class divisions remained clear-cut. The north-south divide was easy to recognise. The so-called 'Establishment' dominated public life. From Eton and Harrow, via Oxford and Cambridge, came the network of political leaders, diplomats, high court judges, bishops and civil servant 'mandarins' who held influence in the upper echelons of British life. The property-owning middle classes lived in the suburbs, tended their gardens and generally voted Conservative, especially the women.

In the areas of heavy industry, in the north, the West Midlands, central Scotland and South Wales, the working classes lived in urban areas close to the factories, were loyal to the trade unions and generally voted Labour, especially men. Social mobility had been increased to some extent by the impact of the war but Britain remained a very class-conscious and deferential society. The class system was very hard to break down.

Many people in the Britain of 1951 were ready for social change. There was a strong sense that the post-war world had to be made better than what had gone before: a fairer Britain, fewer economic inequalities, with less rigid class distinctions and wider educational opportunities. At what speed and in exactly what directions this social change would travel, nobody really knew.

Britain's position in the world

In 1951, Britain's position in the world was deceptive. Outwardly, Britain was a world power, part of the Grand Alliance that had defeated the Axis in the world war and still in possession of a great empire. Many people in Britain were self-consciously proud of having 'won the war'. Britain was one of the five permanent members on the security council of the United Nations and a key ally of the United States in the Cold War. British troops were fighting in the Korean War. British colonial possessions still stretched far and wide around the world. The Royal Navy had a vast reach, matched only by the new American and Soviet superpowers. The Attlee government had committed Britain to maintaining its status as an independent nuclear power. Britain had been a Great Power before the war; now Britain expected to remain 'at the top table' of international affairs.

In reality, Britain had emerged from the world war weakened and impoverished. Britain's role as a colonial power had actually been declining since the First World War; the decision of the Attlee government to withdraw from India in 1947 symbolised Britain's inability to maintain its former imperial status. Disengaging from India was a painful process, involving dreadful inter-ethnic violence, but it was a necessary step. Carrying it through was an important part of the Attlee legacy, particularly as it would have been very difficult for a Conservative government to do so, especially a government led by Winston Churchill.

Militarily and economically, Britain could not compete with the new American and Soviet superpowers. It was the sudden realisation of British weakness in February 1947 that led to the launching of the Marshall Plan to rebuild war-torn Europe, including Britain, through American aid. The idea of Britain as a Great Power was built mostly on illusions. Illusions can take a long time to die, especially when they are warmed by the glow of a hard-won victory in a world war.

1951 was a time when Britain should have been making a fundamental reassessment of its position in the world; scaling down its military commitments, and accepting that the days of imperial grandeur were over. As the European Coal and Steel Community took shape in 1950 and 1951, for example, the door was wide open for Britain to take a leading role in European integration. European politicians seemed eager for Britain to be involved (though they were less enthusiastic for British leadership than politicians in Britain arrogantly supposed). The opportunity was ignored. The eyes of British leaders, of both main political parties, were fixed on the world beyond Europe, on the 'special relationship' with the United States, on the Empire and Commonwealth.

European integration was a fine idea to help the stability and economic recovery of Western Europe – but not Britain's affair. In a speech in New York in 1952, Anthony Eden, the Conservative prime minister, explained why a European federation was: *'something which we know, in our bones, we cannot do. Our thoughts move across the seas to the many communities in which our people play their part. These are our family ties. That is our life: without it we should be no more than some millions of people living on an island off the coast of Europe.'*

The Labour leader, Clem Attlee, was particularly unimpressed by the proposed EEC: *'The Common Market. The so-called Common Market of six nations. Know them all well. Very recently, this country had to spend a great deal of blood and treasure rescuing four of 'em from attacks by the other two.'*

Staying out of the EEC did not seem to be a momentous decision at the time; but within a few years the post-war illusions were shattered by the 1956 Suez Crisis. There was a belated realisation of Britain's reduced power and influence; in 1961, it was decided to apply for membership of the EEC. By then, however, the open door to European integration had been slammed shut by President de Gaulle of France. Looking back, it seems clear that Britain's place in the post-war world was shaped by two momentous decisions. The first was to go ahead with Britain's independent nuclear deterrent. The second was to stand aside from the process that led to the formation of the EEC. For the next half-century, British foreign policy continued to revolve around the consequences of these decisions.

■ Timeline

The colours represent different types of events as follows: political, economic, social and international.

1951	1952	1953	1954	1955	1956	1957
Nationalisation of iron & steel	Death of George VI and accession of Elizabeth II	Mass TV audience for coronation of Elizabeth II	British withdrawal from Egypt	Election victory of Conservatives under Eden	Failure of Anglo-French invasion at Suez	Anthony Eden replaced as prime minister by Harold Macmillan
Festival of Britain	Britain's first atomic bomb test	Steel & transport denationalised		State of emergency declared in Cyprus	Massive financial crisis caused by Suez Crisis	Independence achieved by Ghana and Malaya
Anglo-American relations damaged by Burgess and Maclean affair	Mau Mau rebellion against British rule in Kenya			Launch of ITV as commercial rival to BBC		
Conservative election victory and return of Churchill				British opt-out from plans for the EEC at the Messina Conference		

1966	1967	1969	1970	1971	1972
England win the World Cup at Wembley	Deep cuts in military commitments east of Suez	Voting age reduced to 18	Surprise election victory for Conservatives under Edward Heath	Decimalisation of the currency	'Bloody Sunday' in Derry
Labour election victory with increased majority	Devaluation of sterling by the Wilson government	Start of 'Troubles' in Northern Ireland	Equal Opportunities Act passed	Reform of the divorce laws	Unemployment above 1 million for first time since 1930s
'Swinging London' featured in *Time* magazine	Liberalisation of laws on abortion and homosexuality				
	Enoch Powell's 'Rivers of Blood' speech against mass immigration				

1979	1980	1981	1982	1983	1984	1985	1986
Industrial unrest leads to 'winter of discontent'	Independence granted to Rhodesia (Zimbabwe)	Formation of SDP	Victory in the Falklands War	Conservative victory in the general election	IRA bomb at Brighton	Miners' strike called off amid bitterness	Resignation of Michael Heseltine after the Westland affair
Devolution for Scotland and Wales rejected in referendums		Violent riots in Brixton and Liverpool	Unemployment above 3 million	Michael Foot replaced as Labour leader by Neil Kinnock	Miners' strike & Battle of Orgreave		Deregulation of financial markets in the 'Big Bang'
		Big gains in opinion polls by Liberal-SDP Alliance					

1994	1995	1996	1997	1998	1999	2000
Death of John Smith; Tony Blair becomes Labour leader	Major challenges his own party to a leadership election	Renewal of IRA ceasefire	Landslide election victory 'New Labour'	Good Friday Agreement brings an end to the Troubles in Northern Ireland	Launch of the euro in nine states of the EU but not Britain	Intervention by British forces to stabilise Sierra Leone
First women priests ordained at Bristol	IRA ceasefire suspended and new bombing campaign begins		Death of Princess Diana	Human Rights Act	Devolved parliaments for Scotland and Wales established	
	Peace settlement at Dayton Ohio ends Bosnian War		Hong Kong handed to China		NATO bombing campaign expels Serb forces from Kosovo	

1958	1959	1960	1961	1962	1963	1964	1965
Formation of CND

Serious anti-immigrant rioting in Notting Hill | Sweeping Conservative election victory

The feature film *Sapphire*, dramatises the issue of race relations | Blue Streak missile abandoned in favour of American Polaris

Macmillan's 'wind of change' speech

Independence granted to Cyprus and Nigeria | Britain's application to join the EEC submitted

Cold War tensions intensified by building of the Berlin Wall | Macmillan's ruthless cabinet reshuffle, the 'Night of the Long Knives'

Launch of *That Was The Week It Was* on BBC TV | Britain's EEC application blocked by de Gaulle

Independence granted to Kenya

Profumo Scandal and resignation of Macmillan | Labour election victory

Start of Rhodesia crisis | Death penalty abolished |

1973	1974	1975	1976	1977
Oil-price crisis and energy shortages

British accession to the EEC alongside Ireland and Denmark

Sunningdale Agreement for power-sharing in Northern Ireland

'Three Day Week' imposed | Heath narrowly defeated in February election

Collapse of Sunningdale Agreement after Loyalist Workers' Strike

Victory of Harold Wilson and Labour in the October general election | EEC referendum brings a 2:1 majority for the 'yes' vote

Heath replaced as Conservative leader by Margaret Thatcher | Shock resignation of Wilson; Jim Callaghan becomes prime minister

Britain forced into deep spending cuts by terms of IMF loan | SALT 1 (Strategic Arms Limitation Talks)

Silver Jubilee of Queen Elizabeth II

Start of Concorde flights to New York |

1987	1988	1989	1990	1991	1992	1993
Third election victory of Thatcher

Stock market crash in London and New York | Fall of the Berlin wall and end of the Cold War | First satellite broadcasts by Sky TV

96 Liverpool fans killed in the Hillsborough disaster | Rioting in London against the poll tax

Resignation of Thatcher; John Major becomes prime minister

Unification of Germany agreed at Two-plus-Four talks | Victory of coalition forces in Gulf War | Surprise election victory of Major

Resignation of Kinnock; John Smith becomes Labour leader

'Black Wednesday' forces British withdrawal from the ERM | Rebellion against Maastricht treaty by Conservative Eurosceptics

Downing Street Declaration by John Major and Albert Reynolds |

2001	2002	2003	2004	2005	2006	2007
Labour election victory with big majority

Al Qaeda attacks on New York , 9/11

NATO invasion of Afghanistan and overthrow of the Taliban | UN resolution directed against WMD in Iraq | Invasion of Iraq by US-led coalition forces

Iain Duncan-Smith replaced as Conservative leader by Michael Howard | Publication of the Hutton Report

Expansion of EU to include Hungary, Poland, Slovakia and Slovenia | Third successive election victory for Blair and Labour

David Cameron becomes Conservative leader

56 people killed by terror attacks in London, 7/7 | G8 summit at Heiligendamm | Agreement on power-sharing government for Northern Ireland

Resignation of Blair; Gordon Brown becomes prime minister

Growing financial crisis heralded by collapse of Northern Rock |

The post-war consensus? 1951–64

Politics and the economy, 1951–57

Fig. 1 *A street party to celebrate the coronation of Queen Elizabeth II in 1953*

In this chapter you will learn about:

- the dominance of Labour and the Conservatives in the British two-party political system

- the 'post-war consensus' and how it influenced the Conservative governments in the 1950s

- how politics was affected by the impact of economic recovery and consumerism

- the role and importance of key personalities.

1951 was the most fiercely fought, passionate, neck-and-neck campaign of all the parliamentary elections I contested. But we had almost everything against us – the Bevanite quarrel, the loss of Ernest Bevin and the swing back of votes due to the revival of the anti-Labour propaganda in the national press. The result was very close – Labour won more votes than ever before – but the 1951 election determined the course of British politics for thirteen years afterwards. The Conservative government that won in 1951 was destined to coast along into the economically easy years of the 1950s. Thanks to the tough policies followed by the Attlee governments, there was the first real rise in living standards since the 1930s and a relaxation in restrictions and controls. If Attlee had not felt compelled to call an election in 1951, the Labour government itself might have coasted through to the easy years.

1 *From the memoirs of a Labour cabinet minister, Jay, D., Change and Fortune: A Political Record, 1980*

In 1951, it was not immediately obvious that there would be a long period of Conservative dominance. Some Labour politicians felt convinced they would soon return to power. They regarded Churchill as a tired, old, spent force and believed that the Conservatives would struggle with the intense economic difficulties Britain faced. They were wrong. Between 1951 and 1957, the Conservative governments headed in turn by Churchill, Anthony Eden and Harold Macmillan established the foundations of a complete political dominance: Labour would not return to power for another 13 years. Not even the disastrous humiliation of Anthony Eden in the Suez crisis loosened their grip on power.

1951 was nearly *not* a landmark year because Labour almost won re-election. The total Labour vote in October 1951 was more than the Conservative vote; it was the biggest ever achieved by Labour. If Attlee had delayed calling the election some months longer, by which time the economy had begun to pick up, it is conceivable that Labour might have stayed in power. But Attlee was convinced he could not carry on leading a government that was exhausted by years of strain. The Conservatives *did* win the election and so 1951 took its place as a watershed in British history, the start of the long years of Conservative political dominance.

The Attlee legacy and the post-war consensus

The Britain of 1951 was moulded by its recent history, that is, by the nation's collective memory of three episodes in that history. The first episode was the great depression of the 1930s, seen in 1951 as an awful time of misery and mass unemployment, never to be repeated. The second episode was the world war, regarded in 1951 as a 'good war' in which the nation had come together to defeat the forces of evil by a heroic national effort and shared sacrifice. The third episode was the rebuilding of post-war Britain under Attlee's Labour governments, above all the establishment of the **welfare state**. Public and political opinion in Britain believed that never again should there be anything like the Hungry Thirties or the terrible war that followed. Victory in the war must lead to a better, fairer Britain in the future. This was the basis of the so-called 'post-war consensus'.

> Attlee's governments had been charged with reconstructing a nation a third of whose wealth had melted in the heat of war, which still carried huge, inescapable overseas commitments, and with fostering social justice and industrial modernisation at home. Quite apart from creating a comprehensive system of state-run social insurance, the fusion of myriad hospitals and private practices into a single National Health Service, the transfer of a workforce of 2.3 million people into nationalised industries, the Attlee government also took the first steps towards changing an empire into a commonwealth.

2 From Hennessy, P., *The Prime Minister: The Office and its Holders Since 1945*, 2000

There is a range of different opinions about the Attlee legacy and the post-war consensus. Historians with a social democratic outlook, like Professor Peter Hennessy, regard the Attlee legacy as the foundation stone of all that is best about post-war Britain (see Source 2). Even one of Mrs Thatcher's chancellors (and certainly no socialist), Nigel Lawson is willing to give Attlee credit for setting the direction Britain would follow for a generation (see Source 3).

■ Cross-reference
The Suez crisis is discussed on pages 40–41.

■ Key chronology

The end of Attlee's Labour government, 1950–51

1950	
February	Narrow Labour victory in the general election
June	Start of the Korean War
October	Stafford Cripps replaced as chancellor by Hugh Gaitskell
1951	
January	Huge increases in Britain's defence spending
April	Resignation of Nye Bevan after row over prescription charges
May	Retirement of Ernest Bevin due to ill health
October	Narrow Conservative victory in general election

■ Key terms

Welfare state: the name commonly used to sum up the reforms carried through by the Labour government after 1945, including the National Health Service and the system of social insurance. Critics of the welfare state often use the term 'welfarism' to define what they consider to be an unhealthy dependence on help provided by the state.

The Attlee government of 1945 to 1951 set the political agenda for the next quarter of a century. The two key principles which informed its actions and for which it stood, big government and the drive towards equality, remained virtually unchallenged for more than a generation, the very heart of the post-war consensus'.

3 From a lecture by Conservative politician Nigel Lawson, 'The Tide of Ideas from Attlee to Thatcher', 1988

By 1951, there had undoubtedly been important social reforms. But power had not shifted between the classes. Social transformation had not come. The Labour governments of 1945–51 had not created a socialist commonwealth, nor even taken a step in that direction. It had simply created a mixed economy in which the bulk of industry still lay in private hands. The six years of Labour rule had only marginally shifted the distribution of social power, privilege, wealth, opportunity and security.

> **4** From Coates, D., **The Labour Party and the Struggle for Socialism**, 1975

The illusions and the dreams of 1945 faded away one by one – the imperial and Commonwealth role, the world power role, British industrial genius and the New Jerusalem itself, a dream turned to the dank reality of a segregated, sub-literate, unskilled, unhealthy and institutionalised working class, hanging on the nipple of state paternalism.

> **5** From Barnett, C. **The Audit of War**, 1986

■ Cross-reference

The infighting between Bevanites and Gaitskellites is described on page 19.

R. A. (Rab) Butler is profiled on page 12.

■ Key terms

Nationalisation: state ownership of key industries. The demand for the state to control 'the commanding heights of the economy' had been a central principle of the Labour Party from its beginning. Clause four of the party's constitution spelled out the commitment to nationalisation. After 1945, the Attlee government nationalised many key industries.

The angry denunciation by Coates in his book on the 'struggle for socialism' (see Source 4) shows how left-wing socialists regarded the Attlee years as a lost opportunity, a failure to bring about true equality.

A different, right-wing view of the post-war consensus is that it was a mistaken policy – that the Conservative Party should have broken with it much sooner and prevented Britain from becoming a 'nanny state' overly dependent on welfarism. This is the view trenchantly expressed by Correlli Barnett in *The Audit of War* (see Source 5).

According to Barnett's interpretation, Thatcherism was a necessary correction to the flabby policies followed by her predecessors, Eden, Macmillan and Heath. It is significant, however, that the books by Coates and Barnett both date from the 1970s and the 1980s, when political polarisation in Britain was accelerating. In the 1950s, the post-war consensus was alive and well; accepting it was a key reason for Conservative political dominance.

■ Conservative political dominance, 1951–57

There were several key reasons for the long dominance of the Conservatives after 1951. The first was the reorganisation of the party machine after the dislocation caused by the war and the shock defeat of 1945. Lord Woolton, the party chairman, and R. A. Butler as a policy expert took leading roles in this process. The second

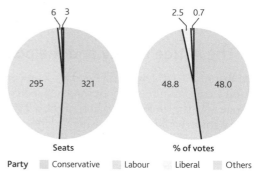

Fig. 2 *General election results, October 1951*

reason was the infighting between Bevanites and Gaitskellites that so badly weakened the Labour Party in opposition. The third perhaps most important reason of all was that 1951 marked the end of 'austerity' and the start of the long post-war boom. The fourth was that the Conservatives recognised the extent of public approval for the legacy of the Attlee governments.

Most Conservatives grasped the political realities of the time. There could be no outright rejection of the welfare state, nor a total reversal of **nationalisation**. Attitudes towards industry, the trade unions and social policy were going to have to be very different from the 1930s because the experiences of the war years had made people far more ready to accept the need for state intervention and planning. The NHS had already assumed iconic status. Partly by conviction and partly by necessity, the new government accepted the existence of the so-called post-war consensus.

■ A closer look

The Conservatives and the post-war consensus

The concept of the post-war consensus is sometimes rather cloudy and difficult to define. It was certainly not unanimous agreement – there were several sharp policy differences between the parties – but there were broad lines of convergence. The central issue was the idea of the mixed economy. The Labour Party had already shown that they did not want all-out socialism and that they accepted private enterprise and the capitalist system, while the Conservatives were quick to denationalise the steel industry and road transport in 1951, they left the rest of Labour's nationalisations alone.

Other key themes included:

- The legacy of national unity and cooperation left by the war; in the wartime coalition ministers from all the major parties had shared the responsibility for handling domestic policies.
- The idea of what Nigel Lawson called 'big government'; many Conservatives were now convinced of the need for government intervention in social and economic policies.
- The importance of maintaining full employment; the bitter memories of the 1930s had been a key issue in the 1945 Labour landslide. Conservatives were very anxious to avoid being seen once again as the 'party of mass unemployment'.
- The importance of the trade unions; the unions had become more powerful and exerted more influence both during the war and also because key industries like coal and the railways had been nationalised. Conservatives wanted a cooperative relationship with the trade union 'barons'.
- The popularity of Labour's welfare reforms, especially the NHS; many Conservatives had changed their minds and were much less hostile to the welfare state.
- The political arithmetic in parliament; the Conservative majority was slender. The Conservative leadership did not feel in a strong enough position to set about dismantling the Attlee legacy, even if they had wanted to. This realism did not please the party faithful at grassroots level, many of whom opposed the consensus all along.

The role of personalities: Churchill, Eden, Butler and Macmillan

At the Conservative party conference in Birmingham in 2008, delegates were asked by Michael Crick of the BBC to play a game called 'Place the Face', putting Britain's post-war prime ministers in order according to their achievements. Overall, the delegates voted Mrs Thatcher second; Anthony Eden came second from bottom; Winston Churchill won by a mile. This outcome did not reflect a very accurate view of post-war British political history. Winston Churchill gained his massive reputation for leading wartime Britain to victory but the Churchill of 1951 to 1955 was hardly Britain's greatest post-war prime minister. Some people think he was not really a prime minister at all in those years, that the man who really led the Conservative government was the acting prime minister, the much-despised Anthony Eden.

Key profile

Anthony Eden

Eden (1897–1977) was a talented politician who had always been thought of as a future prime minister. He was a rising political star in the 1930s and played a key role in the Second World War as Winston Churchill's foreign secretary. On several occasions between 1951 and 1955 he was acting prime minister. He became prime minister in 1955 but was forced to resign in January 1957 after the Suez crisis.

Fig. 3 *Anthony Eden in Downing Street, 1951*

Churchill was indeed an absentee prime minister. One reason was ill health. Churchill was an old man (80 years old when he finally retired in 1955) with many serious ailments. He suffered a serious stroke in 1953 that left him with impaired speech. Few people realised this at the time; those who knew about it said nothing; the 24-hours news culture did not exist. It was only later, in the 1960s, that the publication of the diaries of Churchill's personal physician, Lord Moran, revealed the truth.

There were other reasons for Churchill's inactivity in domestic politics beyond age and illness. Government was very different in the early 1950s from the frenetic 24/7 media-driven politics of 50 years later. The press was much less intrusive. Politics was almost a part-time job; and Churchill's main interests had always been in other things. He thought of himself as an international statesman, not a nuts-and-bolts politician. He spent more time abroad, meeting world leaders or relaxing at his favourite holiday spots such as Marrakesh or Cap d'Antibes than in Downing Street.

Day-to-day government was often left with the acting Prime Minister, Anthony Eden, and key ministers such as Rab Butler, the Chancellor, and Harold Macmillan. On the other hand, even as a part-time prime minister, Churchill's enormous prestige and political ability ensured that he still wielded a lot of power and influence. In his 2000 book, *The Prime Minister*, Peter Hennessy suggested: *'One has to be careful not to overdo the depiction of the old warrior in his final premiership as a kind of walking off-licence-cum-pharmacy.'*

■ Key profiles

R. A. Butler

Rab Butler (1902–82) was famous as 'the best prime minister the Conservatives never had'. He came to prominence as architect of the 1944 Education Act and played a key role in helping the reorganisation of the party and its policies in preparation for returning to power in 1951. He was chancellor from 1951 to 1955 and seen as a possible leader of the party both in 1957 after the fall of Eden and again in 1963 when Macmillan resigned.

Harold Macmillan

Harold Macmillan (1894–1986) was MP for Stockton-on-Tees and was Churchill's military liaison officer during the Second World War. He was a very successful housing minister in Churchill's government from 1951, achieving the ambitious target of 300,000 houses per year. He was foreign secretary in the Eden government. In 1957, he emerged as the new Conservative prime minister after Eden's resignation.

■ Cross-reference
Butler's rivalry with Harold Macmillan is analysed on page 15.

■ Cross-reference
The tensions between Tony Blair and Gordon Brown are described on page 143.

There were tensions within Churchill's government. Butler and Macmillan did not get on well; a rivalry that lasted throughout the 13 years of Conservative rule. Relations also became strained between Churchill and Eden, in ways similar to tensions between Tony Blair and Gordon Brown half a century later. As Churchill's heir-apparent, Eden frequently became impatient. It seemed obvious to him, and to others, that Churchill should step down. Men like Churchill do not step down easily and it may be that Churchill had doubts about Eden's suitability for the top job. Like many leaders-in-waiting, Eden had to endure a long and frustrating time before that happened. When he finally did reach Number Ten, his high expectations were blown away by the Suez crisis and his career ended in failure and disillusionment.

The age of affluence

The Conservative government was lucky in its timing, coming to power just as the beginnings of economic recovery were beginning to show through. From 1952, most economic indicators pointed upwards. Men's weekly wages were going up (£8.30 in 1951 went up to £15.35 ten years later). There were massive increases in private savings. There was a boom in car-ownership. Home-ownership increased, helped by easy access to cheap mortgages. Harold Macmillan, as housing minister, fulfilled the election pledge of getting the construction of new homes above 300,000 per year. The new towns, planned by Labour in the 1940s, such as Stevenage, Crawley, Corby and Cwmbran in South Wales, were rapidly expanding. Farmers did very well economically, encouraged by the continuation of generous state subsidies. Food rationing ended completely in 1954.

The most obvious sign of the new affluence was the surge in ownership of consumer goods – televisions, washing machines, refrigerators and new furniture bought on hire purchase. A visible symbol of the affluence was the advertising industry, especially after ITV launched the age of commercial broadcasting in 1955 and people became accustomed to the glossy adverts during and between popular programmes. In the run-up to the 1955 election, Butler was able to boost Conservative election prospects with a 'give away' budget that provided the middle classes with £134 million in tax cuts.

Fig. 4 *Post-war prosperity: a 1950s refrigerator advertisement*

The 1955 general election

By the time, Butler issued his give-away budget in April 1955, the country was facing new elections. Churchill had finally retired, not long after his 80th birthday. Eden called a general election immediately, seeking his own mandate. It was a relaxed and low-key election campaign. The national press was overwhelmingly in favour of the Conservatives. Most voters were happy with their rising living standards. There was a public mood that might have been described in a later generation as the 'feelgood factor'. Eden was returned as prime minister with a healthy Conservative majority of 70. Clem Attlee had not expected Labour to win in 1955; he retired, after 20 years as Labour leader, to be replaced by Hugh Gaitskell. It is worth noting, however, that 1955 was not a crushing defeat for Labour, whose share of the vote held up well. The two-party system was still in place.

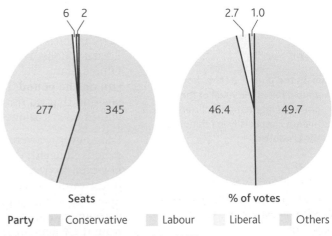

Fig. 5 *General election results, May 1955*

Group activity

Assume you are political advisers to one of the candidates fighting the 1955 election on behalf of the Labour Party. Working in two groups, devise a list of negative points that should be included to attack the Conservatives and a list of positive points about the policies Labour will bring in if they are elected.

Hugh Gaitskell

Gaitskell (1906–63) was chancellor in Clement Attlee's government in 1951. It was his decision to introduce prescription charges, partly to fund the Korean War, that led to the resignation of Nye Bevan and the start of a long-running party split. The conflict between Gaitskellites and Bevanites was to prove a serious problem for Labour throughout Gaitskell's time as leader from 1955 to 1963. These divisions were made worse by rows over nuclear disarmament. Gaitskell struggled to make an impression against the Prime Minister, Harold Macmillan, but might well have led Labour to eventual victory but for his sudden death in 1963.

From Eden to Macmillan

When he at last took power in his own right in 1955, there were high hopes for Eden's government. One of his party colleagues, Lord Hailsham, looked forward in 1955 to '*a real post-war government, led by a prime minister who represented contemporary manhood, rather than the pre-First World War generation*'. There was optimism about Eden's progressive ideas in domestic affairs, his belief in a property-owning democracy and industrial partnership. On the other hand, almost all of Eden's political career had been in foreign affairs and he had little direct experience of domestic politics.

Ironically, the cause of Eden's downfall was foreign affairs. His decision to launch military action against the new nationalist leader of Egypt, Colonel Nasser, in October 1956 ended in disaster. The Anglo-French military operation had to be called off in humiliating circumstances, with Britain being virtually commanded to withdraw by American pressure.

Suez was first and foremost a diplomatic and military fiasco, a turning point for Britain's illusions of imperial power. But it was also a political crisis. Eden suddenly seemed weak, all at sea in the area of policy he was supposedly a master. He came under heavy attack from the Labour Party in parliament and from sections of the national press, notably the *Manchester Guardian*. In denying his collusion with France and Israel, Eden had lied to the House of Commons. His prestige was badly tarnished.

Suez also split the Conservative Party. The Colonial Minister, Anthony Nutting, resigned from the cabinet. There was a rebellion by nearly forty Conservative MPs. The chief whip, Edward Heath, was responsible for keeping the party in line but Heath himself was strongly opposed to Eden's actions. Worst of all for the government, the pressure from the United States had exposed Britain's financial weakness and started a **run on the pound**. It was recognition of Britain's vulnerable financial position that led the Chancellor, Harold Macmillan, to lead the campaign within Eden's cabinet for Britain to abort the Suez invasion.

Eden never recovered from Suez, though it was on the grounds of serious ill health that he resigned early in 1957. The Conservative Party, however, recovered with remarkable speed. Harold Macmillan emerged as prime minister, despite the fact that he had originally been a prominent 'hawk' in favour of the Suez intervention. Party unity was restored, without lasting splits. Economic prosperity continued to gain approval from the voters. In 1959, Macmillan, by now nicknamed 'Supermac', led the Conservatives to another comfortable election victory.

The foreign policy aspects of the Suez crisis are covered in Chapter 4.

Run on the pound: a term describing a rapid fall in the value of the pound in international currency markets, especially in relation to the US dollar.

On the surface, it seemed surprising that Harold Macmillan should establish such a strong political grip so swiftly in 1957, but there were several factors working in his favour. There was the continuing affluence of the consumer society, keeping voters contented. The Labour Party under Hugh Gaitskell had internal problems of its own. There was also the remarkable ability of the Conservative Party to manage changes of leadership without too much blood being spilt in power struggles.

The Conservatives at that time had no mechanism for any leadership election; leaders just 'emerged' from discussions behind closed doors. It eventually became clear that Macmillan's main rival, R.A. Butler, did not have enough support among the party rank-and-file. Macmillan was seen as a safe choice, with few enemies. Perhaps above all, the main cause of the crisis, Anthony Eden, had disappeared from the political scene with brutal suddenness; the crisis disappeared with him. While Suez hung over British foreign policy like a dark cloud for the next fifty years, Suez made hardly a dent in Conservative political dominance at home.

A closer look

Why Macmillan and not Butler?

It has often been suggested that Rab Butler was 'the best prime minister we never had'. By 1957, Butler had immense experience. He had been the architect of the education reforms brought in by the wartime coalition government. He had played a key role in revitalising Conservative policies during the years of opposition after 1945. He was chancellor in Churchill's government from 1951. When Anthony Eden was out of action through illness after Suez, Butler took over as acting prime minister. Eden confidently expected Butler to be chosen as his successor; so did Butler. Yet he was overlooked in favour of Harold Macmillan. In 1963, he was overlooked again, this time in favour of Lord Home. Why?

One reason was that Macmillan was a formidable rival. He had made a great political success as housing minister, delivering the ambitious 300,000 new houses a year promised in the 1951 manifesto. Macmillan was also more of a showman than Butler. The main problem was that Butler was not nearly as popular in the Conservative Party as he was with the country. The vast majority of Eden's cabinet preferred Macmillan; only three supported Butler. Many backbenchers resented Butler as 'too clever by half' – a negative intention, to 'Stop Butler', had an important influence.

For those with long memories, there were also ghosts from the past: the memories of appeasement (giving into Hitler's aggressive demands) and mass unemployment in the 1930s. Macmillan had been a dissenter over both issues and had voted to remove Neville Chamberlain in 1940. Butler, however, had been closely linked to the policy of appeasement. In the end, the key factor may be that Butler just lacked the killer instinct, which Macmillan certainly did not.

Activity

Group discussion

Working in two groups, make a list of the reasons why the Conservatives became so politically dominant between 1951 and 1957 and why the Labour Party was so unsuccessful. Arrange the top three factors in each list in order of importance.

Activity

Class debate

Write a list of the arguments for or against the view that 'From 1951, the Conservative Party was the natural party of government'. Present your speeches to the class and take a vote on whether you agree or not.

Summary question

Explain why there was a 'post-war consensus' in British politics from 1951.

Post-war prosperity and Conservative dominance, 1957–64

Fig. 1 *Advertising consumer goods in the 1950s*

Let's be frank about it; most of our people have never had it so good. Go around the country, go to individual towns, go to the farms, and you will see a state of prosperity such as we have never had in my lifetime – nor indeed ever in the history of this country. What is beginning to worry some of us, 'Is it too good to be true?', or perhaps I should say, 'Is it too good to last?' For amidst all this prosperity there is one problem that has troubled us ever since the war. It is the problem of rising prices. Our concern today is, 'Can prices be steadied while at the same time we maintain full employment in an expanding economy?' For if inflation prices us out of world markets we shall be back in the old nightmare of unemployment. The older ones among you will know what this meant. I hope the younger ones never have to learn it.

1   *Harold Macmillan addressing a large audience at Bedford football ground, July 1957*

Despite the Suez fiasco, the Conservative government maintained its political dominance after 1957, supported by rising living standards. This 'age of affluence' was the subject of Macmillan's famous 'never had it so good' speech (see source 1), but Macmillan intended his speech to have a double message. He was pleased about the spread of affluence, and was happy for the Conservative government to be given credit for it, but most of his speech was a stern warning about the perils of inflation and the 'nightmare of unemployment'. Few remember this; everybody remembers the line 'never had it so good'. The rise in consumer prosperity was a key reason why Macmillan was able to win a thumping victory in the 1959 election. At the same time, the Labour Party's internal divisions boiled over, making Hugh Gaitskell's job as party leader almost impossible. Only from 1962, when the government was hit by economic setbacks and by damaging scandals, did the political tide begin to turn.

◼ 'Supermac': the Conservative government under Harold Macmillan, 1957–63

Almost immediately after his emergence as the new Conservative prime minister in 1957, Harold Macmillan commanded a remarkable aura of confidence and political mastery. For five years, Macmillan appeared to be in full control of affairs. The post-war economic boom was continuing. The Labour Party was in disarray, increasingly preoccupied with its own internal battles. Macmillan seemed to have the media in the palm of his hand, using the new political opportunities provided by television with flair. Many observers noted his theatrical style: he was compared with puppet masters, with conjurors, with actors of the Edwardian era. For historians, the task is to evaluate how much substance there was behind the style.

Macmillan was a man of many contradictions. Famous for his elegance and calm, he was actually physically sick with nerves before big speeches. Outwardly he seemed sunny and full of dry humour, inwardly he was prone to long fits of depression. Aristocratic in his dress and demeanour, the very image of a 'Tory toff', he actually had quite radical views on social justice. The *Sunday Times* journalist James Margach thought Macmillan was, with Attlee, '*one of the two most left-wing prime ministers of my forty years reporting politics*'. Clem Attlee said in 1951 that Macmillan had very nearly joined the Labour Party in the 1930s and would have become party leader if he had done so.

Macmillan's politics were moulded by two world wars and the great depression. He had been badly wounded on the Somme in 1916. In the 1930s he was MP for Stockton-on-Tees in the depressed north-east. His social and political views in the 1950s were classic post-war consensus. A television interview in 1963 revealed his 'common touch': '*I usually drive down to Sussex on Saturday mornings and I find my car in a line of family cars, filled with fathers, mothers, children, uncles, aunts, all making their way to the seaside. Ten years ago, most of them would not have had cars, would have spent their weekends in the back-streets and would have seen the seaside, if at all, once a year.*'

Macmillan and most of his cabinet, such as Rab Butler, Minister of Labour, Iain Macleod, and Education Secretary, Edward Boyle, were capable and efficient political managers, in tune with public opinion. The Suez crisis did not have any lasting effect on underlying electoral support for the Conservatives. In October 1959, after just more than eighteen months in power, Macmillan was able to call a general election at a time of his own choosing, when the economic situation was very favourable. The result was a comfortable and predictable victory, pushing the Conservative parliamentary majority up to 100 seats.

◼ **Key chronology**

Britain, 1957–64

1957 New Conservative government under Macmillan

1958 Formation of CND
Resignation of Thorneycroft

1959 Conservatives re-elected with majority of 100

1961 British application to join EEC

1962 Macmillan's cabinet reshuffle, 'Night of the Long Knives'

1963 Death of Gaitskell, replaced by Harold Wilson

Profumo affair
Resignation of Macmillan

1964 Narrow Labour victory in general election

◼ **Cross-reference**

The political impact of the Suez crisis is outlined on pages 40–43.

Fig. 2 *Conservative poster from the 1959 general election*

■ Cross-reference

Monetarism is discussed on page 86, with reference to Mrs Thatcher's governments from 1979.

■ Key terms

'Stop-go' economics: the economics of 'stop-go' derived its name from the tensions between an expanding economy, with low interest rates and rising consumer spending ('go') and the results of the economy over-heating, with wages and imports exceeding productivity and exports, necessitating a deliberate slowing down, or deflating of the economy ('stop') through higher interest rates and spending cuts.

Sterling: a term used by economists for the British currency – the pound sterling.

■ Activity

Revision exercise

Use the evidence in this chapter to write a brief explanation of the importance of economic factors for strength of support for the Conservative government in 1959.

The general election of 1959

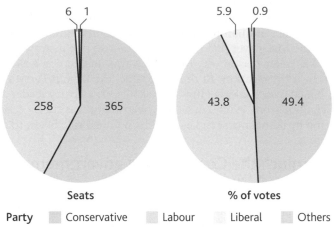

Fig. 3 *General election results, October 1959*

Viewed in retrospect, it appeared to many people that the Conservatives had been sailing towards an inevitable victory almost from the moment Macmillan replaced Eden as prime minister. In reality, it was not quite so straightforward. In 1957 and 1958, the new government faced serious economic and political problems.

In the summer of 1957, there was a major financial crisis. Inflation was rising because wages were running far ahead of productivity. There was also a run on the pound, with the danger that the pound would have to be devalued against the US dollar. Macmillan's chancellor, Peter Thorneycroft, believed in what a later generation would have called 'monetarism': he wanted to limit wage increases and to cut the money supply. Other cabinet ministers, led by Iain Macleod, strongly opposed such a policy because it would lead to increased unemployment and cutbacks in housing.

The crisis and the divisions in the cabinet carried on throughout the summer of 1957. It was a row that symbolised the problems of **'stop-go' economics**: the disagreements over what to do about it were to keep on rumbling in the Conservative Party until (and after) Mrs Thatcher committed herself to monetarist policies in the early 1980s. Macmillan, however, was a very different leader from Mrs Thatcher. He sided with those who wanted to keep up an expansionist economic policy. When Thorneycroft proposed drastic spending cuts in 1958, Macmillan overruled him. Thorneycroft resigned, together with his junior ministers, Enoch Powell and Nigel Birch. The post-war consensus had won again.

This crisis did not do lasting harm to Macmillan's position, which improved dramatically by 1959. Typically, he shrugged off the resignations of Thorneycroft and Powell as *'a little local difficulty'*. **Sterling** regained its value against the dollar. The economy expanded so much that the budget of April 1959 provided tax cuts of £370 million – even more than the Butler 'election give-away' budget of 1955. The general air of consumer affluence reflected in the budget is generally accepted as the key factor in Macmillan's comfortable re-election in October 1959, but it is important to analyse other issues, especially the reasons why the Labour Party was unable to challenge more strongly.

■ The Labour Party and its internal divisions, 1957–63

The Labour Party had only narrowly lost the 1951 election. The total Labour vote, 14 million, was actually larger than in any of Labour's election victories, even including the 1997 landslide. Many Labour activists believed they might soon return to power. In fact, the Labour Party was already suffering from deep internal problems; these problems intensified during the 1950s. Clem Attlee continued as leader until 1955 but the great wartime generation of Labour leaders was ageing and often in poor health. Attlee's most important lieutenant, Ernest Bevin, had died in 1951. Party unity had been well maintained while in government but there was a growing split in the party, both in ideology and in personalities.

The key figures in this split were Aneurin ('Nye') Bevan and Hugh Gaitskell, who was considered by most people in the party to be the logical choice to succeed Attlee as party leader when the time came. The clash between Bevanites and Gaitskellites did not reach its peak until later but it seriously harmed the effectiveness of Labour's opposition to the Conservative government.

■ Key profile

Aneurin Bevan

Nye Bevan (1897–1960) had been minister of health in the Attlee government and was the architect of the NHS. He was was a charismatic public speaker and a hero to the Labour left. He was also a hate-figure to Conservatives (he called them *'lower than vermin'* in a 1948 speech), to sections of the national press and to many in his own party. When Bevan resigned from the government in 1951 to protest against the introduction of prescription charges, he gained the support of many Labour MPs and trade unionists but became a political enemy of Hugh Gaitskell, the chancellor who had pushed through prescription charges.

■ Activity

Thinking point

Write a letter to be sent to the editor of the *Daily Mirror*, to express the view that Hugh Gaitskell is the wrong person to be leader of the Labour Party in 1957. (The *Mirror* traditionally supported Labour).

At the time of the Suez crisis in 1956, the Labour Party had seemed to be on the attack. Hugh Gaitskell, leader since Attlee retired in 1955, seemed likely to benefit from the disgrace of Anthony Eden and boost Labour's electoral prospects. If there had been a general election early in 1957, this might well have happened. The Suez affair, however, did not split the Conservative Party. Harold Macmillan quickly re-established party unity and proved himself to be a commanding prime minister. The Labour opposition had few targets to hit. At the same time, maintaining party unity was increasingly difficult for Gaitskell.

Hugh Gaitskell was always associated with the right wing of the Labour Party and was regarded with suspicion by the Labour left. Disagreements, and personal feuds, between 'Gaitskellites' and 'Bevanites' became an almost permanent feature of Labour in opposition after 1951. Gaitskell was the obvious choice as party leader after Attlee. Some Bevanites rejoined the party mainstream, including Harold Wilson, who became Gaitskell's shadow chancellor but the fault-line dividing the party was papered over, not really bridged.

Labour did enter the 1959 election campaign with some optimism. Gaitskell was a confident and effective campaigner, promoting moderate policies that Labour thought would be popular with voters. The extent of

Fig. 4 *CND on the march to Aldermaston, Easter 1958*

the crushing defeat for Labour was a genuine surprise as well as a disappointment. On election night, the historian Alan Bullock, well known for his regular appearances on BBC as a panellist in *The Brains Trust*, commented gloomily that: *'For the past fifteen years the country has been moving towards equality; now this process may start going backwards'*. Bullock was not necessarily wrong in his judgement, just premature.

After the 1959 defeat, splits in the Labour movement widened. Two key factors combined to bring this about: growing opposition to the party leadership from the trade unions and the simmering divisions over Britain's nuclear weapons. Britain's first tests of the atomic bomb happened in 1952. As the technology advanced, the more powerful hydrogen bomb was tested in 1957, right at the time when controversy over Britain's foreign policy was at a height over Suez. CND (the Campaign for Nuclear Disarmament) was formed in 1958.

CND rapidly became the most powerful pressure group in Britain, backed by many intellectuals and mobilising middle class protesters to demand that Britain should go ahead with **unilateral disarmament**. 8,000 people took part in a demonstration at the weapons research base at Aldermaston in Berkshire in 1958; a second march on Aldermaston in 1959 was even bigger. CND's 'unilateralism' became a powerful magnet for anti-government protest, almost a substitute for opposition in parliament. Many Labour left-wingers joined in. The links between CND and the Labour left may well have turned some voters away from Labour in the 1959 election.

At the same time, the trade unions were starting to challenge the Labour leadership. Until the late 1950s, the unions had been happy with full employment and their leaders were essentially moderates. In 1956, however, a left-winger, Frank Cousins, became leader of one of the most powerful unions, the TGWU (Transport and General Workers). Cousins then led fierce union opposition to Gaitskell over Britain's nuclear weapons.

■ Key terms

Unilateral disarmament: the policy of renouncing use and possession of nuclear weapons without waiting for any international consultation or agreement.

■ Key profile

Frank Cousins

Frank Cousins (1927–92) became leader of the TGWU in 1956. In 1958, he led an unsuccessful bus strike against the Macmillan government. In the Labour party conference in October 1960, Cousins bitterly opposed Gaitskell's leadership of the Labour movement, specifically over nuclear weapons. Gaitskell later re-established some control and Labour did not become a unilateralist party but Cousins had led the unions into taking left-wing positions hostile to the party leadership. These divisions carried on into the 1970s and 1980s.

The battles over the future direction of the Labour Party were fought out at the annual party conferences at Blackpool in 1959 and at Scarborough in 1960. The Scarborough conference became a legend in Labour's history because of Hugh Gaitskell's emotional speech in which he promised to *'fight and fight again to save the party we love'*, after he was defeated over nuclear disarmament. The 1959 conference is not so well remembered but was perhaps equally important because it was in 1959 that the Labour Party missed the opportunity to modernise. Sometimes the history of things that do *not* happen is very significant.

At the 1959 conference, held just before the general election, Gaitskell put forward the idea of abolishing clause four of the party constitution, the clause that committed the party to nationalisation. Gaitskell was impressed with the way the moderate socialists in West Germany, the SPD, had dumped their commitments to Marxist ideas in their party conference at Bad Godesberg earlier in 1959. It soon became clear, however, that opposition from the left wing and from some union leaders would be fierce; Gaitskell backed down without putting it to the vote.

It may well be true that Gaitskell was right to back down because the issue would have split the party. Even so, it remains an important historical question how differently British politics might have developed if Labour had followed the German SPD example in 1959. The Labour split happened anyway, tearing the party to pieces in the 1980s. It was only in 1994, 25 years after Bad Godesberg, that Tony Blair finally convinced the Labour movement to abandon clause four and to fully commit itself to social democracy.

Labour's political position slowly improved after 1960. There was a cultural shift in the country that made public opinion less satisfied with affluence and more critical of government, symbolised in print by the rise of the satirical journal *Private Eye* and on television by the popularity of *That Was The Week That Was*.

By 1962, some of the 'Supermac' magic seemed to be wearing off. The government had to deal with some unexpected political problems and with the more traditional difficulties of the balance of payments and an over-heated economy. When Hugh Gaitskell died suddenly in 1963, his successor, Harold Wilson, took up the leadership at a time when Labour's electoral prospects were vastly better.

■ The end of Conservative dominance, 1962–64

Harold Macmillan's nickname, 'Supermac', reflected his sure touch in politics and his flair for presentation. From 1962, however, Macmillan's smooth mastery began to slip. Macmillan's own classic explanation of the causes of political ups and downs had always been: *'Events, dear boy, events'*. In 1962 and 1963, numerous 'events', economic, political and personal, came together to weaken his grip on government. In October 1963, Macmillan resigned as prime minister. The Conservative Party faced a divisive power struggle to succeed him. Meanwhile, the death of Hugh Gaitskell in January 1963 had opened the way for Labour to elect a new and formidable leader, Harold Wilson. The balance of power between the main parties was shifting.

■ **Cross-reference**

Nationalisation and clause four are covered on page 21.

■ **Cross-reference**

These cultural trends are covered in Chapter 4.

■ **Exploring the detail**

The balance of payments

The balance of payments is a vital issue for almost all governments. A balance of payments surplus (more money coming in from exports and the 'invisible earnings' of the financial sector than money going out on imports) is good thing. A balance of payments deficit (more money going out on imports than is being received from exports) gives governments a serious problem in economic policy.

The problems of economic modernisation, 1960–63

The Age of Affluence did not come to an end in the early 1960s but the government faced difficulty and frustration in its economic policies. Hopes of a radical modernisation of the economy were never really fulfilled. The intended transformation of Britain's infrastructure made stuttering progress. By the late 1950s, it was becoming clear that economic growth in Europe, especially West Germany, was leaving Britain behind and that trade with the Empire and Commonwealth was not sufficient to keep up. Macmillan reversed his party's previous policy and decided it was essential for Britain's economy to be joined with Europe's.

In 1959, Britain took the lead in forming the European Free Trade Area (EFTA) but the new organisation was not able to match the economic growth of the EEC. In 1961, the Macmillan government submitted Britain's application to join the EEC. Three key economic factors were behind the application: the hope of boosting industrial production for a large-scale export market; the hope that industrial efficiency would be increased by competition; and the hope that economic growth would be stimulated by the rapid economic expansion already racing ahead in the EEC.

The 1961 application was a symbol of the sense of failure in bringing about economic modernisation. The British economy was still growing and living standards were still going up – but the cycle of 'stop-go' economics had not been broken. Economic growth too often led to the over-heating of the economy through excessive, expensive imports and rising wage demands. Britain continued to slip behind foreign competitors such as West Germany, the United States and Japan. The problems that had caused Peter Thorneycroft and Enoch Powell to resign in 1958 were still there.

> We have slithered from one crisis to another. Sometimes it has been the balance of payments crisis and sometimes it has been an exchange crisis. It is a picture of a nation in full retreat from its responsibilities. It is the road to ruin. I do not believe that the question is whether we should use bank rate or physical controls; to tell the truth, neither of them works very well. The simple truth is that we have been spending beyond our means.

2   *From a speech in parliament by the Chancellor, Peter Thorneycroft, January 1958*

In 1961, worries about the economy over-heating forced the government to introduce a 'pay pause' to hold down wage inflation, and to ask for a loan from the IMF (International Monetary Fund). The economic difficulties facing the Conservatives by 1962 were familiar ones: the balance of payments problem and the economics of 'stop-go'. In February 1962, Macmillan set up the NEDC (National Economic Development Council) in an attempt to get economic cooperation between government, employers and unions.

In the **Night of the Long Knives** reshuffle of 1962, Macmillan replaced his chancellor, Selwyn Lloyd, with Reginald Maudling, thought to be a rising star in the party. Maudling attempted to avoid the threat of rising unemployment through tax concessions and a policy of 'expansion without inflation'; the result was that the balance of payments continued to deteriorate, with imports running well ahead of exports and rising inflation. This left a difficult inheritance for Wilson's Labour government in 1964.

■ **Cross-reference**

'Stop-go' economics are explained on page 18.

■ **Key terms**

Night of the Long Knives: a label given by journalists to Harold Macmillan's cabinet reshuffle in July 1962, comparing the reshuffle to the original 'Night of the Long Knives' in 1934 when Adolf Hitler murdered many of his own supporters including the SA chief Ernst Roehm. In Macmillan's purge, he sacked seven senior ministers including his chancellor, Selwyn Lloyd.

■ **Key profile**

Reginald Maudling

Maudling (1917–79) was a liberal Conservative who had cabinet experience since 1959, at the board of trade and as colonial secretary, before becoming chancellor of the exchequer under Macmillan and Douglas-Home. He was considered a possible future party leader (Harold Wilson claimed he was the only candidate he was afraid of) but missed out in the leadership struggle of 1963 and again when Edward Heath became leader in 1965. He was later home secretary from 1970 to 1972 before his career was ended by a financial scandal.

The rejection of Britain's application to join the EEC in January 1963 was a serious setback for Macmillan's economic policies. In his memoirs, Edward Heath claimed that he never saw Macmillan as bitterly depressed as he was after de Gaulle's veto. In his diaries, Macmillan himself wrote: *'All our policies, at home and abroad are in ruins. European unity is no more; French domination of Europe is the new and alarming feature; the popularity of our government is declining. We have lost everything.'* Later that year, the publication of the Beeching Report, recommending massive cuts in Britain's rail network, showed continuing concerns over economic modernisation; it also provoked a lot of public outrage. The government was no longer surfing on a wave of prosperity and economic success.

■ **Cross-reference**

The reasons why the 1961 application was rejected are covered on page 46.

■ **A closer look**

The debate over Britain's economic decline

To historians such as Correlli Barnett, author of *The Lost Victory* (1995), the crises of the 1970s were the inevitable culmination of long-term economic decline. British governments had failed to control public spending, or to face down wage demands from the unions. British industry had failed to restructure and invest in modern equipment. Britain's share of world trade had declined steadily from a quarter in 1951 to a tenth by 1975. Technical education had been neglected. Productivity was low compared with foreign competitors. Nationalisation had been a big mistake. Governments, Conservative as well as Labour, had intervened too often to prop up failing industries. Too much emphasis on full employment had led to constant problems with inflation. The painful economic reforms introduced by Mrs Thatcher after 1979 were both necessary and overdue.

There is clearly a lot of evidence to support this critical view of the post-war British economy. Three prime ministers, Macmillan, Wilson and Heath, had entered Downing Street full of determination to accelerate the modernisation of the British economy; all three had left office frustrated by the failure to achieve more. Yet it has to be said that there is also much evidence to dispute the theory of 'continuous decline'. Seen from other perspectives, the post-war era can be regarded as a 'Golden Age'. Living standards rose steadily; the rate of economic growth was consistently higher than it had been between 1900 and 1939; unemployment, the curse of the 1930s, averaged 2 per cent during the 'Golden Age'. Year by year, Britain was becoming a more prosperous and equal society.

Even the unfavourable comparison with foreign competitors can seem misleading. The two countries far ahead of Britain in growth and modernisation were Germany and Japan. Both countries had been so devastated by the Second World War that they had no alternative but complete restructuring of their economies; and neither had been permitted to rebuild their military strength. If Britain's defence spending (an annual average of 7 per cent of GDP) is taken into account, the overall economic performance compared with West Germany and Japan does not look so bad.

In the end, the debate is about politics and ideology as much as it is about economics. For historians like Peter Hennessy and economists like Larry Elliott, the 'Golden Age' really did mark a generation of progress; Mrs Thatcher's radical policies in the 1980s were excessively severe and often unnecessary. For Thatcherite economists such as Patrick Minford, drastic action was the only and essential way to drag Britain out of decline and to impose greater competitiveness through market forces and deregulation.

■ Activity

Thinking point

Explain why there is so much disagreement among historians about the causes of Britain's economic decline.

Political problems and the fall of Macmillan, 1962–63

Macmillan's command over his government faltered in 1962. The key political event was brutal reshuffle known as the 'Night of the Long Knives'. Macmillan's purge of his cabinet was intended to rejuvenate the government but it actually weakened it. Macmillan was made to seem clumsy and out-of-touch. Even so, the damage was hardly fatal. Macmillan might well have regained his authority but for more unexpected 'events'.

The first personal disaster to strike Macmillan in 1963 was the Profumo affair. This was a lurid scandal, combining sex, spying and high politics – it was given sensational treatment by the press – but the damage to Macmillan was not just the side effects of an embarrassing scandal. The politician at the centre of attention was Macmillan's defence secretary, John Profumo. In his statements to parliament, and in his personal assurances to the Prime Minister, Profumo lied about his actions. A public inquiry, headed by a high court judge kept the affair in the headlines for weeks on end. The political impact of the Profumo affair was actually short-lived but the image of Macmillan as old and out-of-touch was reinforced.

■ Cross-reference

The social impact of the Profumo scandal is covered on page 36.

Macmillan's position was finally undermined by a serious illness; a major abdominal operation that kept him in hospital for weeks in the autumn of 1963. He was still in hospital when he informed the Queen of his decision to resign in October. (Macmillan actually recovered better and faster than expected; he was tempted to reconsider his resignation but by then it was too late).

Macmillan had not prepared the way for anyone to succeed him. There was strong opposition to the two most obvious candidates, Rab Butler and Lord Hailsham. In the end, a compromise candidate, Lord Home emerged. Using the recently-passed Peerage Act, he renounced his peerage to become plain Sir Alec Douglas-Home, and thus able to take his place in the House of Commons. The whole business made the Conservative

Party seem trapped in a bygone age, sharply contrasting with the new Labour leader and his promises to take Britain forward into the '*white heat of the technological revolution*'.

"THANK GOODNESS, WE EVOLVE OUR LEADER IN OUR OWN WAY AND DON'T ELECT HIM DEMOCRATICALLY LIKE THOSE SOCIALISTS!"

Fig. 5 *The emergence of a new Conservative leader after the 'customary processes of consultation'. Cartoon by Vicky in the* Evening Standard, *October 1963 (left to right: Lord Poole, Rab Butler, Quintin Hogg, Sir Alec Douglas-Home, Iain Macleod, Reginald Maudling, Edward Heath)*

Did you know?

The Peerage Act of 1963 provided for hereditary peers in the House of Lords to renounce their noble titles and thus become 'ordinary people' eligible to sit in the House of Commons. In previous generations, it had been quite usual for a prime minister to sit in the Lords. In the more egalitarian 1960s, this changed. Two key candidates for the Conservative leadership took advantage of the Peerage Act. Lord Home became Sir Alec Douglas-Home and Lord Hailsham became Quintin Hogg. On the Labour side, Viscount Stansgate became plain Tony Benn.

Key profile

Sir Alec Douglas-Home

Lord Home (1903–95) was a Scottish aristocrat who had had a long career as a diplomat, closely associated with the policy of appeasement in the 1930s. He was very reluctant to run for the Conservative leadership and had to be persuaded it was his duty. In the social climate of 1963 he was an easy target for the satirists in *Private Eye* and on *That Was The Week That Was* but it is often forgotten that he very nearly led the Conservatives to victory in the close-run election of 1964.

The general election of 1964

The 1964 election was a close-run contest. Despite the problems affecting the Conservatives and the low public approval for Sir Alec Douglas-Home, Labour squeezed to victory by only three seats.

Many were factors running against the Conservatives:

- There had been a run of scandals and 'events' in 1962–63.
- There was the sense of a power vacuum following the resignation of Macmillan and the doubts over choosing his successor.

■ There was a sense of growing impatience with the old 'Establishment' and desire for generational change that showed through *Private Eye* and *That Was The Week That Was*.

■ There was increased support for Labour. Harold Wilson was a strong political campaigner, confident in dealing with the media and more focused and succinct than Gaitskell, who had sometimes been an impressive and passionate speaker but was too often long-winded, trying to make many points at once.

■ The split between Bevanites and Gaitskellites was over, with both the key personalities now dead.

■ Labour could exploit the powerful public mood that it was 'time for a change' – the Labour election slogan, *'Thirteen years of Tory misrule'* proved very effective.

There was one other key factor whose impact has often been underrated by historians; this was the 'Liberal revival'. The Liberal Party had seemed as dead as Monty Python's parrot ever since 1951. The Liberals bumbled through the post-war era, attracting merely 2.5 per cent of the vote and never winning more than six seats. After 1960, however, the Liberals began to show some signs of life under a capable leader, Jo Grimond. In 1962, there was a stunning surprise when the Liberals won a by-election in the safe Conservative seat of Orpington in Kent.

This did not lead to an instant transformation of the party's prospects but it was evidence of some softening in the Conservative vote. In the 1964 election, the Liberals still won only nine seats, but the Liberal share of the total vote almost doubled. This was a pre-echo of the future Liberal revival after 1964. It is also possible that votes taken by Liberals from Conservative candidates may have just tipped the balance in such a close election race.

Activity

Revision exercise

Using the evidence of this chapter and that in Chapter 3, make a list of reasons why the Labour Party won the general election of 1964.

Using the same evidence, make a list of reasons why the Labour victory was by such a narrow margin.

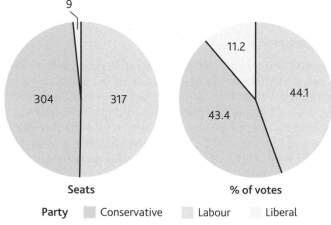

Fig. 6 *General election results, October 1964*

Summary question

Why did the Conservative Party dominate British politics from 1951 to 1964?

3 British society, 1951–64

Fig. 1 *Results of a social revolution? School playground, c. 1970*

In this chapter you will learn about:

- the causes and extent of social tensions, including immigration, criminality and violence

- changes in secondary education and their impact on the class system

- changing attitudes to class in culture and the media.

Much of the Britain of 1951 has disappeared. [In 1951] you might climb into your Austin Sheerline for a visit to the Midland Bank, stopping off at a Lyons to read your *News Chronicle,* or *Picture Post* while smoking a Capstan, looking forward to your weekend visit to the Speedway by tram. The people you see around you look different. Few schoolboys are without a cap and shorts. Young girls have home-made dresses and, it is earnestly hoped, have never heard of sexual intercourse. Every woman seems to be a housewife; corsets and hats are worn, but trousers hardly ever.

But there were signs of social change everywhere – from disaffected teenagers to the rise of home-grown crime dynasties and the first wide-eyed Caribbean immigrants. There was also boredom and frustration. Working class Britain was getting richer but was still housed in dreadful old homes, excluded from higher education, and deprived of any jobs but hard and boring ones. Eventually, the lid would blow off.

1   *From Marr, A., **A History of Modern Britain**, 2007*

Britain in 1951 was a country still moulded by the Second World War. There were widespread visible signs of war damage. Wartime rationing was only just coming to an end. Young men had to spend two years on National Service. Much of British social life looked to the past. Regional and class loyalties were strong; it was usually easy to recognise people's origins and social background from their dress or accent. These class attitudes were reinforced by the familiar stereotypes that featured in films and on the radio.

Yet, then again, British society in 1951 was not static or frozen in time. The experiences of the war had caused significant social change; so had the introduction of the welfare state in the post-war years. Many of the people who attended the Festival of Britain in 1951 felt that they were on the edge of a new modern world, a world of technological and social progress. Children born in the 'baby boom' after the war would grow up in a very different society than that of their parents' generation. In the years to 1964, there were to be significant shifts in population, growing social tensions including immigration and violence, and changes in attitudes to class.

Key terms

Demographic change: a change in the population trend. Demography, the study of population, tracks the increase in the overall population through birth rates, death rates and migration. Demography involves the analysis of shifts in the population, changes according to age, or movement between regions, or mobility between the classes.

New Commonwealth: those countries which had recently gained independence, India, Pakistan, the West Indies and so on, as compared to the 'Old Commonwealth' countries like Australia, New Zealand, Canada and South Africa. The term was a useful, indirect way of differentiating between non-white and white populations.

A closer look

Demographic change, 1951–64

Three key factors created **demographic change** in Britain after 1951. The first was health and life expectancy. Birth rates ran consistently ahead of death rates throughout the post-war era. Medical treatment improved under the welfare state; standards of nutrition and hygiene also improved steadily. The second factor was inward migration. There was a continuing flow of arrivals from the Irish Republic. Starting in 1948, about 250,000 immigrants arrived in Britain from the West Indies and other parts of the **New Commonwealth**.

What is often forgotten, however, is that there was also considerable outward migration from Britain. In the 1950s, Australia was particularly keen to attract new citizens, offering assisted passages and help with jobs and housing. There was also a steady flow of British emigrants to North America. In the 1950s, Britain received a total of 676,000 immigrants seeking permanent residence, while 1.32 million Britons left for a new life abroad. In the 1960s, the total inward migration was 1.25 million and outward migration was 1.92 million.

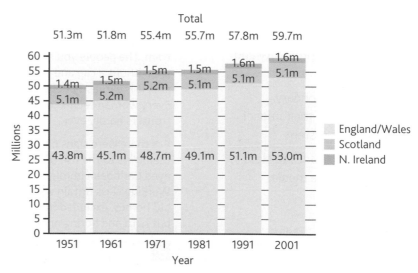

Fig. 2 *British population statistics, 1951–2001*

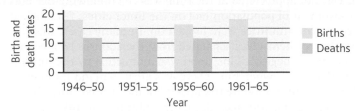

Fig. 3 *Birth and death rates per thousand (England and Wales), 1946–65*

Population change was not only a question of numbers. It was also a matter of how and where people lived. The difference between town and country was much more sharply drawn. The countryside was still dominated by agriculture (which had been boosted by government subsidies) and rural areas were not yet faced by the creeping urbanisation that was to threaten village life later on. Most people lived in communities with a strong sense of local identity, close to their extended families. This situation was about to change, as various forms of social mobility, above all the impact of mass car ownership, started to drain the population away from town centres.

Fig. 4 *Urban populations in Britain, 1951*

Britain's **infrastructure** was run-down and badly needed modernising. Another important factor was housing. There was a desperate need for housing development to replace war damage and to deal with the decay of the housing stock that had been neglected for the previous decade. From 1951, the Conservative government set the ambitious target of building 300,000 new homes every year. Local government spent millions on clearing pre-war slums and building new towns on green field sites – such as Harlow in Essex and Kirkby on Merseyside.

Activity

Statistical analysis

Use your own knowledge and Figures 2 to 4 to reach a judgement on the following questions:

1. To what extent and why did the population of England and Wales increase between 1951 and 1965?

2. Why did the population of Scotland and Northern Ireland remain so constant?

3. Why did the population of most British cities decline after 1961 when the overall population was increasing?

Key terms

Infrastructure: the physical environment of a modern developed society including the network of communications, such as roads, railways, airports and telecommunications, the industrial base, the public buildings, the schools and the housing stock.

Did you know?

People living in council houses and rented accommodation substantially outnumbered private homeowners in Britain in the 1950s. The decision of the Thatcher government in 1980 to encourage the mass sale of council houses to their tenants represented a significant social change.

What was not appreciated at the time was the hollowing-out effect this movement of population had on the inner cities. Established traditional communities were broken up. In many cases, town centres found themselves separated from the suburbs by a belt of dereliction and neglect. This trend was intensified by the impact of the private car ownership. There was great demand for new roads to be built, including the novelty of motorways, already well established in countries like Germany and Italy but unknown in Britain. Car travel changed ideas of holidays and leisure. Commuting by car began to push housing developments further outside towns and cities.

Fig. 5 *The Mini car*

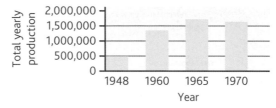

Fig. 6 *Car production in Britain, 1948–70*

Construction of the M1 (London–Birmingham) began in 1958. Work on the M6 (Midlands–north-west) commenced soon afterwards. Between 1957 and 1963, 1,200 miles of new or upgraded main roads were completed. Roads were in, railways were out of fashion. British Railways, nationalised in 1948, struggled vainly to modernise the rail system. The Beeching Report of 1963 recommended the closure of more than 30 per cent of the rail network because roads offered a cheaper and more flexible alternative. Hundreds of branch lines and thousands of stations were axed. It remains a matter of controversy between 'Romantics' and 'Realists' whether or not the Beeching cuts went too far. Whichever side is right, the Beeching cuts caused quite fundamental social change, leaving many rural areas isolated.

Activity

Thinking point

Using the evidence of this study list the **five** key aspects of demographic change that would be the cause of social change and social tensions in the 1950s and early 1960s.

Social tensions, 1951–64

The social impact of immigration, including race riots

Fig. 7 *A group of well-wishers greet new arrivals from the West Indies at London's Waterloo Station, 1961*

NO IRISH, NO BLACKS, NO DOGS

2	
	Notice on the front door of a guest house in Birmingham, 1955

Of the great demographic changes taking place in post-war Britain, immigration was not the biggest or most significant factor, but it did become an issue of intense public concern. Britain's imperial history had linked the nation closely to the multiracial peoples of the Commonwealth. These ties had been strengthened by the war. At Queen Elizabeth II's coronation in 1953, there was evident enthusiasm for the Commonwealth ideal. Such ideas had to be balanced, however, against fears of Britain having to absorb too many new citizens at once. The New Commonwealth (i.e. 'coloured') immigrants who followed in the wake of West Indian migrants who arrived on the *Empire Windrush* in 1948, were both a cause of social change and a cause of social tensions.

By 1958, about 210,000 Commonwealth immigrants had settled in Britain. 75 per cent of them were male, working to support families back home. The largest number came from the West Indies, though the numbers coming from India and Pakistan was beginning to rise. In the urban areas where the new arrivals were concentrated, there were instances of friction and resentment against immigrants. The discredited leader of British fascism, Oswald Mosley, tried to use the issue to exploit the issue by printing thousands of racist leaflets on behalf of his so-called Union Movement.

Exploring the detail

The *Empire Windrush*

The *Empire Windrush* sailed from Kingston, Jamaica, to London in May 1948, carrying 492 migrant workers seeking a new life in Britain. Although the numbers were small, the *Windrush* voyage became a symbol of a new wave of Afro Caribbean immigration into Britain. In the following decade, about 150,000 immigrants from the West Indies arrived in Britain. The *Windrush* story is covered well by Robert Winder in *Bloody Foreigners* (2004).

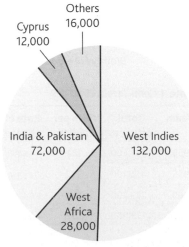

Others 16,000
Cyprus 12,000
India & Pakistan 72,000
West Indies 132,000
West Africa 28,000

Fig. 8 *New Commonwealth immigration, 1951–60*

The authorities regarded immigration as economically desirable (immigrants filled many important low-wage jobs) and hoped that the social tensions would ease gradually over time. In 1958, serious race riots, especially in Notting Hill in west London in August, altered perceptions. The rate of New Commonwealth immigration speeded up. Government policy changed. The result was the Commonwealth Immigrants Act of 1962, limiting immigration through a system of work permits.

■ A closer look

The Notting Hill riots, 1958

The race riots in Notting Hill in west London in August 1958 were preceded by a weekend of violence in Nottingham, in which gangs of white youths went on what they called 'nigger hunts' after pub brawls. A week later, there were outbreaks of serious violence in Notting Hill, an area that had become very run-down and had a large concentration of people from the Caribbean. One of the problems of the area was the number of unscrupulous landlords exploiting overcrowded and badly maintained housing.

At first, the violence was mostly white youths attacking West Indians; later there was some concerted violence in the other direction. The police were unprepared and lacked experience of dealing with race riots. A local resident, Labour politician Tony Benn, described the menacing atmosphere (see Source 3).

Everyone was standing out in front of their doors in the hot sultry air just waiting for something to happen. The next day I toured the area before breakfast and saw the corrugated iron behind the windows of the prefabs where the coloured families live. The use of petrol bombs and iron bars is appalling.

Eventually the tension was broken by a huge thunderstorm.

The Notting Hill riots brought to national attention a problem that had been simmering for a long time. Politicians began to consider how to intervene in a problem they would have preferred to leave alone. In 1962, the Commonwealth Immigrants Act was passed, followed by the Race Relations Act of 1965.

 3

Tony Benn, quoted in Winder, R.,
Bloody Foreigners, 2004

Public attitudes to immigration were mixed. Immigrants were all too aware of the prejudices and discrimination against them; but they kept coming. There were many unpleasant examples of outright racism from the host communities, but also a general feeling of tolerance and 'getting along'. There was reluctance to use legislation to control immigration from countries with close historic links to Britain and the Labour Party strongly opposed the 1962 Act, but Labour did not repeal it after the 1964 election. Government and local communities muddled along towards a multicultural society without any clear sense of direction.

Violence, criminality and hooliganism

One of the concerns expressed about immigration was fear of crime. Public anxieties were often aroused by unfair and inaccurate reports of criminal behaviour by immigrants. In fact, violent crime in Britain was mostly home-grown. By the mid-1950s, 'Teddy boys' had become part of the social fabric and previous norms of law-abiding behaviour were breaking down.

Britain was a remarkably law-abiding society in the early 1950s, more so than at any time in the post-war era. During the war, social dislocation and the blackout had led to a sharp rise in crime but this proved to be only a blip. From 1951 to 1955, criminal behaviour dipped down again. From the mid-1950s, however, there was a crime wave; the number of criminal offences more than doubled between 1955 and 1965. Two prominent examples of the rise in crime and disorder were the Kray Twins and the clashes between 'Mods' and 'Rockers'.

Table 1 *Crime levels, 1950–65*

Years	Total offences	Rate per million	Rate of change
1950	461,400	12.1	− 4.8%
1955	438,100	11.2	− 5.1%
1960	743,700	18.5	+ 64.4%
1965	1,133,900	28.3	+ 53.0%

Reggie and Ronnie Kray grew up in a culture of boxing and street fighting in London's East End and began their full-scale criminal career after they were jailed for repeatedly deserting from National Service duty. By the late 1950s the Kray twins had a reputation for extreme violence and had built up a crime empire of clubs and 'property development'. They became outwardly respectable, associating with celebrities like the film stars Diana Dors and Barbara Windsor. The Krays did not reach their peak of notoriety until after 1964, but their rise reflected the changing attitudes to crime among some sections of society.

The Mods and Rockers were not organised criminals. The disorder they caused was that of a new, aggressive youth culture, disrespectful of authority and spoiling for a fight. Young men fighting in the street was hardly new; brawls outside pubs were already a familiar part of the scene in almost any town on Saturday nights. By the early 1960s, people were also getting used to the new phenomenon of football hooligans, causing disturbances outside football grounds and vandalising trains.

The Mods and Rockers, however, attracted a lot of attention because of their peculiar emphasis on 'style'. Rockers rode heavy motorcycles, wore leather and listened to rock and roll music. Mods rode scooters, wore smart suits and preferred 'sophisticated' pop music. Rockers saw Mods as snobbish wimps; Mods looked down on Rockers as scruffy and old-fashioned. There were numerous clashes between Mods and Rockers in the early 1960s but the event that caused a national sensation was the large-scale, organised rioting in south coast holiday resorts, Clacton, Margate and Brighton, in May 1964.

In Brighton, the fighting went on for two days, with large contingents of police struggling to restore order. The public reaction to these events has been described as a moral panic. Politicians, churchmen and the media went overboard, with hysterical descriptions of knife-wielding hooligans undermining the very foundations of society. The actual levels of violence were vastly exaggerated.

One of the reasons it was difficult for people to understand the rise in crime and disorder was that it was taking place at a time of affluence and personal prosperity. Another puzzle was that it occurred against the background of National Service, which had been set up in the hope that it would instil discipline into Britain's young men. Whatever the reasons, British society was slowly getting accustomed to the emergence of a new youth culture.

Fig. 9 *'The trouble with young people today': fighting between Mods and Rockers at Margate, 1964*

Exploring the detail

Teddy boys

The nickname 'Teddy boys' was derived from the Edwardian fashions, such as long coats, narrow trousers and winklepicker shoes, worn by young males. Like 'hoodies' fifty years later, the dress sense and behaviour of the 'Teddy boys' was seen as a challenge to older people and their ideas about social order.

Exploring the detail

National Service

National Service conscripted young men for two years in military uniform. It was introduced in 1947 and eventually abandoned in 1960. For many, the experience was unwelcome and unrewarding: a regimented existence marked by boredom and square-bashing. For others, it opened new opportunities for travel, training, higher education and possibly a new career.

The debate over secondary education

Another potentially divisive aspect of social change was education, especially secondary schools.

For most people, the distinctive feature of education in the fifties was selection: the 'Eleven Plus' examination that decided whether a child's future would be in a grammar school (about 30 per cent of pupils) or in a secondary modern school (more than 60 per cent). The 1944 Education Act had aimed to produce a 'tripartite system' giving equal status to grammar schools, technical schools and the secondary moderns, but this never materialised in practice. Only a handful of technical schools were established and secondary modern schools quickly came to be regarded as receptacles for children who failed the Eleven Plus.

The Eleven Plus was a hotly debated issue for the middle classes. Many saw the test as essentially unfair and also inefficient. Many saw it as a waste of talent and human potential. The psychological strain placed on children by parents could be awful. For the Labour opposition, Anthony Crosland began working on plans for comprehensive schools. Edward Boyle, the Education Secretary from 1962 to 1964, was ready to consider new initiatives, in order to get away from the Eleven Plus and to learn from foreign countries such as Sweden and the United States. At the same time, the government commissioned the Robbins Report of 1962, which led to a massive expansion of higher education. Existing universities took in greater numbers. New universities sprang up in Lancaster, Warwick, York and elsewhere.

■ Key profile

Anthony Crosland

Crosland (1918–77) was the leading social democrat thinker in the Labour Party, with little enthusiasm for old-style Marxism. He was a keen supporter of comprehensive schools. He became education secretary after Labour won the 1964 election. In 1965, Crosland issued Circular 10/65, ordering local authorities to draw up plans switching to a comprehensive system.

It needs to be remembered that in the early 1960s, many people saw comprehensive education as modern and progressive, likely to bring better economic performance as well as more equality. Some local authorities, led by Leicestershire, experimented with a three-tier system, setting up middle schools for the 9–13 age group and avoiding the Eleven Plus altogether. When Labour came to power in 1964 it was evident that secondary school education was becoming a major social issue. Only later, after 1970, did it become a political battleground.

Changing attitudes to class

Britain in 1951 was a deferential and conformist society, with an ingrained respect for authority. It was easy to recognise class distinctions from people's dress or way of speaking. Class loyalties were very strong within the political parties. By the late 1950s, there were signs of a shift in attitudes, hinting at the gradual breakdown of old social restrictions and a loss of deference. The Suez crisis of 1956 exposed blatant lying and manipulation by the government. The rise of CND from 1958 encouraged the tendency to

■ Activity

Class debate

Using the source material in this chapter, assemble appropriate evidence to support a speech to be given during the 1964 general election. You should argue for or against the view that: 'Current social trends indicate an alarming decline in morality and behaviour, especially amongst our youth.'

challenge authority. Perhaps above all, new trends in culture and the media opened the way for a more individualist and less conformist society, less willing to follow the lead set by Britain's 'Establishment'.

The idea of the Establishment referred to the informal networks that connected the social and political elites. There was a perception of privileged people (overwhelmingly male) who were inside a charmed circle, who had influence who 'knew the people who mattered'. The Establishment included the aristocracy, barristers and High Court judges, civil service mandarins, diplomats, Anglican bishops and senior officers in the armed forces. Most were very well off, but wealth was less important than background and connections. The natural progression was from the most exclusive private boarding schools, to the most prestigious colleges at Oxford or Cambridge and thence into positions of power and influence. The table below gives one brief glimpse into this pathway to the top.

Table 2 *The 'Establishment' and Britain's post-war prime ministers, 1950–2007*

Date of office	Prime ministers	Leaders of the opposition
1950–51	(L) **Clement Attlee** Haileybury and Oxford	(C) **Winston Churchill** Harrow and Sandhurst
1951–55	(C) **Winston Churchill**	(L) **Clement Attlee**
1955–57	(C) **Anthony Eden** Eton and Oxford	(L) **Hugh Gaitskell** Winchester and Oxford
1957–63	(C) **Harold Macmillan** Eton and Oxford	(L) **Hugh Gaitskell**
1963–64	(C) **Alec Douglas-Home** Eton and Oxford	(L) **Harold Wilson** *Wirral GS* and Oxford
1964–70	(L) **Harold Wilson**	(C) **Edward Heath** *Chatham House GS* and Oxford
1970–74	(C) **Edward Heath**	(L) **Harold Wilson**
1974–76	(L) **Harold Wilson**	(C) **Edward Heath**
1976–79	(L) **James Callaghan** *Portsmouth Northern*	(C) **Margaret Thatcher** *Grantham GS* and Oxford
1979–90	(C) **Margaret Thatcher**	(L) **Michael Foot** *Leighton Park S* and Oxford
		(L) **Neil Kinnock** *Lewis School* and Cardiff
1990–97	(C) **John Major** *Rutlish GS*	(L) **Tony Blair** Fettes and Oxford
1997–2007	(L) **Tony Blair**	(C) **William Hague** *Wath-on-Dearne CS* and Oxford
2007	(L) **Gordon Brown** *Kirkcaldy HS* and Edinburgh	(C) **Iain Duncan Smith** HMS Conway and Sandhurst
		(C) **Michael Howard** *Llanelli GS* and Cambridge
		(C) **David Cameron** Eton and Oxford

* State schools indicated in italics

Cross-reference

The extent of social change by 2007 is covered in Chapter 16 and in the conclusion.

Activity

Revision exercise

Analyse the evidence about in the educational background of Britain's political leaders, both Conservative and Labour, between 1951 and 2007. Construct two graphs, one for each party, to trace the patterns of attendance at private or state schools and at Oxbridge.

1 What changing trends can be detected over the period?

2 How significant are the differences between the two parties?

The left-wingers in the Labour movement had long battled against the class system. They had wanted the Attlee government to abolish private schools, along with the House of Lords. Moderates believed in opening up the route to the top levels of society to make it a meritocracy, especially by reforming the education system. It was among the middle classes that this change was most marked and many of the most scathing attacks on the Establishment came from people with the same education and background as the targets they were aiming at.

In the early 1960s, these ideas were getting a new lease of life. The mocking humour of the 'satire boom' showed a dramatic loss of deference towards those in authority. One event in 1963 symbolised the shifting attitudes towards class and privilege that was taking place. The Profumo affair was a political scandal that brought down a cabinet minister and rocked the Macmillan government. But it was also a barometer of social change and suggested that Britain was becoming a less deferential, less class-ridden society.

■ Cross-reference

The political aspects of the Profumo affair are covered on page 24.

■ Cross-reference

The Cold War is discussed on pages 123–125.

■ A closer look

The Profumo affair

In one sense, the Profumo affair was all about politics. John Profumo, the Defence Secretary, was trapped by a sex scandal. He lied about his involvement, both to parliament and to the Prime Minister. He resigned in disgrace. The Conservative government was weakened. The girl in the scandal, Christine Keeler, was also sleeping with a Soviet spy called Ivanov, which raised questions about possible leaks of Cold War secrets. The Profumo scandal came just after other spy scandals, such as the Vassall affair, had been revealed. A public enquiry was held under Lord Denning.

The greater significance of the Profumo affair, however, was what it revealed about Britain's changing society. The security aspects were not very serious. They provided an ideal excuse for the popular press to go after every juicy detail of the sexual behaviour of those involved, including Lord Astor (who owned Cliveden, the stately home where Profumo first encountered Keeler, swimming naked in the swimming pool) and other prominent figures. Christine Keeler and her friend, Mandy Rice-Davies, became celebrities. The press became notably less deferential and more intrusive. Previous tactics used by governments to prevent publication of sensitive or embarrassing information no longer worked.

Fig. 10 *Christine Keeler after giving evidence at the Old Bailey, June 1963*

Private Eye showed the new irreverent style by comparing Macmillan's Britain with the fall of the Roman Empire:

By the early days of the year 1963, the twilight of the British Empire provided a sorry spectacle of collapse and decay on every hand. ... After years of an uneasy indulgence, the people were restless and dissatisfied. ... Wild rumours flew nightly through the capital. Of strange and wild happenings at country villas out in the country. Of orgies and philanderings involving some of the richest and most powerful men in the land. ... All these happenings brought the capital into a frenzy of speculation that was far from healthy for the continued reign of Macmillan, and the scribes and pamphleteers were only the leaders and articulators of the hostility and contempt aroused by the Government in the hearts of the great mass of the people.

4	*From Booker, D., 'The Last Days of Emperor Macmillan', **Private Eye**, 5 April 1963, quoted in Sandbrook D., **White Heat**, 2006*

In 1965, the funeral of Winston Churchill provided the occasion for an Establishment spectacular, bidding farewell to the great statesman and war hero of the last generation. By this time, however, the social dominance of the Establishment was beginning to be challenged. British society was becoming less deferential, as could be seen in the new wave of disrespectful satire in the press, television and the theatre. Developments in secondary education and the expansion of the universities opened new opportunities for the children of the middle classes. Attitudes to class in the Britain of 1965 had already changed considerably from those that had prevailed in 1951.

■ A closer look

Changing attitudes in culture and the media, 1951–64

The simmering social tensions were increasingly reflected in culture and the media. In the early 1950s, deference to authority was still strong. Mass entertainment, which mostly meant the cinema and the BBC (ITV began broadcasting in 1955) was mostly very cosy and reassuring. There were huge radio audiences for programmes like *The Archers* and *The Navy Lark*, which got a regular audience of 20 million listeners when it began in 1958. The diet of feature films was dominated by war epics like *The Cruel Sea* and *The Dam Busters*; and by Ealing comedies such as *The Lavender Hill Mob* and *The Titfield Thunderbolt*. Such films often reinforced existing attitudes to class. On the other hand, the influence of cinema was starting to decline by 1964. Cinema attendances fell steadily as television took over more and more households.

As time went on, culture began to reflect current society. Gang violence was chillingly portrayed in Anthony Burgess's 1962 novel *A Clockwork Orange*. The alienation of young working-class males was the theme of several films, especially *Saturday Night and Sunday Morning*, a big hit in 1960.

Table 3 *The cinema, 1951–64*

Year	Number of cinemas	Attendances per week (millions)
1951	4,581	26.2
1953	4,542	24.7
1955	4,483	22.7
1957	4,194	17.6
1959	3,414	11.2
1960	3,034	9.6
1962	2,421	7.6
1964	2,057	6.6

Racial tension was the theme of *Sapphire*, a 1959 crime thriller with a then rather daring portrayal of sex and violence. On television, the cosy and comforting police series *Dixon of Dock Green* was shouldered aside by the gritty realism of *Z Cars* set in a new town on Merseyside. Television also produced campaigning programmes designed to raise controversy about social issues, such as *Cathy Come Home*, a powerful drama about homelessness by Ken Loach in 1962.

There was also a drive to break down censorship and social taboos. Several plays and films pushed out the boundaries in portraying sex on screen or dealing more openly with issues like homosexuality or back-street abortions. In 1962, Penguin Books caused a storm by publishing a paperback edition of D.H. Lawrence's sexually explicit novel *Lady Chatterley's Lover*. The result was a high-profile court case under the Obscenity Act.

There was also a 'satire boom'. Peter Cook, Dudley Moore, Jonathan Miller and Alan Bennett made a big impact with their satirical stage show *Beyond The Fringe*. From 1961, *Private Eye* rapidly established a loyal following for its witty disrespect for the great and famous. In 1962, *That Was The Week That Was* made its debut on BBC television, delighting half the nation and scandalising the other half. The cultural tide did not only flow in one direction. There was a middle-class backlash against the new 'immorality and depravity', led by Mary Whitehouse and supported by parts of the national press. In general, the majority opinion in Britain was socially conservative and much of Britain's popular culture remained in the same old groove. The class system may have been dented by the shifts in social attitudes but it was certainly not broken.

■ Cross-reference

British society between 1959 and 1975 is covered in entertaining depth by Sally Waller's book *A Sixties Social Revolution?* in the Nelson Thornes AS History series.

■ Key profile

Mrs Mary Whitehouse

Mrs Whitehouse (1910–2001) was a Birmingham housewife. In 1963, she began her own 'moral crusade' against what she saw as a 'tide of immorality and indecency' in Britain at that time; her crusade was directed in particular at the director-general of the BBC, Sir Hugh Greene. Mrs Whitehouse gained a lot of public support when she launched her Clean Up TV campaign in 1964. In 1965, she founded the National Viewers and Listeners Association.

■ Summary question

In what ways did post-war prosperity bring social change in Britain between 1951 and 1964?

4   Britain, Europe and the world, 1951–64

Fig. 1 *Queen Elizabeth II and Prince Philip greeted by 14,000 schoolchildren on a royal tour to Malta, 1954*

In this chapter you will learn about:

- why Britain retreated from her imperial role and accepted the need for decolonisation

- the impact of the Suez upon Britain's position in the world

- the 'wind of change' in Africa

- the reasons why Britain was not involved in the process of European integration between 1955 and 1963.

Britain has lost an empire and has not yet found a role.

1   *US diplomat Dean Acheson, in a report to Washington, 1950*

The core of our policy is the Atlantic Alliance. Our main task in the next decade will be to maintain, and to make even closer, the association between North America, the United Kingdom and the continental countries of Western Europe. We must therefore work to ensure continuation of the United States presence in Europe and the development of an economic and political community of interests embracing both the United States and Western Europe. We must also do all we can to strengthen the Commonwealth, which can be a valuable instrument for maintaining our influence as a Power with worldwide interests and for promoting our ideals, and can form a bridge between the Western world and the developing countries of Asia and Africa.

2   *From **The Future Policy Study**, February 1960*

■ Key chronology

Britain and the world, 1951–64

1951 Attlee government committed to British nuclear deterrent

1955 Messina conference

1956 British pull-back from Suez

Hungarian rising crushed by Soviet forces

1957 EEC formed by the Treaty of Rome

1960 Failure of Blue Streak missile programme

1963 Rejection of Britain's application to join the EEC

■ Exploring the detail

The Mau Mau rebellion

The Mau Mau revolt in Kenya was one of several violent nationalist uprisings against British colonial rule after 1945. The leader of the revolt, Jomo Kenyatta, was imprisoned by the authorities but later emerged as president of an independent Kenya. In the 1950s, the struggle led to great bitterness on both sides. The Mau Mau fighters were accused of committing atrocities; on the other hand, revelations about brutal treatment of captives held at the Hola prison camp badly damaged Britain's reputation. Kenya was granted independence in 1963.

■ Key chronology

Decolonisation, 1947–64

1947 Withdrawal from India

1952 Start of Mau Mau rebellion in Kenya

1954 British withdrawal from Egypt

1956 Failure of military intervention at Suez

1957 Independence granted to Ghana

1960 Macmillan's 'wind of change' speech

1960 Independence granted to Nigeria and Cyprus

1961 South Africa's exit from the Commonwealth

1963 Independence granted to Kenya

By 1951, Britain had already had to face up to the prospect of imperial decline. This decline had begun after the First World War but it was the Second World War that left Britain badly damaged, burdened with massive debts, and in the shadow of two new military superpowers. In 1947, Britain's ambassador in Washington had to inform the Americans that the country faced bankruptcy and would have to withdraw from commitments in Greece, Turkey and Palestine. In the same year, independence was granted to India and Pakistan, marking Britain's 'retreat from empire'.

Illusions, however, can take a long time to die. Political and public opinion was slow to recognise Britain's reduced position in the world, or to see the implications for the future. This slow realisation had profound consequences. It delayed Britain's involvement in European integration until 1973, when it could easily have begun twenty years earlier. It was only after the humiliating failure of the Anglo-French military intervention at Suez in 1956 that Britain's inability to act like a great power began to be realised.

Imperial illusions also held back the process of decolonisation. Only in 1960, with Harold Macmillan's 'wind of change' speech, did the British people begin to come to terms with the need to let go of colonies in Africa. Even after 1960, these illusions kept British defence spending at impossibly high levels, including the massive costs of the independent nuclear deterrent. And the illusions influenced British ideas about the 'special relationship' with the United States and Britain's role in the Cold War. By 1964, many of these illusions had been blown away, but by no means all of them. Britain had still not yet found a new role.

■ Adjusting to the post-war world

Britain's declining imperial role: Empire and Commonwealth, 1951–64

By 1951, Britain's retreat from empire had already begun. The decision to withdraw from India in 1947 was the most dramatic example of this. During the 1950s, the pressures of colonial independence movements became harder and harder to contain. British forces found themselves fighting against national independence movements in Malaya, Kenya and Cyprus. Nor was it only Britain who faced these pressures: France faced even bigger challenges in Vietnam and in Algeria; Belgium and Portugal had to deal with revolts in their African colonies.

In the early 1950s, Britain's rulers believed they could manage a gradual transition from the Empire to the new Commonwealth and that colonial resistance movements could be controlled until their peoples were 'ready' for independence. Nobody then had any idea of the sudden rush to independence that was waiting to happen. In Malaya, for example, British forces fought a long and ultimately successful counter-insurgency campaign to defeat Communist guerrilla forces. When the Mau Mau rebellion broke out in Kenya in 1952, it was assumed that military repression would succeed against the Mau Mau, too. At that time, independence for Kenya was unthinkable – but that was before Suez.

The Suez crisis of 1956

The Suez Canal was one of the keystones of Britain's overseas empire and trade routes. It was because of the Canal, bought by Britain in 1875, soon after it was completed, that Britain became the ruling power in Egypt during the 1880s. The Suez Canal was the main artery connecting trade routes from the Mediterranean through to the Indian Ocean and beyond to Asia, Australia and New Zealand. Above all, the Suez Canal was the vital route for oil shipments: 80 per cent of Western Europe's oil imports passed through the canal.

The emergence of Egyptian independence under a new nationalist leader, Colonel Nasser, was deeply worrying for Britain's strategic interests. When Nasser nationalised the Suez Canal Company in July 1956, his action was seen as a provocation Britain could not accept or ignore.

Fig. 2 *Hero or villain of Suez? Gamel Abd al-Nasser*

A closer look

Colonel Nasser and the Suez Canal

Gamel Abd al-Nasser was the leader of a nationalist revolt against the old Egyptian monarchy. He was keen to see British influence removed and to establish full independence; though it is possible that he would have preferred to do this without open confrontation if Britain and the United States had been willing to negotiate. This seemed possible, especially as Britain and the United States were involved in financing the massive Aswan high dam project aimed at harnessing the River Nile for economic development.

The American government was lukewarm about the Aswan project, however, and Nasser began considering alternative offers from the USSR. In July 1956, Nasser acted unilaterally to force the issue. He announced the nationalisation of the Suez Canal Company. One of his stated reasons was to use the revenues from the Suez Canal to provide finance for the Aswan Dam. By carrying out the nationalisation, Nasser issued a direct challenge to British and European interests. His action also seemed to place Egypt on the Soviet side of the Cold War. For Britain, there was no question of simply accepting the nationalisation. It had to be reversed, either by diplomacy or by military force.

Did you know?

The Suez Canal was built mostly by French engineers, backed by French investors, and was completed in 1869. In 1875, the British government organised a *coup* by which the majority shareholding in the Suez Canal Company was purchased on Britain's behalf. From 1882, Britain became the occupying power in Egypt, and stationed troops in the canal zone to ensure the canal remained under British control.

The personality of Anthony Eden was a key factor in the British response to Colonel Nasser's action in taking over the canal. Eden prided himself on his mastery of foreign policy. He still believed in Britain as an imperial power. He was also a man who had fiercely opposed appeasement in the 1930s. Eden was quick to see Nasser as *'an evil dictator who could not be allowed to get away with unprovoked aggression'*. He had little faith that diplomacy would work. Eden and several of his policy advisers thought Nasser would be a danger to stability in Africa. Most of Eden's cabinet, including the Chancellor, Harold Macmillan, were minded to take drastic action and not wait for a long, slow diplomatic process.

The Suez situation is beginning to slip out of our hands. I try not to think we have 'missed the bus' – it has taken such a long time to get our military arrangements into shape. But we must win this struggle by one means or another. Nasser may well try to preach Holy War in the Middle East. *Without oil, and the profits from oil*, neither the UK nor Western Europe can survive.

| 3 | *From the diaries of Harold Mamillan, 4 October 1956* |

Eden's natural instinct to use force was encouraged by both France and Israel. The French government was fearful of Nasser's influence undermining French colonies in North Africa. Israel was keen to make a pre-emptive military strike against Egypt as part of the ongoing struggle for survival. The result was collusion in a conspiracy. A top-secret meeting was held at Sèvres, in Paris, at which Britain, France and Israel agreed a plan of action. Israeli forces would invade Egypt; British and French forces would then intervene. The excuse for intervention would be to enforce peace on Egypt and Israel; the real effect would be to seize control of the Suez Canal zone. The details of this plan were concealed from most of the cabinet and from the Americans.

This plan was put into operation on 29 October when the Israeli attack was launched. The Anglo-French invasion followed a day later. The military action did not go as smoothly as planned, though it might well have succeeded in the end. It caused a storm of political protest in Britain, even though it took a long time for the full details of the secrecy and deception to come out.

It was not the opposition from political and public opinion within Britain that halted Eden's Suez adventure in its tracks. It was pressure from the United States.

■ **Cross-reference**

The impact of the Suez crisis on domestic politics is covered on page 14.

On 29 October, the Israelis began their offensive. On 31 October, British bombers went into action against Egyptian airfields, an action of dubious morality since Britain was supposedly only trying to separate the Israeli and Egyptian forces. President Eisenhower's original reaction was astonishment, then anger that the British had reverted to gunboat diplomacy, accompanied by deception of their closest ally. 'I've never seen great powers make such a mess and *botch* of things', Ike exploded. 'Of course, there's just nobody I'd rather have fighting alongside me than the British, but *this* thing!'

Eisenhower telephoned Downing Street. The call was taken by Eden's press secretary. 'Is that you, Anthony?' the angry voice inquired. 'Well, this is President Eisenhower and I can only presume that you have gone mad!'

| 4 | *From Dimbleby D., and Reynolds, D., **An Ocean Apart**, 1988* |

The Joint Intelligence Committee had warned Eden that the United States might take a negative view of military intervention at Suez. On the other hand there was evidence that the American state department, headed by John Foster Dulles, was willing to accept British seizure of the canal as long as it was done quickly. Eden had gone ahead anyway, convinced that he was right; he never changed his mind about this, even after it had turned into a disaster and ruined his career. But Britain was simply not strong enough in 1956 to stand up to American pressure; Britain was plunged into a serious financial crisis. Harold Macmillan, one of the strongest supporters of the invasion, was the first to realise that it was essential to pull out, even though this meant accepting failure and humiliation. Anthony Eden's career ended in a painful anti-climax. Britain's position in the world now had to go through a fundamental reassessment.

It is important to understand why the Suez invasion happened. One leading member of Eden's government, Peter Thorneycroft, remembered in 1993:

> I think it's important to remember how overpowering Anthony Eden's position was. He was not only prime minister but he was considered to be the greatest prime minister we'd had for a long time and the greatest foreign policy expert that we'd had for a long time. It's always difficult to challenge a prime minister, but to challenge a prime minister on foreign policy if that's his real strength, well is very difficult indeed.

5   *From an interview with Peter Thorneycroft, quoted in Hennessy, P.,*
***The Prime Minister**, 2000*

This obviously holds a lot of truth but there was more to it than Anthony Eden. Many people in Britain still had illusions of imperial grandeur before Suez. Afterwards, lessons began to be learned.

The wind of change

After the Suez fiasco, British policymakers began to reconsider the pace of decolonisation. In 1957, Ghana (formerly the Gold Coast) became the first of Britain's African colonies to be granted independence. Malaya also gained independence in 1957, followed by the West Indies Federation in 1958 and a rush of others, including Nigeria and Cyprus in 1960, Tanganyika and Sierra Leone in 1961, Uganda in 1962, Kenya in 1963. The accelerating pace of this rush to independence was the subject of Harold Macmillan's most famous speech on foreign affairs, at Cape Town in South Africa in 1960, known ever since as the 'wind of change' speech.

In Cape Town, Macmillan was addressing a white audience, mostly believers in **apartheid**. He was trying to convince them of the need to face reality. His main audience, however, was not present: he was speaking over the heads of those in the hall, to the Commonwealth, to public and political opinion at home in Britain. Macmillan himself knew that it was a momentous speech – he was sick with nerves beforehand. Two key questions arise: Why had Macmillan come to believe that change was so irresistible? How successfully did Britain react to it?

The answer to the first question can be found in Macmillan's recollections as an old man, looking back at a conversation with the British Governor General in Nigeria in 1960, not long before the Cape Town speech:

> I asked him: 'Are these people ready for independence?' and he said, 'No, of course not.'
>
> 'When will they be ready?' He said, 'Twenty years, twenty-five years.'
>
> 'What do you recommend me to do?' He said, 'Give it to them at once.'
>
> 'Well, doesn't that seem strange?' 'Well', he said, 'If they were twenty years well spent, learning administration, getting experience, I would say wait. But what will happen? All the intelligent ones will become rebels. I shall have to put them in prison. There will be violence, bitterness, hatred. We shall simply have twenty years of repression. They'd better start learning to rule themselves at once.'
> I thought that was very sensible.

6   *Quoted in Hennessy, P., **Having It So Good**, 2006*

 Activity

Revision exercise

Compare the evidence in this chapter about Britain's invasion of Suez in 1956 with the evidence in Chapter 16 on the invasion of Iraq in 2003. Make a list of the similarities and the differences between the motives and actions of Anthony Eden and Tony Blair.

Key terms

Apartheid: a rigid system of segregation on racial grounds.

Exploring the detail

Macmillan and the wind of change

Before 1960, the central aim of British imperial policy was to defeat nationalist revolts and to maintain control over Britain's African colonies. Other European colonial powers, including Belgium, France and Portugal, were fighting similar wars against nationalist uprisings. Macmillan's speech at Cape Town, describing the 'wind of change' blowing through the whole African continent was a significant change of policy, calling for decolonisation and recognition of independence movements.

Fig. 3 *President of Tanganyika, Julius Nyerere greets General Sir Richard Turnbull, the British Governor of Tanganyika, prior the proclamation of the country's independence with the new name, Tanzania, 1961*

Activity

Source analysis

Read the description of Macmillan's conversation with the Governor General in Nigeria carefully. Evaluate its strengths and weaknesses as historical evidence about the wind of change.

The difficult struggle to contain the Mau Mau rebellion in Kenya reinforced Macmillan's view of the need to recognise and adapt to the wind of change. Iain Macleod, the Colonial Secretary, was also convinced of the need to speed up the movement towards independence. In retrospect, the policy followed by Macmillan and Macleod was extremely successful. The process did not always go as planned, but British decolonisation was completed more swiftly and with far less violence than was the case with other colonial powers such as Belgium and Portugal. By 1964, the transition from empire to commonwealth seemed to represent a significant achievement.

Key profile

Iain Macleod

Iain Macleod (1913–70) was a 'One Nation Tory'. He was a minister of health under Eden and was a key member of Macmillan's cabinet, first as minister of labour and then as colonial secretary. He was considered a possible candidate for the party leadership in 1963. He resigned from the government when
Sir Alec Douglas-Home became prime minister.

Britain and Europe, 1955–63

When the process leading towards European integration began, there was an open opportunity for Britain to take a central role. The Schuman Plan of 1950 set out the proposals for a Coal and Steel Community that would integrate French and German heavy industry in order to promote rapid economic reconstruction and also to bind together the historic enemies, France and Germany, and eliminate the dangers of future wars between them.

The Schuman Plan was to be the foundation of economic cooperation across Western Europe. This scheme was strongly supported by Britain and the United States as an important contribution to the security of Europe as the Cold War took shape. At any time up to 1957, there was an open door for British entry to the EEC; but Britain saw European integration as something vitally important for continental Europe, not for Britain. In a remarkably short space of time, however, British attitudes changed.

In 1959, Britain took the lead in the formation of the European Free Trade Area (EFTA) linking the economies of Britain, Denmark, Norway, Austria, Portugal and Switzerland. This was only moderately successful and Britain submitted an application for membership of the EEC in 1961. There were economic considerations influencing the decision to apply but also important foreign policy aims. Britain wanted to keep her position in three areas of world affairs: Europe, the Commonwealth and the United States. The Americans were very much in favour of Britain joining the EEC. Britain was determined to keep her links to the Commonwealth; although this made the negotiations with the EEC extremely complex and difficult.

By 1961, however, European integration was already leaving Britain behind. The EEC was under the domination of the partnership between France and Germany. The French president from 1958, Charles de Gaulle, was determined to protect this partnership from 'les Anglo-Saxons' (Britain and, through Britain, the influence of the United States). The British application was rejected in 1963, as was a later application from Wilson's Labour government in 1967. Only in 1973, after de Gaulle had departed the scene, was Britain able to join, by which time many commentators suggested Britain had 'missed the European bus'.

Cross-reference

British attitudes to Europe in the early 1950s are covered on pages 163–165.

The open door, 1951–57

The question of why Britain stood aside from European integration is both important and complicated, but it was a decision that reflected a national consensus. There were very few politicians or journalists in favour of Britain taking up the leadership role in Europe that was on offer. The Labour Party was suspicious of the free-market principles behind the Common Market. The response of the Labour politician, Herbert Morrison was that: *the Durham miners won't wear it, I'm afraid*. The vast majority of Conservatives regarded the preservation of traditional trade links with Australia, Canada and New Zealand as far more important than Europe.

The thinking of many people in Britain was also coloured by memories of the war. Britain had 'won the war'. The Germans had been deadly wartime enemies; France had been overrun and occupied. The key political leaders in Britain, Attlee, Churchill, Eden, were all men of the wartime generation. There was little enthusiasm for what was going on in continental Europe and many people still had illusions about Britain being a great world power. The economic advantages of the EEC were disregarded. British foreign policy, therefore, was to encourage European integration from the sidelines but not to get involved.

The EEC took shape at an international conference at Messina, in Sicily, in 1955. The six member states, France, West Germany, Italy and the 'Benelux countries' (Belgium, Netherlands and Luxembourg) hammered out the complex arrangements for a Common Market and the bureaucracy that would run it. A British delegation on behalf of the Foreign Minister, Harold

Macmillan, was present at Messina to observe and encourage but not to join. The agreements made at Messina in 1955 were then developed in detail and the Treaty of Rome launched the EEC, without Britain, in January 1957.

At that time, it was not clear how successful 'The Six' would become. British foreign policy was focused on the Cold War, on the Empire and the Commonwealth, on the 'special relationship' with the United States. But a few months before the treaty of Rome was signed, the Suez crisis had provided a shock to the system. Within a very short space of time, British attitudes began to shift.

Locked outside, 1958–63

The fundamental reason why Britain changed its mind about the EEC was economic: the realisation that the patterns of trade that had existed in the 1930s were no longer sufficient for Britain to keep pace with continental Europe, especially the 'economic miracle' occurring in West Germany. But there were also important foreign policy issues involved, both in the reasons why Britain applied for membership and, above all, in the reasons why that application was rejected.

The United States was keen to see Britain join the EEC for strategic reasons, seeing Britain as a vital link between Europe and Americans. The massive crisis over Berlin in 1958 accentuated this. Belief in Britain's imperial power had been shaken by Suez and by the accelerating pace of decolonisation in Africa. The shift in British policy became apparent in May 1960, when Britain became one of the seven founder members of EFTA (European Free Trade Association) alongside Denmark, Norway, Sweden, Austria, Switzerland and Portugal. It was hoped that this 'Outer Seven' would provide an effective alternative to the six original members of the EEC but such hopes were never really fulfilled. Less than a year later Britain applied to join the EEC.

Having taken the decision to apply for membership in 1961, the Macmillan government then faced a massive task in negotiating the terms of entry. The EEC had already developed detailed economic structures, especially the Common Agricultural Policy, that Britain found difficult to conform to. It was also hugely difficult to negotiate special exemptions for Britain's Commonwealth trade partners, such as lamb exports from New Zealand, which would have been blocked by EEC rules. These complex negotiations took many months of hard bargaining, led on the British side by Macmillan's chief negotiator, the patient and persistent Edward Heath.

These negotiations at last seemed to have reached a successful conclusion in January 1963; but at the last moment the whole process was derailed by the French president, Charles de Gaulle, who exercised France's right of veto and blocked Britain's application.

> When the Brussels negotiations resumed in January 1963 we were all very optimistic and an official English translation of the draft treaty was arranged. The French foreign minister was not present; we were told he had to attend de Gaulle's press conference. I concluded the meeting in an upbeat mood, saying: 'We all seem to be in complete agreement'.
>
> Immediately afterwards we were told what de Gaulle had said in his press conference. He claimed the negotiations had shown that Britain could not adapt to the ways of the Six; and criticised Britain's unwillingness to give up its 'special political and military relations' with the United States. We were all astonished and very worried about the future.

7

*From Heath, E., **The Course Of My Life**, 1998*

Cross-reference

The political calculations behind Britain's application to join the EEC are covered in Chapter 2.

Cross-reference

The idea of Britain providing a 'transatlantic bridge' between Europe and the United State was also a strong influence on the policies of Tony Blair after 1997; see Chapter 16.

Key profile

Charles de Gaulle

De Gaulle (1894–1970) came to fame as leader of the Free French forces who fought on after France surrendered in 1940. He had many rows with his main allies, Winston Churchill and Franklin Roosevelt, and remained suspicious of 'les Anglo-Saxons', especially the Americans, in his later career. He led France through the transition from dictatorship to democracy after the liberation of France in 1944 but then suddenly retired in 1946. He remained in the political wilderness until 1958, when he returned as president under a new constitution.

De Gaulle's intervention was a bombshell. The other five members of the EEC were as shocked and disappointed as the British negotiating team but were unable to persuade de Gaulle to carry on with the negotiations. His intervention caused bad relations between France and Britain for some time; and it was France's veto that blocked Britain's next application for membership, in 1967.

Britain's position in the world by 1964

In 1951 Britain was already deeply embroiled in the Cold War. British troops were fighting in the Korean War as part of the United Nations force opposing North Korea. Britain had become a founder member of NATO in 1949 and substantial contingents of British troops were stationed in West Germany. There was close cooperation between Britain and the United States on nuclear weapons development and the sharing of intelligence secrets.

There were numerous occasions, such as the Burgess and Maclean affair, when the 'special relationship' was placed under strain. Britain sometimes resented American pressure pushing Britain to join the EEC. The 1956 Suez crisis adversely affected Anglo-American relations for a considerable time.

Fig. 4 *A special relationship? Harold Macmillan and John F. Kennedy at Downing Street, June 1963*

Overall, however, Britain and the United States remained close allies in the Cold War. Harold Macmillan was involved in plans for a summit conference with Soviet leader Nikita Khrushchev in 1960; and he established a particularly good relationship with President Eisenhower's successor, John F. Kennedy. Their partnership had a lot to do with the success of the negotiations for the Test Ban Treaty of 1963, limiting the testing of nuclear weapons. In many respects, Britain had kept its place at the international 'top table'.

On the other hand, Britain was still militarily overstretched and very dependent on American power. This was demonstrated by the costs of Britain's independent nuclear deterrent. In 1960, Britain's own rocket project, Blue Streak, had to be abandoned. It was replaced by dependence on the American Polaris submarine weapons system. When the Wilson government came to power in 1964 it had to confront the need for deep cuts in Britain's military commitments.

Activity

Thinking point

'President de Gaulle was the single most important factor in Britain's exclusion from the process of European integration between 1951 and 1963.'

Make a double list – in the left column, outline the main reasons for agreeing with the statement; in the right column, outline the reasons for arguing that the statement is wrong. Then decide which list you find more convincing.

Exploring the detail

The Burgess and Maclean affair

Guy Burgess and Donald Maclean were highly placed officers in British intelligence. They defected to the Soviet Union in 1951. For years afterwards, there were concerns about finding the 'Third Man' who has tipped them off. The revelation that British spies had been leaking vital secrets to Moscow deeply worried the Americans, who became much less ready to share intelligence secrets with Britain.

Activity

Revision exercise

Look at the timeline of the key events in British foreign affairs between 1951 and 1964 on page 40. Make a list of the **five** key factors shaping British foreign policy during this time, and explain their importance.

Cross-reference

An extract from the *Future Policy Study* appears in Source 2 on page 39.

The most significant change in Britain's role in the world concerned the Empire and Commonwealth. Disengaging from colonial responsibilities had gone a long way by 1964. Independence had been granted to a wide range of Britain's former colonial territories, from Ghana to Cyprus to Singapore. The wind of change was indeed blowing hard by 1964. The Commonwealth was a seemingly thriving organisation. Yet the legacy of the imperial past was still hard to shake off. There were still intractable problems, such as achieving a long-term settlement for issues such as Rhodesia, Gibraltar, Hong Kong or the Falkland Islands.

The *Future Policy Study* presented to Harold Macmillan's cabinet in 1960 showed Britain had accepted some but not all the implications of the retreat from empire. The sentimental myths about Britain's glorious imperial past were hard to shake off. Part of the reason for the failure of Britain's application to join the EEC, on both sides, lay in the perceptions of Britain as a country still tied to dreams of empire. In 1964, long after he said it, Dean Acheson's phrase that *'Britain has lost an empire and has not yet found a role'* seemed as true as ever.

Learning outcomes

In this section, you have looked at the development of Britain during the crucial years of adjustment to the realities of the post-war world. At home, this adjustment was marked by the return of the political dominance of the Conservatives and by a period of full employment and rising living standards in an 'age of affluence'. Socially, the legacy of the Second World War was carried forward by the welfare state and the 'post-war consensus'. Abroad, the adjustments to Britain' new position in the world were more painful as the retreat from empire accelerated and as it became clear that Britain was overshadowed by the new superpowers.

Practice question

'The foreign policy failures of British governments in the years 1951 to 1964 were due to a lack of realism about Britain's position in the post-war world.' Assess the validity of this view.

(45 marks)

Study tip Questions like this require a coherent overall argument showing the ability to evaluate alternative views in order to reach a conclusion, together with a secure grasp of chronology and context. A good answer would need to be decisive in supporting or refuting the key quotation, but the answer needs to be more than a list of reasons. A long answer full of detailed information in the right order may not score as well as a shorter answer that is more structured and shows differentiation. Any attempt to be comprehensive would lead to problems. A selective approach is vital, showing a synoptic awareness of the whole period 1951 to 1964 but supporting the main argument with precisely selected evidence. An answer to this question may well benefit from an understanding of various historical interpretations; but this does *not* mean a lengthy list of second-hand references to historical works and their authors. The more effective approach is to differentiate between the various perspectives.

5 Politics and the economy, 1964–70

Fig. 1 *Barbara Castle, Employment Secretary in the Wilson government at the time of the row over* In Place of Strife

In this chapter you will learn about:

- the strengths and weaknesses of the Labour government, 1964–66

- the policies and achievements of the Wilson's Labour government, 1966–70

- how government interventions affected the British economy

- the reasons why the Conservatives won a surprise victory in 1970.

I want to speak to you today about a new Britain and how we intend to bring home to our people the excitement there will be in building it. For 1964 is the year in which we can take our destiny into our own hands. Since the war, the world has been rushing forward at an unprecedented and exhilarating speed. In two decades, the scientists have made more progress than in the past two thousand years. They have made it possible for mankind to reach out to the stars and to bring abundance from the earth. They have made it possible to end the dark ages of poverty.

This is what 1964 can mean. A chance for change. A chance to sweep away the grouse-moor conception of Tory leadership and refit Britain with a new image, a new confidence.

1

From a speech by Harold Wilson,
Birmingham Town Hall, January 1964

The Labour government, 1964–70

1964

October Victory in the general election

1965

July Crosland plan for comprehensive schools

September Launch of George Brown's National Plan

1966

March Labour re-election victory

July State of emergency due to seamen's strike

December UN sanctions against Rhodesia

1967

November Devaluation crisis

November Rejection of Britain's application to join EEC

1970

June Wilson government defeated in general election

Wilson's skills were mainly suitable for the politics of survival. He was personally popular, both in parliament and in the country. He constantly out-manoeuvred the Tories and made Heath seem humourless and even foolish. It was clear that Wilson was the master of his own party and that Labour was able to weather its internal storms. The question remained whether Wilson could ever be master of the nation, whether Labour could move out of its own bunker to take control of domestic and international events.

2

From Morgan, K. O., The People's Peace: British History 1945–1990, 1992

When Harold Wilson entered Downing Street in 1964, his government was welcomed with considerable optimism and public goodwill. Labour seemed to be more in touch with the social and cultural trends of the sixties. One of Wilson's most effective campaign speeches had promised Britain would catch up with 'the white heat' of technological change. This sense of a fresh start provided the impetus for Labour to consolidate its position with a thumping victory in 1966.

The results of Labour's ambitious policy programme were disappointing. Economic policies ran into trouble, symbolised by a major devaluation crisis in 1967. From 1966 to 1969, the government lagged well behind the Conservatives in the opinion polls. There was a sense of frustration that Labour had been 'blown off course'. The Conservatives returned to power in 1970 and Labour went back into the political wilderness again. Many in the party blamed Wilson's indecisive leadership for wasting its golden opportunity. Although Wilson was to return to power in 1974, by then, the country faced huge economic problems and deep social divisions.

Reaching a balanced judgement on the Labour government of 1964–70 remains difficult. There were many achievements in social policy: comprehensive schools, the Open University, liberalisation of the laws on abortion and homosexuality. After the early stumbles, economic policy was under firm control by 1970 under the direction of Roy Jenkins as chancellor. If Wilson had won in 1970, his government might have gone on to achieve great things. As it was, the electoral defeat left Labour's supporters feeling cheated; they were quick to contrast the muddles and delays of Wilson's six years with the purpose and effectiveness of Attlee after 1945.

■ The Labour government, 1964–70

The Wilson government seemed well suited to the tasks it faced from 1964. Smoking a pipe, calm, with a reassuringly 'normal' Yorkshire accent, Harold Wilson had a classless image far removed from the Old Etonian style of Eden, Macmillan and Douglas-Home. He was the first prime minister educated at state secondary school. Wilson was a relaxed and skilful performer on television. Edward Heath, who became leader of the Conservative opposition in 1965, found it very difficult to compete with Wilson's air of political authority. Wilson seemed even stronger after his convincing election victory in 1966.

Wilson also seemed to be in tune with modern trends. He had a genuine commitment to science and technology. He created a new government department of technology and strengthened the department of education and science. The 1963 Robbins Report on higher education was implemented; by 1966 seven new universities (Sussex, East Anglia, Kent, York, Essex, Lancaster and Warwick) were up and running. Colleges of advanced technology were given extra funding for expansion. A lot of scientists were employed as government advisers. There was a similar modernising approach to social issues. Roy Jenkins, Home Secretary from 1965, promoted liberalisation. Parliament voted against capital punishment in 1965. A new Race Relations Act was passed.

■ Key profile

Roy Jenkins

Jenkins (1920–2003) was from the right wing of the Labour Party. Many people thought he was more of a liberal than a socialist. He was also an accomplished historian whose books included biographies of W. E. Gladstone and Winston Churchill. He played a leading role in the Wilson government from 1964, first as home secretary and then as chancellor. Jenkins was very pro-European and resigned from Labour's shadow cabinet in 1972 after clashing with Wilson over the EEC. In 1981, Jenkins was one of the founders of the Social Democratic Party.

Reorganisation of economic policy was less successful. Many Labour ministers put this down to factors outside the government's control: to the difficult balance of payments situation inherited from the outgoing Conservatives, and also to the obstructive, anti-Labour attitudes they felt existed among senior civil servants and at the Bank of England. Other people felt that Labour simply made a mess of their attempts to restructure the economy, especially the National Plan introduced by George Brown in 1965.

From 1964, Wilson was worried about his small parliamentary majority. Wilson also showed a lot of anxiety (some would say paranoia) about what he felt was biased, hostile coverage by the BBC and by the national press. In March 1966, he called a general election to try to consolidate his political position.

■ Cross-reference

Labour's economic policies and the National Plan are covered on page 53.

The general election, 1966

Despite the frustrations over economic policies, Labour achieved a decisive victory in 1966. The new Conservative leader, Edward Heath, had a stiff, awkward manner and found it difficult to connect with voters

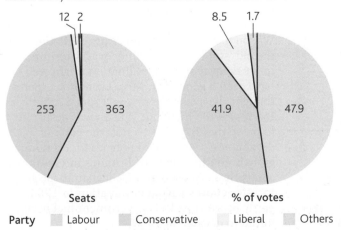

Fig. 2 *General election results, March 1966*

or to enthuse his own party; he was easily outshone by Wilson's superior skill and experience as a campaigner. Labour was still regarded as a fresh start after *'thirteen years of Tory misrule'*. After a low-key election campaign, Labour obtained a large majority of 98 seats. Labour's share of the vote was the biggest since 1945.

The clear-cut election win in 1966 might have been expected to boost Wilson's government with a feeling of greater permanence and confidence. It didn't. Even on election night, Wilson was showing his sense of persecution by refusing to give any interviews to the BBC. He remained very sensitive to criticism from within the Labour Party, often relying on his 'kitchen cabinet' of close personal advisers more than on ministers. For the next three years the Labour government struggled to assert its authority, facing one problem after another in dealing with industrial relations and the economy.

■ **Cross-reference**

The British economy from 1951–64 is discussed on page 23.

■ **Exploring the detail**

Wilson's 'kitchen cabinet'

Wilson relied heavily on a personal team of trusted advisers from outside the government and civil service. In this, he was consciously copying the American model: President Kennedy's White House staff. Wilson's team was dominated by the personality of Marcia Williams, his 'personal political secretary'. Others who took part in the informal discussions in the kitchen at 10 Downing Street included economic advisers and a few 'inner circle' MPs. Many people felt that the 'kitchen cabinet' reinforced Wilson's suspicions of party rivalries and prevented ministers from having access to him.

■ **Key terms**

GDP: Gross Domestic Product, a term used by economists for the total value of a nation's economy.

■ The British economy, 1964–70

Modernisation of the British economy was one of the key priorities for the Labour government. By 1964, it was widely accepted that Britain was lagging behind more advanced economies such as West Germany and Japan. The affluence of the post-war boom was not reflected in productivity or growth rates. Britain's economy was apparently trapped in the cycle of 'stop-go', with bursts of prosperity always leading to inflation, pressure on the pound and regular crises over the balance of payments. Reorganising the economy to break out of this cycle was the aim of Wilson's government in 1964, just as it had been for the Macmillan government before him and for the Heath government after 1970.

Fig. 3 *A relaxed political style: Harold Wilson at Number 10*

When Labour came to power in 1964, there was a serious balance of payments crisis waiting for them. The deficit was £400 million, the worst since the Second World War. The two classic economic solutions to this kind of problem were deflation or devaluation. Wilson did not want to do either. Deflation was the old 'stop-go' approach he was determined to break away from. Devaluation might well have been a good idea. Most economic experts thought the exchange rate in 1964, $2.80 to the £, was too high, but Wilson was desperate to prove that Labour was not 'the party of devaluation'. He wanted policies for economic growth, to catch up with Britain's international competitors. Wilson and Callaghan made a massive effort to avoid devaluation in 1964, partly because Attlee's government had been forced to devalue in 1949.

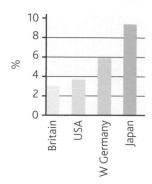

Fig. 4 *Average growth in* **GDP**, *1950–73*

The drive for economic expansion led to the creation of a new department of economic affairs (DEA) led by George Brown. There were two problems with this approach. One was that the new DEA overlapped with the Treasury and the role of the Chancellor, James Callaghan. Civil servants found it difficult to know which boss they should be listening to. The second problem was George Brown.

Key profiles

George Brown

George Brown (1914–85) was deputy leader of the Labour Party from 1960 to 1970. He lost by 88–115 to Harold Wilson in the race to succeed Gaitskell as leader in 1963. Brown had strong support from the trade unions, but many people in the party regarded him as too unpredictable. He had a serious drink problem and frequently clashed with his cabinet colleagues. He was strongly pro-Europe. From 1964, he was in charge of the DEA and Labour's National Plan for the economy but he was moved to the foreign office in 1966. He resigned from the cabinet in 1968 after a blazing row with Wilson.

James Callaghan

'Sunny Jim' Callaghan (1912–2005) was a natural conciliator. He entered parliament as MP for Cardiff in 1945. Harold Wilson appointed him chancellor in 1964; later on, he served as both foreign secretary and home secretary, becoming one of the few men to have held the three top cabinet posts. Associated with the centre-right of the party but with excellent links to the union bosses, Callaghan was the obvious choice to succeed Wilson as prime minister in 1976.

George Brown was impulsive and lacked consistency – partly because of his notorious drink problem. On the other hand, he was an energetic and able politician. A leader in *The Times* suggested that *'Lord George Brown drunk is a better man than the Prime Minister sober'*. Brown's National Plan was agreed after extensive consultations with industry and the unions but it did not have united government support; Brown and the DEA were virtually in competition with the Chancellor, James Callaghan, and the orthodox economists at the Treasury. It is easy to blame Brown for the confusion that followed but the real problem may have been political, caused by Harold Wilson trying to keep key personalities happy rather than pick the best team for the job.

After the 1966 election Brown was moved sideways to the foreign office and the DEA faded away. The government brought in a **prices and incomes policy** to keep down inflation. But there was another sterling crisis in 1966, caused in part by a long and bitter strike by the National Union of Seamen. In 1967, there was a major docks strike, affecting London and Merseyside. This time, the sterling crisis threatened to run out of control. In November 1967, the government decided on devaluation: the pound dropped by 14 per cent to $2.40.

The devaluation crisis damaged Labour's credibility. A few weeks later, Britain's second application to join the EEC was rejected. Just as in 1963, President de Gaulle played a decisive role. The application to join the EEC had been made above all on economic grounds. Wilson was lukewarm about Europe and much of his party hated the idea of joining. Having the application rejected hard on the heels of the devaluation crisis made the government's economic policies look futile.

Key terms

Prices and incomes policy: government intervention to set limits on price rises and to call for wage restraint in negotiations between unions and employers. In 1966, the Wilson government set up the Prices and Incomes Board to implement this.

Cross-reference

Britain's application to join the EEC is covered on page 22 and on page 46.

In fact, the economic situation improved markedly from this low point. Callaghan's replacement as chancellor was Roy Jenkins, who had been strongly in favour of devaluation in 1964. Jenkins used deflationary methods. He raised taxes and tightened up government spending in all areas of the economy, giving top priority to improving the balance of payments. These tough measures made the government unpopular but, by 1969, Jenkins had achieved a balance of payments surplus. The improvement in the economic situation from 1969 was a key factor in making Labour confident of victory in the 1970 general election. By that time, however, Labour had also run into serious problems in industrial relations.

The Labour government and the trade unions

One of the key elements in the post-war consensus was the influence of the trade unions. Since the war, all governments, Conservative as well as Labour, had seen it as essential to maintain full employment and to keep the unions happy. In opinion polls in the 1960s, nearly 60 per cent of people said they had a favourable view of the unions. Both Macmillan and Wilson had relied on union cooperation when they brought in their prices and incomes policies. In 1964, Wilson made the trade unionist Frank Cousins minister of technology. Wilson also relied on keeping a good relationship with the TUC.

In 1966 and 1967, this previously cosy relationship began to fall apart. The big strikes by the seamen and the dockers caused massive problems for the government. These strikes also showed how the old-style union bosses were losing some of their control. A lot of strikes started with **'wildcat' strikes** by local activists who would not take orders from the top. The Conservative opposition under Edward Heath announced a policy they called *A Fair Deal at Work*. Wilson and his new employment minister, Barbara Castle, started planning to use the law to limit unofficial strikes, even though this would cause uproar on the Labour left.

Key terms

'Wildcat' strikes: sudden, unofficial local disputes begun without reference to the national leadership.

A closer look

In Place of Strife, 1969

Barbara Castle was a fiery personality from the Bevanite wing of the party. She believed strongly in a powerful trade union movement but she was also convinced of the need for it to act responsibly. In January 1969, Castle produced her white paper, *In Place of Strife*. In many ways, Castle's policy proposals would strengthen the unions in dealing with employers, but three aspects of her plans were seen as too radical:

- There was to be a 28-day 'cooling off' period before a strike went ahead.
- The government could impose a settlement when unions were in dispute with each other in 'demarcation disputes'.
- Strike ballots could be imposed.

An industrial relations court would be able to prosecute people who broke the rules. Voters liked these proposals and Labour's standing in the polls went up. The unions and the Labour left hated them. There was a storm of protest from unions and MPs, including the powerful boss of the National Union of Mineworkers (NUM), Joe Gormley, and the Home Secretary, James Callaghan. At least 50 Labour MPS were ready to rebel. People with long memories warned of a party split as bad as the one that had destroyed Ramsay MacDonald in 1931.

The row went on for months until Wilson gave in. Mrs Castle was left high and dry. In June 1969, the TUC negotiated a face-saving compromise but everyone knew it was really a humiliating climb-down by the government. Reform of the unions was left to be tackled by later Conservative governments in ways much more damaging to the unions than *In Place of Strife* would have been.

Activity

Creative thinking

Imagine you are a political adviser to the Labour government in 1969. Working in groups, devise a list of negative points that support the case for abandoning *In Place of Strife*; and a list of reasons why it is essential to push the policy through.

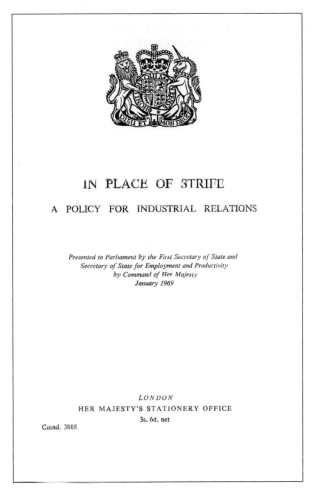

IN PLACE OF STRIFE

A POLICY FOR INDUSTRIAL RELATIONS

Presented to Parliament by the First Secretary of State and Secretary of State for Employment and Productivity by Command of Her Majesty January 1969

LONDON
HER MAJESTY'S STATIONERY OFFICE
3s. 6d. net

Cmnd. 3888

Fig. 5 The white paper *In Place of Strife*, 1969

By 1969, the Labour Party had seen its new version of British socialism collapse. An economic theory that could not be made to work had been at the heart of Wilson's message in 1964. Abandoning that message left an ideological gap that neither Wilson, nor Callaghan, nor Foot, nor Kinnock were able to fill.

*From Pimlott, B., **Harold Wilson**, 1992*

The row over *In Place of Strife* was one of many setbacks for the Wilson government in 1969. There were also serious problems over Rhodesia and Northern Ireland. Even so, Wilson's political situation was looking much stronger in 1970, especially as the economy improved. When Wilson decided to call a general election for April 1970, he was very confident of winning.

Labour's defeat in the general election of 1970

At the time, the victory of Edward Heath and the Conservatives in 1970 was a stunning surprise. The Wilson government had apparently come through its difficult times in 1967–69. The new chancellor, Roy Jenkins, was credited with achieving economic and financial stability, allowing Labour to call the election at a time of its own choosing. Harold Wilson was considered to be a master campaigner, far more experienced and more popular than Heath. Perhaps the result should not have been so unexpected. Beneath the surface, Heath had greater strengths than he was given credit for and Labour's position in 1970 was actually quite fragile.

Between 1966 and 1969, Wilson's government had suffered a series of setbacks and real or perceived failures. The Conservatives were consistently ahead in the opinion polls throughout this time, even though Heath's personal approval ratings were not impressive. Although Labour's polls improved sharply in the spring of 1970, this did not reflect a complete turnaround. The Conservatives did quite well in the local government elections. Special polls in the key marginal constituencies showed a narrow Tory lead. Edward Heath told anyone in his party who would listen to him that he was confident of winning.

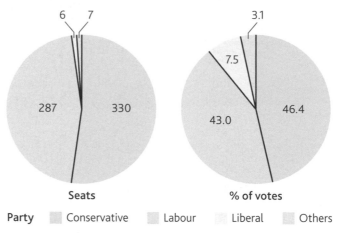

Fig. 6 *General election results, June 1970*

Cross-reference

More detail on Enoch Powell's stance on immigration and the 'rivers of blood' speech can be found on pages 70–71.

Activity

Group discussion

Make lists of the reasons why:

1 the Conservatives won in 1970

2 Labour lost in 1970.

Select three factors in each list in order of importance.

Activity

Class debate

Make a list of the arguments for and against the view: 'Between 1964 and 1970, Harold Wilson's government squandered its opportunity to make Labour the natural party of government in Britain'

One feature of Edward Heath's determination (some would say obstinacy) in the 1970 campaign is the way he resisted pressure from within his own party to make immigration an election issue. Heath had sacked Enoch Powell from the shadow cabinet in 1968 after his 'rivers of blood' speech. He refused to let Powell take part in the election campaign, even though he would have clearly have boosted the Conservative vote in several key constituencies. The immigration issue did not go away, however (nor did the problem of Enoch Powell) and tensions over immigration remained very divisive within the Conservative Party after Heath came to power.

Heath felt his election victory would enable him to run a strong government, committed to modernising Britain. He did not know, nor did anyone else, that he had come to power just in time for the economic and political earthquake that was going to hit Britain in 1973–74 as the long post-war boom came to an end.

Summary question

Assess the extent to which the Wilson government achieved its objectives by 1970.

6 Political crisis and the end of the post-war boom, 1970–75

'By gum, lads, I wouldn't be in Ted's shoes for all the cans in Thatcher's cupboard !'

Fig. 1 *Harold Wilson and his loyal cabinet colleagues at the time of the Conservative leadership contest in 1975, according to Emmwood of the Daily Mail (left to right: Tony Benn, Michael Foot, Peter Shore, the Prime Minister, Jim Callaghan, Denis Healey)*

In this chapter you will learn about:

■ the aims and policies of the Heath government, 1970–74

■ the problems in the economy and the impact of the oil price crisis of 1973

■ the circumstances in which Labour returned to power in 1974.

From first to last, Heath was trying to breathe new life, economic vitality especially, into the post-war settlement. In 1973, he declared: 'The alternative to expansion is not, as some seem to suppose, an England of quiet market towns and trains puffing peacefully between villages. The alternative is slums, dangerous roads, old factories cramped schools and stunted lives.' There spoke a Grade 1 listed Post-war Settler. When he went to see the Queen on 4th March 1974, Heath was not alone. The post-war consensus, too, went with him to resign.

1   *From Hennessy, P.,* **The Prime Minister**, *2000*

Edward Heath's place in history was shaped by the events of 1973–75. In those years, he achieved success in his determined efforts to secure British membership of the EEC, and seeing that confirmed by the

Britain, 1970–75

1970 New Conservative government under Edward Heath

1971 Decimalisation of the currency

1972 'Bloody Sunday' in Northern Ireland

1973 OPEC oil crisis

British entry to the EEC

Miners' strike and imposition of three-day week

1974 February general election and fall of Heath

Collapse of Sunningdale Agreement for Northern Ireland

Inconclusive October general election

1975 Victory for 'yes' vote in EEC referendum

Heath replaced as party leader by Mrs Thatcher

Fig. 1 *The problems of dealing with Northern Ireland: Edward Heath in conflict with an Irish lephrechaun*

1975 referendum. At the same time, his career ended in failure with a massive economic and political crisis from 1973 culminating in electoral defeat in 1974 and his replacement as party leader by Mrs Thatcher in 1975. History is usually written by the winning side: after 1975, Heath's reputation took a battering from supporters of Thatcherism who repudiated much of his legacy, especially on Europe. Heath also became notorious for the 'Long Sulk' that lasted from his downfall in 1975 to the demise of Margaret Thatcher in 1990.

In fact, Heath was a formidable politician. He was a prime minister with a clear and detailed programme of policies for the modernisation of Britain. He came close to success in his attempt to secure a political solution in Northern Ireland. But Heath's bad luck was that his time in office coincided with the end of the long post-war boom in 1973 and the economic and political crisis that followed. What happened to Britain between 1970 and 1975 marks a time of transition from the era of Attlee, Macmillan and the post-war consensus to the era of Thatcher and Blair. Mrs Thatcher, in particular, hangs over the years 1970–75 like a dark cloud; it is hard to reach a judgement about the Heath years without first taking a decisive view of the impact of Thatcherism.

■ The Conservative government, 1970–73

Edward Heath always claimed to be the only person in British politics who was not surprised by his election victory in 1970. Heath had already been leader of the opposition for five years, longer than any Conservative leader since the war apart from Churchill. He was often perceived to be rather stiff and prickly in dealing with people and had been overshadowed by the more fluent political skills of Harold Wilson. Like Wilson, he had been educated at state schools; he came from a different social background from the Old Etonians who had previously dominated the Conservatives. Unlike Wilson, he was never seen as devious or given to plots and intrigue; many of his colleagues regarded him as too honest for his own good, not skilful enough in pleasing political allies. Heath was good at policies but not at politics.

Edward Heath's cabinet included a number of able politicians, not all of them conspicuous for their loyalty to the Prime Minister. Among those who strongly supported Heath were the Chancellor, Anthony Barber, the Northern Ireland Secretary, Willie Whitelaw and the Employment Minister, Jim Prior. Those who were lukewarm about Heath's economic policies included Sir Keith Joseph and the Education Secretary, Margaret Thatcher.

■ Key profile

Margaret Thatcher

Margaret Hilda Roberts (born 1925) from Grantham in Lincolnshire married a wealthy businessman, Denis Thatcher. She became MP for Finchley in 1959. She gained her first cabinet post in 1970, as education secretary in Edward Heath's government. In 1975, she emerged as the surprise candidate challenging Heath for the party leadership. She became prime minister after the 1979 general election and dominated British politics for the next eleven years.

Heath was well prepared for government. He had spent his time in opposition developing detailed policies, especially on industrial relations and economic modernisation. For another of his main aims, securing

Britain's entry to the EEC, he knew the issues inside out, having been the chief negotiator in 1961–63. In January 1970, the Conservatives held a conference at Selsdon Park to approve Heath's policy programme. The Selsdon meeting set out a number of tough approaches to economic problems, many of them influenced by the ideas of Sir Keith Joseph, such as allowing inefficient businesses to go bankrupt and not prop them up with state aid.

Key profile

Sir Keith Joseph

Joseph (1918–94) was Conservative MP for Leeds North East from 1956 to 1987. He held posts in the cabinets of four prime ministers between 1961 and 1986. He was a deep thinker on economic policy, with strong views on the need for free-market policies. He was considered to be a candidate to rival Edward Heath in 1975 but eventually gave his support to Margaret Thatcher instead. He had much influence on her early policy decisions from 1979.

Because of his famous 'U-turn' in 1972, a myth took hold that Heath had too easily given up on his aims and objectives, that he lacked a clear sense of direction. This was not the case. Heath's government was to some extent blown off course by economic circumstances, but Heath's political aims, including a belief in 'One Nation Toryism' and the post-war consensus, remained consistent. The Selsdon Park programme had never been intended to be an all out repudiation of consensus politics.

In the end, the fate of Heath's government was decided by economic issues, above all by the consequences of the 1973 OPEC oil price crisis and the miners' strike of 1974. His first priorities, however, were British entry into the EEC and what to do about the 'troubles' in Northern Ireland.

Negotiating the terms of Britain's entry into Europe was a relatively easy issue. Heath's main political task was to gain parliamentary approval. There were doubters in the Conservative Party, especially those who believed strongly in the Commonwealth. The Labour Party was also badly divided on the issue of Europe. There were committed pro-marketeers, such as Roy Jenkins, but the Labour left was mostly hostile. The party leadership was neither for nor against but was obsessed with party unity. In the end, 69 rebel Labour MPs helped the Conservative government to win the decisive Commons vote. The Labour Party was badly split. Wilson could only keep a semblance of unity by promising a national referendum as and when Labour came back to power. Heath's persistence had at last brought Britain into Europe but a cloud of uncertainty still hung over the issues.

The incoming Heath government inherited huge problems in Northern Ireland. There was an explosion of sectarian violence, the British army was struggling to keep the peace and the political situation in Belfast was close to complete breakdown. Edward Heath's government made strenuous attempts to find a political solution. These efforts came close to success in the Sunningdale Agreement of 1973 but ultimately failed. It is impossible to know whether the Sunningdale Agreement would have established a workable solution to the problems of Northern Ireland if Heath had not been distracted by the economic and political crisis at home. At the time, however, it did seem that Heath's typically tough and persistent negotiating style might well have achieved success but for the bad timing of the economic crisis that undermined him.

Cross-reference

An explanation of 'One Nation Tories' can be found on page 2.

Exploring the detail

The U-turn

Edward Heath's 'U-turn' in 1971–72 was his retreat from the free-enterprise economic principles his government had tried to follow from 1970. Heath's desire to maintain full employment led him to give state aid to key industries, especially Rolls Royce. This policy was heavily criticised by Enoch Powell, Sir Keith Joseph and, later, Margaret Thatcher, all of whom opposed state intervention in industry.

Cross-reference

The foreign policy aspects of British entry to the EEC are covered in Chapter 8.

Britain's previous applications in 1961 and 1967 are outlined on page 78.

The issue of Northern Ireland, 1969–74

Fig. 3 *British paratroopers in the streets of Derry, 1972*

Since late 1968, the civil rights movement in Northern Ireland had challenged the old 'Stormont Ascendancy' – the domination of the Belfast parliament and the whole socio-economic system in Northern Ireland by Protestant Unionism. In 1969 and early in 1970, there was serious sectarian violence. The Wilson government sent in the British Army to keep the peace. Northern Ireland had not been much noticed by people on the 'mainland' since Ireland was partitioned in 1922. Now it was centre stage.

Since 1912, the Ulster Unionists had always been part of the Conservative & Unionist Party but now Heath felt he had to force the Unionist politicians in Belfast to accept change. At first, Heath backed the Belfast government's leader, Brian Faulkner. In 1971, Heath went along with Faulkner's policy of internment, locking up terror suspects without trial, but the policy was ineffective as a security measure and it alienated the nationalist communities. The British Army came to be regarded as an enemy occupying power. Then, on 'Bloody Sunday' in January 1972, attempts to control a demonstration in Derry ended with British soldiers firing live ammunition. Thirteen civilians were killed.

The worsening situation led Heath to suspend the Stormont parliament and to bring in direct rule from Westminster. Heath's policy was not only to try to defeat the IRA, as the unionists and loyalists wanted, but to look for a permanent political solution. In 1973, Heath and Willie Whitelaw achieved the Sunningdale Agreement, a complex plan for a power-sharing government. Extremists, both republicans and loyalists, denounced Sunningdale as a sell-out, but there seemed a good chance of achieving a settlement.

The prospects of a settlement, however, were undermined by political crisis in mainland Britain – first the miners' strike and then the February 1974 election in which Heath lost power. Loyalist opponents of power sharing organised an Ulster workers' strike that brought the whole province to a standstill. The Sunningdale Agreement collapsed and the cycle of sectarian violence and political stalemate went on for another 24 years.

Willie Whitelaw

Whitelaw (1918–99) was an old-style upper-class Conservative with centrist ideas similar to those of Harold Macmillan. He was appointed Northern Ireland secretary in 1971 and was a highly effective negotiator in the talks over power-sharing at Sunningdale and afterwards. In December 1973, he was suddenly moved to the department of employment in an attempt to get a compromise solution to the miners' strike. In the 1980s, to the surprise of many observers, he became a loyal deputy prime minister to Mrs Thatcher.

The problems of economic modernisation, 1970–73

It is ironic that it was economic issues and industrial relations that brought Edward Heath to political disaster. This was an area of policy in which Heath was better prepared than any post-war Conservative leader. He had a genuine commitment to economic modernisation and had put together unusually detailed plans to make it happen. But almost from the time he came to power, Heath's government ran into difficulties over the economy.

Heath had hoped his first choice as chancellor, the able and experienced Iain Macleod, might do for his government what Roy Jenkins had done for Wilson's, but Macleod's sudden death in 1970, at the age of 56, removed a key asset from his team. The new chancellor, Anthony Barber, introduced tax cuts and cuts in public spending. One small but controversial aspect of these cuts was the ending of free school milk. The row over this was the first time the then little-known minister of education, Mrs Thatcher, came into the public eye. The 'Barber boom' began, with a rapid rise in wage inflation.

Many people blamed the steep rise in wages on the power of the unions and their willingness to hold the country to ransom through strike action. Inflation was not accompanied by economic growth. Unemployment actually went up, something that was highly unusual at the same time as inflation. This led to the invention of a new word, '**stagflation**'. The government had wanted to reduce state intervention in industry but now felt compelled to take action. The prestigious engineering firm, Rolls Royce, had to be nationalised in 1971. Government money was poured in to prevent Upper Clyde Shipbuilders going to the wall. This was the famous 'U-turn'.

In 1971, the government also brought in the Industrial Relations Act. This was very similar to Barbara Castle's proposals in her white paper, *In Place of Strife*. It set up an Industrial Relations Court and provided for strike ballots and a 'cooling off period' before official strikes could begin. The policy did not work as expected. Both the Trades Union Congress (TUC) and the Confederation of British Industry (CBI) were opposed to it. The Industrial Relations Court proved ineffective in dealing with disputes. For the first time since the 1930s, unemployment in Britain rose above one million. There were major strikes in 1972: by the miners in January and by the railwaymen three months later.

The miners' strike lasted six weeks, at a time of harsh winter weather. The strike virtually stopped the movement of coal around the country. Industry nationwide was placed on a three-day week to conserve energy supplies. The NUM leader, Joe Gormley, was a moderate Lancastrian with

■ **Key terms**

Stagflation: a word invented by economists to describe the unusual combination of inflation and stagnant economic growth (which often produces unemployment) occurring at the same time.

■ **Cross-reference**

For Barbara Castle's *In Place of Strife*, refer back to page 54.

Fig. 3 *Lancashire versus Yorkshire: Joe Gormley and Arthur Scargill, 1972*

■ Cross-reference

The later conflict between the miners and the government is covered on pages 111–2.

■ **Key terms**

Parliamentary private secretary (PPS): a job carried out by a junior MP. The main role of a PPS is to keep the PM in touch with backbench opinion.

OPEC: the Organisation of Petroleum Exporting Countries, a cartel formed under the leadership of Saudi Arabia to protect the interests of oil-exporting countries from the power of the advanced industrial economies. The OPEC countries agreed to fix levels of production in order to prevent prices from falling too low when oil supplies were plentiful.

■ **Exploring the detail**

The three-day week

On 13 December 1973, the government imposed the three-day week on business and industry in order to conserve electricity supplies in view of the threatened miners' strike. The order for the three-day week was to come into force on 1 January 1974.

■ Cross-reference

For more on the three-day week, see page 73.

a good sense of public relations. He negotiated a generous wage settlement, accompanied by other concessions. The strike looked like a clear victory for the miners against the employers and against the government. It encouraged many left-wingers to see industrial action as a political weapon, not just a way of bargaining for better pay and conditions. It also encouraged a right-wing backlash against excessive union power.

The post-war consensus was fraying at the edges in 1972 but it is often forgotten that the government seemed to be making a good recovery in 1973. In *Finest and Darkest Hours*, Kevin Jefferys emphasises the improvements in Heath' position:

■ There was wide support for stages one and two of his prices and incomes policy: limits on wage increases imposed by the government's pay board in line with rises in the cost of living.

■ The number of working days lost through strike action was cut in half compared with 1972.

■ There was a lot of government investment to boost the economy.

■ Unemployment dropped sharply, to about 500,000.

■ North Sea oil was due to come on stream in the next few years.

■ The government started to become more popular, drawing about level with Labour in the opinion polls.

'If no horrors occur', Heath's **parliamentary private secretary (PPS)** Douglas Hurd wrote in his diary in autumn 1973, *'this time next year might be best to have an election'*. But horrors did indeed occur.

The economic and political crisis of 1973–74

The end of the long post-war boom was symbolised by the oil price crisis of 1973 and the energy crisis that followed. This economic crisis then became a political crisis when the coal strike turned into a confrontation between the NUM and the government. It ceased to be an industrial dispute about wages and conditions and became a struggle to decide 'who governs Britain?' The answer to this question turned out to be: 'not Edward Heath'. The result was a lengthy period of political turmoil, leading to two general elections in the same year – the first time since the great constitutional crisis of 1910–11.

The trigger for the economic crisis in October 1973 was the Yom Kippur War in the Middle East, the third Arab–Israeli war since the formation of Israel in 1948. The war prompted **OPEC** to declare an oil embargo. Exports suddenly stopped. The price rocketed up to four times the usual levels. Long queues formed outside petrol stations. This was the context for the NUM to demand a huge new pay rise in November 1973. At a time when Heath was deeply concerned about oil supplies, about the economy, about his prices and incomes policy and about the talks over a political settlement in Northern Ireland. In December, the government announced the imposition of the three-day week. The stage was set for a dramatic struggle between the NUM and the government.

■ **A closer look**

Who governs Britain? The government against the miners, 1974

The NUM had a special place in the trade union movement since the General Strike in 1926. The dirty and dangerous job miners did was guaranteed to gain a lot of public sympathy. Many people felt the NUM had a good case for improved pay and conditions to match recent rises in other industries, even though the NUM had won a big pay award after their 1972 strike. The victory in 1972 had also convinced many in the union that its industrial muscle was strong enough to get its own way, not just against the employers but against the government.

The government was equally determined. Joe Gormley was a moderate but the leaders of the NUM also included a communist, Mick McGahey, and the radical leader of the Yorkshire miners, Arthur Scargill. There was a sense that the NUM was directly challenging the power of a democratically elected government. Heath still hoped for compromise. He moved Willie Whitelaw from the Northern Ireland office to be minister of employment so he could use his famous powers of persuasion on Joe Gormley. This failed. In January 1974, the NUM called a national strike.

There was massive support for the strike among the miners, even from moderate areas like Nottinghamshire. Heath and the government were not willing to give up on phase 3 of the prices and incomes policy. The shortage of coal, together with rising oil prices led to a balance-of-payments crisis. Heath called a general election for 28 February 1974, intending the central issue of the election to be 'who governs Britain?' For most of the campaign, the opinion polls favoured the Conservatives but the final result showed a small swing against them. Labour won five more seats than the Tories. Indirectly, the miners' strike had indeed brought down the government.

Cross-reference

The career and significance of Arthur Scargill is covered further in Chapter 9.

The general election result of February 1974 was very inconclusive, leading to a 'hung parliament' in which no party had an overall majority. This reinforced the idea that 1974 was a political crisis not just an economic one. The two-party system had not produced the usual clear-cut outcome. Labour was the biggest single party, by five seats, but it was by no means certain that Wilson would lead the next government.

One key feature of this election was the increase in representation for other parties. The Liberal Party had continued its comeback from the political dead and now had 14 seats. Nationalist parties from Scotland, Wales and Northern Ireland had 23 seats. If Edward Heath could gain the support of some of these other parties he would be able to continue as prime minister. If the Ulster Unionists had continued their traditional support for the Conservative Party, Heath would have won anyway. But times had changed, symbolised by the fact that Enoch Powell had now joined the Unionists and had campaigned fiercely against Heath. For a few days, Heath attempted to make a deal with the Liberals but failed. On 4 March 1974, Harold Wilson was back in power.

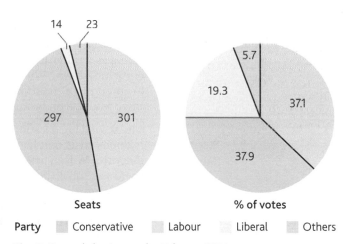

Fig. 5 General election results, February 1974

Creative thinking

Write a letter to be sent to the editor of the *Daily Telegraph* in February 1974 to express the view that Edward Heath was personally to blame for the defeat of Conservative Party in the general election.

■ Key terms

Working majority: enough votes in the House of Commons to defeat all other parties even if they combine together. If this is not possible, the situation is known as a 'hung parliament'. 1974 was the first time there had been a hung parliament in modern times.

After February 1974, things could never be the same again. The outcome of the election gave Unionists in Northern Ireland a veto over any constitutional changes, and saw advances for the Scottish Nationalists. Future governments would be confronted with threats to the stability of Britain from the non-English parts of the United Kingdom. The success of the Liberals also confirmed the new volatility of the electorate and the weakening of the two-party system. Above all, uncertain times lay ahead for the economy. What began to look like the 'Golden Age' in the 1950s and 1960s was fading in the memory.

2   *From Jefferys, K., Finest and Darkest Hours, 2002*

■ Labour's return to power, 1974

When the Labour government came back into power in March 1974, Harold Wilson was in a much less promising position than he had been in 1964. There was little chance of having a free hand in parliament because Labour had to depend on support from other parties to get legislation through parliament. The economic situation was awful. The Labour Party was less united than ever. Wilson himself was older, less energetic and less certain of the way he wanted to govern. He was anxious to call another election as soon as possible in order to obtain a **working majority**.

In 1974, Wilson planned to have a less frenetic, less personalised style. *'No presidential nonsense this time,'* he told one of his close advisers, Bernard Donoghue, *'no first hundred days, and no beer and sandwiches at No 10 to solve crises.'* He was going to be *'a sweeper in defence'*, he said, *'not a striker in attack'*.

Wilson had some urgent decisions to take in March 1974. The first was how to carry on in parliament: by making a deal with the Liberals, or by acting as a minority government, effectively daring the other parties to bring him down? Wilson decided on the second option. He didn't want to enter into a coalition and make a lot of compromises and he was sure there would soon be another election anyway.

The second big question was what to do about the economic and industrial relations crisis that had caused Heath's fall and which Labour now inherited. Wilson acted quickly. The Industrial Relations Act and the pay board were abolished. The trade unions were sent a clear message that the government was not looking for any confrontations. Wilson's new chancellor, Denis Healey, issued two budgets, first in March and then in July, aiming to deal with the economic crisis without annoying the unions.

By now the tanks of the unions were fanning out over open country as they faced Harold Wilson, a general they had already once defeated, commanding an army that was divided and under siege. Michael Foot, at the department of employment, resembled a baron in the Wars of the Roses: one could never be sure which side he was on. The miners won another 22 per cent pay rise and weekly wages nationally rose by 33 per cent in 1975.

3   *From Annan, N., Our Age: The Generation that made Post-war Britain, 1990*

In October 1974, Wilson felt safe enough to call a new election. Voters still associated Heath and the Conservatives with the three-day week and conflict with the miners; they were not much impressed with Heath's new idea that there should be a government of national unity. Wilson won his working majority, but only just. Labour gained 18 seats. The Conservatives lost 21. Labour's overall majority was only three, but their lead over the Conservatives was 42.

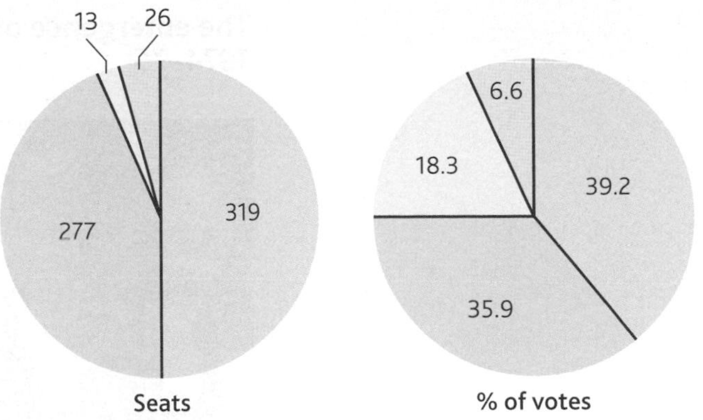

It seemed to many observers that Wilson's main aim in his second term was self-preservation and the avoidance of disasters. There was nothing like the desire for innovation and modernisation that had been there in 1964. This obsession with domestic politics and party unity showed through in the EEC referendum that Wilson called in 1975. Wilson had been against British membership in 1972. Now he let the referendum campaign go ahead, more as a device to stop splits in the Labour Party than because of any deep commitment on his part.

By 1975, voter support for Britain staying in the EEC was much stronger than before. The economic mess the country was in seemed to prove Britain needed to be in, for its own economic survival. Most of the press was strongly in favour. The 'yes' campaign was well financed by business supporters. Politicians at the head of the 'yes' campaign, such as Edward Heath and Roy Jenkins, made a bigger impression on public opinion than those leading the 'no' campaign, such as Michael Foot and Enoch Powell.

Fig. 6 *General election results, October 1974*

Party: Conservative Labour Liberal Others

Seats: 13, 26, 277, 319

% of votes: 6.6, 18.3, 39.2, 35.9

Cross-reference

Michael Foot's career as Labour leader from 1979 to 1983 is covered in Chapter 9.

■ **Key profile**

Michael Foot

Michael Foot (born 1913) was a popular and respected left-winger, a great admirer (and biographer) of Aneurin Bevan. He was a talented journalist, with a regular column in the *Daily Herald*. He was thought of as a radical, whose natural home was always on the back benches. His first experience of being in the government was as Wilson's minister of employment in 1974. He strongly supported CND and he was fervently opposed to Britain joining the EEC. He became leader of the Labour Party in 1980, after Labour's defeat by Mrs Thatcher.

17 million voted 'yes' in July 1975; 8 million voted 'no'. Britain's membership was confirmed. Wilson had successfully avoided a Labour split. In the years that followed, Europe was no longer such a divisive issue for the Labour Party. Ironically, it would be the Conservative Party that suffered more and more from divisions over Europe, especially in the later stages of the reign of Mrs Thatcher.

 Activity

Revision exercise

Use the evidence in this chapter and the evidence in Chapter 5 to write a paragraph explaining the reasons why Britain's membership of the EEC came about between 1971 and 1975 but not before.

Did you know?

Enoch Powell was sacked from the Conservative shadow cabinet by Edward Heath in 1968 after making a speech on the dangers of immigration in Birmingham. This speech caused a public sensation and was known ever afterwards as the 'rivers of blood' speech. Powell got a lot of public support but was kept on the fringes of Heath's Conservative government. In 1974, he fought the election as an Ulster Unionist, directly attacking Heath and calling for the Conservatives to lose power. His position as a political outsider meant that he was not as effective in the EEC referendum campaign as he could otherwise have been.

The emergence of Margaret Thatcher as Conservative leader, 1974–75

Fig. 7 *New Conservative woman: Margaret Thatcher outside the House of Commons after winning the party leadership, February 1975*

Some historical events seem different afterwards from the way they did at the time. In 1975, nobody knew or guessed what a dominating political figure Margaret Thatcher was going to turn into. Her rise was also totally unexpected; nobody had previously considered her to be a potential leader. The Margaret Thatcher who emerged as Edward Heath's challenger in 1974–75 looked different, sounded different and had many different ideas from the prime minister who dominated British politics in the 1980s.

Cross-reference

The political dominance of Mrs Thatcher as prime minister is covered in Chapter 9.

Heath seemed to be in a strong position, despite having lost three of the four elections he fought against Harold Wilson in eight years. All the shadow cabinet made it clear they would not run against him. Several backbench MPs, however, were determined to force a leadership contest. The problem was finding a candidate. Enoch Powell was no longer a Conservative. Keith Joseph thought about running but then withdrew. This left an opportunity for Mrs Thatcher, who would have supported Joseph because she agreed with his ideas on the free-market economy. Her promises on policy were generally to the right of Heath and Macmillan (she was sympathetic to the monetarist policies put forward by Powell and Joseph) but she was certainly not yet anti-Europe. Later in 1975 she worked enthusiastically for a 'yes' vote in the EEC referendum.

Cross-reference

Sir Keith Joseph is profiled on page 59.

Monetarism is outlined on pages 86 and 90.

Mrs Thatcher seemed to have little chance of toppling Heath. She had only brief experience in the cabinet, as minister for education. Many of the people who did support her only did so reluctantly, because there was nobody else in the frame. Mrs Thatcher did not win because of a sudden surge of positive support for her, or her specific policies, but she and her campaign manager, Airey Neave, cleverly exploited the sense that things were going badly wrong, both with the party and with the country.

Key profile

Airey Neave

Airey Neave (1916–79) was a war hero, famous for escaping from the high security POW camp at Colditz Castle in 1942. He was on the right wing of the Conservative Party and a strong supporter of Ulster unionism. He was Mrs Thatcher's campaign manager in her leadership bid in 1975 and became an influential adviser afterwards. He was murdered by an IRA car bomb in 1979.

Another factor was Heath's inability to win over the doubters. He underrated Thatcher, and, even if he had campaigned urgently, he was not very good at schmoozing. Some Conservatives were saying 'anyone but Ted'; others were persuaded by Mrs Thatcher's obvious self-confidence and conviction. Mrs Thatcher won 130 votes on the first ballot. Heath got only 119 and immediately resigned. New candidates, who had not run before because of their loyalty to Heath, emerged but Mrs Thatcher had gained too much momentum to be stopped. She got 146 votes on the second ballot; her nearest rival, Willie Whitelaw, got 79. To the amazement of the party and the media, the Conservatives now had a leader who might become Britain's first-ever woman prime minister.

After her victory, Mrs Thatcher got the support of most of the party. Willie Whitelaw became a loyal deputy prime minister. Most of Heath's shadow cabinet stayed on. According to Mrs Thatcher, she offered Edward Heath a senior position but he turned it down; Heath's autobiography states firmly she did not. He withdrew to the sidelines, in a huff that lasted fifteen years. It was some consolation to him that his most important policy achievement, joining the EEC, was vindicated in June 1975 when there were 19 million yes votes in the EEC referendum held by the Labour government. The Heath era was over and the Thatcher era was about to begin.

Summary question

Why did the British economy face such difficulties in the early 1970s?

7 British society, 1964–75

Fig. 1 *Meat porters in London demonstrating support for Enoch Powell after his 'rivers of blood' speech, April 1968*

The social fabric had been kept intact because of high and advancing living standards for the population as a whole. But evidence mounted up in the 1960s that economic pressures were adding to social tensions. Rising inflation was accompanied by growing unemployment. By 1973, it was clear that the economic problems of Britain were having more general consequences. Britain seemed to have become 'the new sick man of Europe'. In retaliation for declining living standards, the unions replied with collective industrial power. The background to the February 1974 election was a widening mood of protest, a reluctance to accept traditional disciplines, and trade union pressure for enormous wage rises.

1

From Morgan, K. O., The Twentieth Century, 1984

Britain in 1964 was a country just beginning to get used to the idea of the 'affluent society'. The new Labour government was determined to get away from the old 'Establishment' ways. There was a lot talk about new beginnings and the 'white heat of the technological revolution'. Of course, a lot of the social changes now being noticed had already started in the middle of the 1950s; in much of the Britain of 1964 continuity was more apparent than change.

There were certainly signs of changing attitudes, especially in respect of young people and women, at least the middle class, educated ones. The respectful, deferential society of the post-war era was giving way to a more open society, one that was more concerned with individual freedom of expression, more likely to go on demonstrations. There was also a vocal backlash against it from social conservatives who disapproved of the 'breakdown in morality'. The Sixties was the time of the generation gap.

The old two-party Britain found all this difficult to cope with. The divisions within the main parties widened in the 1970s. More and more people began turning away from traditional loyalties. This was reflected in the increased voting support for other parties and extra-parliamentary pressure groups. The Liberals and the nationalist parties in Scotland, Wales and Northern Ireland all gained ground in the two-election year of 1974. Organisations like Shelter and Oxfam came to prominence. 1968 showed the power of protest demonstrations. The environmental movement took off. All this was reflected in the harder edges of culture.

A closer look

Demographic change, 1964–75

Three key factors affected the patterns of population growth and movement in Britain after 1964. One was the continued influx of immigrants. Another factor was the accelerated shift of population to the new housing developments and council estates that were replacing the old urban areas affected by slum clearance and urban redevelopment. This process had begun before 1964, of course, but it was in the late 1960s and the 1970s that its effects were most apparent. The third factor was the impact of road transport and private car ownership. New roads frequently had the effect of fragmenting established communities; and commuting by car accelerated the 'flight to the suburbs' and the spread of urban blight in the inner cities.

Fig. 2 Urban population in Britain, 1971

Table 1 *Population statistics*

Year	Total UK population (millions)
1960	52.4
1970	55.6
1980	56.3

The population of Britain increased from 50 million in 1951 to 56 million by 1975. It is important to note, however, that this increase was not steady or consistent. There were periods of faster growth and periods of stagnation. In the 1970s, population statistics showed no year-on-year increases; in the three years from 1975 to 1978 the population actually began to fall. These fluctuations in the population reflected the economic and social background of the time.

■ Social trends, 1964–75

The impact of immigration

Table 2 *Growth of ethnic groups in Britain, 1951–2001*

Year	Caribbean	Indian	Pakistani	Bangladeshi
1951	28,000	31,000	10,000	2,000
1971	548,000	375,000	119,000	23,000
1991	501,000	840,000	477,000	164,000
2001	529,000	984,000	675,000	257,000

The continuing influx of immigrants from the New Commonwealth meant that the social tensions experienced in the late 1950s and early 1960s did not go away. In opposition, the Labour Party had attacked Conservative policies aimed at limiting immigration but in 1965, now in power, the Wilson government put forward a white paper proposing further controls on immigration. At the same time, the government attempted to outlaw race discrimination and set up the Race Relations Board to implement this.

In February 1968, alarm over the sudden influx of Kenyan Asians prompted the government to pass a new Commonwealth Immigration Act, limiting the right of return to Britain for non-white Commonwealth citizens. It was the furore over the arrival of the Kenyan Asians that prompted Enoch Powell to make his notorious 'rivers of blood' speech in April 1968.

■ **Cross-reference**

The importance of immigration as a social and political issue is covered on pages 28–29.

The political impact of Powell's views on immigration is covered in Chapter 6.

Fig. 3 *Asian immigrants in a northern town, late 1960s*

Here is one of my constituents, a decent ordinary fellow in my own town of Wolverhampton, telling me that the country will not be worth living in for his children. I simply do not have the right to shrug my shoulders. What he is saying, hundreds of thousands are saying and thinking in the areas that are undergoing the total transformation to which there is no parallel in a thousand years of British history. For reasons they could not comprehend, on which they were never consulted, they found themselves made strangers in their own country. We must be mad, literally mad to allow the annual inflow of 50,000 dependants. So insane are we that we actually permit unmarried persons to immigrate for the purpose of founding families with spouses they have never seen. As I look ahead, I am filled with foreboding. Like the Roman prophet, *'I see the Tiber foaming with much blood'*.

| 2 | *From a speech by Enoch Powell to the Conservative Political Centre at the Midland Hotel Birmingham, April 1968* |

There was a lot of inflammatory language in Powell's speech and he was strongly condemned by the liberal establishment. Edward Heath not only sacked him from the shadow cabinet but never spoke to him again. The reaction from public opinion was very different. There were strikes by dockers and meat porters in London and a protest march to Downing Street. A Gallup poll found 75 per cent supporting what Powell had said.

Enoch Powell was not really a racist, more a sentimental imperialist who wanted to turn the clock back. He was genuinely concerned that Britain was creating race relations problems like those that were causing social upheaval in the United States at that time. But there is no question that he had stirred up (some would say pandered to) powerful racist feelings in parts of Britain. In the next few years, immigration remained a contentious social and political issue. The Heath government introduced a new Immigration Act in 1971.

On the other hand, the political leaders of the country remained committed to managing immigration and maintaining social cohesion. The relatively smooth assimilation of sudden surges of migration by Asian refugees from Kenya and Uganda, followed by a similar number of Vietnamese 'boat people' in the early 1970s, seemed to prove that Britain both needed the economic contribution of new migrants and was able to cope with the social consequences. There were no rivers of blood.

 A closer look

The arrival of the Ugandan Asians

Between 1968 and 1972, Britain faced two surges of Commonwealth migration. In 1968, Jomo Kenyatta, leader of Kenya since independence in 1963, enforced a policy of Africanisation, denying rights to the Asian minority. About 1,000 a month fled to Britain. When the British government moved to limit this migration by its Commonwealth Immigration Act, more Kenyan Asians decided to move quickly, ahead of any ban. In the first two months of 1968, 13,000 came to Britain.

In 1972, the eccentric military dictator, Idi Amin, announced that he had had a dream that instructed him to give the Ugandan Asians three months to emigrate. There were 50,000 Asians, mostly shopkeepers and small businessmen, who held British passports.

Under the 1968 quota, 3,000 were allowed to enter Britain in any one year. The government set up the Ugandan Resettlement Board, using military camps as holding centres and linking with volunteer groups to assist the immigrants find homes to go to. 28,000 came in all, settling mostly in Leicester, Birmingham, Bradford and west London. Leicester rapidly became almost a model city for multi-ethnic integration. It was estimated that 30,000 new jobs were created in the city.

In each case, the end result was the successful assimilation of the new arrivals into British society; but only after considerable anxieties about possible strains on community relations. There were numerous instances of racial discrimination against them but mostly in the short term. So many were skilled and self-reliant that they assimilated easily. *'I never fell back on the state for any kind of support,'* said one immigrant, Manzoor Moghal, *'I wanted to explode this myth that Asians were scroungers.'*

The impact on communities of industrial disputes

By the 1970s, the nature of industrial disputes had begun to change. The traditional union leaders had been part of the post-war consensus. They had achieved improvements in pay and conditions by collective bargaining with employers. They were often invited to Number Ten for beer and sandwiches. Two trends emerged: government became more involved, with strikes becoming more 'political' and union leaders began to lose control of the local memberships, as more and more wildcat strikes occurred. From 1970, the number of working days lost through strikes increased sharply, reaching exceptional levels in the crisis years of 1972, 1974 and 1979.

Key terms

Flying pickets: busloads of activists sent to the scene of local disputes to support strikers by pressuring workers to walk out and by blockading places of work to force closures. Flying pickets were often accused of intimidation and violence.

Cross-reference

The political impact of the miners' strikes in 1972–74 is covered in Chapter 6. Arthur Scargill is profiled on page 99.

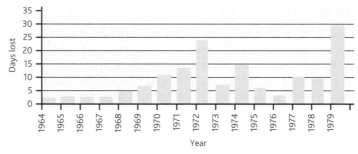

Fig. 4 *Working days lost to industrial action, 1964–79*

Many strikes in the 1970s were reactions against long-term industrial change. This was particularly true of miners facing the contraction of the coal industry. Between 1972 and 1974, the miners were involved in a series of confrontations with their employers and with the government. Younger, more radical union leaders and the use of more radical tactics by strikers, such as **flying pickets**, changed the nature of industrial action.

Together with the impact of the 1973 OPEC oil price crisis, these confrontations led to a major energy crisis. One result of this was the polarisation of society, with many working class communities feeling that their way of life was under siege. For the nation as a whole, the combination of the oil crisis and major industrial disputes meant learning to live with the three-day week.

Table 3 *Coal industry statistics, 1955–86*

Year	Output (millions of tons)	Total workforce	Number of pits
1955	221.6m	695,000	850
1968	170.9m	391,900	378
1976	123.8m	247,100	241
1986	104.5m	154,600	133

Fig. 5 *Saving energy: living with the three-day week*

The three-day week was imposed by the Heath government to conserve electricity in response to a wave of industrial action by engineers, dockers and firemen and the looming threat of a national coal strike in the middle of an energy crisis. Restrictions included fuel rationing, a speed limit of 50 mph on all roads, and deep cuts in the heating and lighting of public buildings and commercial premises. Many industries laid off workers and there was a huge surge in the number of people signing up for temporary unemployment payments.

The three-day week brought about a change of government and also changed public attitudes. Union militancy was strengthened but so was the public reaction against it. The social tensions revealed in 1973–74 did not disappear after the arrival of a Labour government ready to give in to union demands. In the winter of discontent of 1979 and above all in the miners' strike of 1984–85, these tensions boiled over into another bitter era of confrontation with employers, government and the police.

The birth of environmentalism

The great protest movement of the late 1950s and the early 1960s was the Campaign for Nuclear Disarmament. CND was a forerunner of other movements that worked outside the traditional framework of politics and tried to involve people in direct action. The huge anti-war protests in 1968 outside the American Embassy in Grosvenor Square were part of this trend. This provided the background for the emergence of what became known as the environmental movement. Environmentalism covered a multitude of issues affecting the planet: industrial pollution, protection of wildlife, organic farming, and the dangers from radiation and nuclear waste. A new word, 'ecology', entered the vocabulary, defining the health of the natural environment.

In 1962, *Silent Spring*, by the American biologist Rachel Carson, had an enormous international impact. The book sounded the alarm about the decline in birds and other wildlife in the farming countryside. The root cause was attributed to overuse of chemical pesticides, especially DDT. The interest stirred up by *Silent Spring* was one aspect of a series of

Cross-reference

For details of the winter of discontent look ahead to Chapter 11. The miners' strike of 1984–85 is detailed on pages 111–112.

Key chronology

Industrial unrest, winter 1973–74

1973
October — Rash of strikes against government pay policy
November — NUM overtime ban; State of emergency declared
December — Imposition of three-day week

1974
January — 1.5 million on temporary unemployment benefit
February — Start of miners' strike
March — Three-day week ended by Labour government

Activity

Thinking point

Using the evidence of this chapter, list the **five** key aspects of economic change that caused social tensions in the late 1960s and early 1970s.

uncoordinated developments, all linked by the theme of keeping nature green and protecting against the contamination caused by various forms of human activity.

In 1963, the Hunt Saboteurs organisation was formed to carry out direct action against the cruelty of foxhunting. In 1967, the wreck of a giant oil tanker, *Torrey Canyon*, caused a massive oil spill and polluted a stretch of the coastline of south-west England. After other similar incidents, there were passionate demands to clean up the oil industry. Where the original drive behind CND had been pacifist protest against atomic weapons, a new form of anti-nuclear protests campaigned against the use of nuclear power to generate electricity because of the long-term dangers in dealing with radioactive nuclear waste. In 1968, a campaigning book, *The Population Bomb* by Paul Ehrlich, dramatised the threat to the environment from over-population.

In the early 1970s, these disparate environmental protests began to coalesce into organised campaigns. Friends of the Earth was formed in the United States in 1969 and expanded to include Britain, France and Sweden in 1971. The British Ecology Party (later the Green Party) was formed in 1973. The more radical Greenpeace organisation was founded in Vancouver, Canada in 1971, to campaign against whaling. Greenpeace UK was formed in 1977. Direct action was an issue that split the environmental movement. Animal rights protesters carried out violent attacks on pharmaceutical laboratories from 1973. The Animal Liberation Front, formed in 1976, adopted extreme violence: letter bombs were sent to politicians, including Mrs Thatcher, in 1984.

Alongside environmental pressure groups, there was a general increase in interest in the natural environment and the need for conservation. Television programmes, many made at the BBC Natural History Unit in Bristol, did a lot to raise awareness. In 1979, David Attenborough's *Life On Earth* series used new techniques of colour photography and gained massive television audiences worldwide. In the same year, the British thinker James Lovelock gained many adherents for his fascinating *Gaia* theory, about the interconnectedness of all ecological issues. By the end of the 1970s, environmentalism had carved a permanent place on the political scene.

By 1975, the post-war consensus was breaking down and the age of affluence, at least temporarily, had come to an end. Britain seemed to be losing its social cohesion. There were rising crime levels and a large rise in sociologists analysing the ills of society. The debate over immigration intensified. The trade union movement lost some of its old solidarity, with the grip of the traditional moderate union leaderships increasingly challenged by wildcat strikes and a new breed of union activists looking for political confrontation typified by Arthur Scargill and his flying pickets.

■ Summary question

In what ways did environmental issues influence society in Britain between 1964 and 1975?

8

Britain, Europe and the world, 1964–75

Fig. 1 *No meeting of minds: Harold Wilson and Ian Smith all at sea on board HMS Fearless, 1965*

In this chapter you will learn about:

■ how Britain continued the process of decolonisation and retreat from her imperial role

■ how the problem of Rhodesia caused difficulties for Britain

■ the reasons why it was not until 1973 that Britain entered the EEC

■ the extent to which Britain's position in the world had changed by 1975.

Cross-reference

For the beginnings of decolonisation and the wind of change, look back to pages 40–44.

Chapter 4 also outlines the relationship between Britain and the USA and between Britain and Europe from 1951–64.

By 1975, the Empire was formally over. All that was left was a scattering of individual outposts and impoverished islands too weak to enjoy independence and a few last colonial governors in places like Hong Kong and Bermuda. In the Middle East, British rule ended after a nasty little war in Aden. There remained that strange half-life empire called the Commonwealth, an illogical world-straddling organisation that embraced republics, despotisms and democracies, slavish admirers of Britain and frank opponents, as well as all the former white dominions still loyal to the Crown.

1 *From Marr, A., A History of Modern Britain, 2007*

By 1964, the wind of change had brought independence to eighteen New Commonwealth states, with many more about to follow. The Wilson government could reasonably hope that the complicated process of Britain's 'retreat from empire' might carry on smoothly. This would mean not only granting independence to the colonial peoples who had not yet achieved it, but also reducing Britain's military responsibilities, especially 'east of Suez', but political and public opinion still clung to the illusion that Britain had an important world role.

Britain's 'special relationship' with the United States was another awkward question. Britain had tried to join the EEC in 1961–63 and the Wilson government was about to make another application in 1967.

■ Key chronology

Britain and the world, 1964–75

1964 Escalation of the Vietnam War

1965 UDI proclaimed for southern Rhodesia

1967 British pull-back from east of Suez

1968 Hungarian rising crushed by Soviet forces

1971 British forces withdrawn from Arabian Gulf

1973 Britain's accession to the EEC
Yom Kippur War
OPEC oil price crisis

1975 End of Vietnam War

■ Cross-reference

Macmillan's 1960 speech is covered on page 44.

Apartheid is defined on page 43.

As Britain moved closer to Europe, people speculated about what the effect would be on the Atlantic alliance. The expansion of America's war in Vietnam from 1964 sharpened this debate. Should Britain give direct military support to the United States (as President Johnson was urging), or not?

By 1975, most of these issues were resolved. Britain disengaged from overseas bases. The influence of CND waned and the Labour Party continued its acceptance of the nuclear deterrent. Britain avoided direct involvement in the Vietnam War. President de Gaulle left the political scene in 1969 and the way was opened for British accession to the EEC. The issue that was not resolved was southern Rhodesia. The biggest headache in British foreign policy in these years was not caused by Charles de Gaulle or Lyndon Johnson or any other world figure, but by an obscure farmer and ex-RAF fighter pilot from Salisbury in southern Rhodesia called Ian Smith.

■ Britain's world role

Empire and commonwealth: Britain and Rhodesia, 1964–75

What Harold Macmillan called the 'wind of change' in his speech at Cape Town in 1960 was welcomed as a force for good throughout most of Africa – everywhere north of the Zambezi river. In southern Africa, however, it was seen as a challenge and a threat, which after all, was why Macmillan had chosen Cape Town as the place to make his speech in the first place. His main target was not the colonial peoples yearning for independence but the white minority regimes who thought they could stand against the wind of change. They were not persuaded.

In 1961, South Africa left the Commonwealth and moved further and faster towards apartheid. In 1963, the Federation of Rhodesia and Nyasaland broke up into its three separate entities. In 1964, northern Rhodesia became the new independent state of Zambia; Nyasaland became independent Malawi. Southern Rhodesia hoped for independence at the same time but Britain made it clear that this could not happen until majority rule replaced the political domination by the white population. A political row blew up when Ian Smith became prime minister. In 1965, Smith rushed into UDI (Unilateral Declaration of Independence) for Rhodesia. Smith was absolutely committed to perpetuating white rule: he said *'I do not believe in black majority rule in Rhodesia in a thousand years.'*

The result was a direct challenge to Harold Wilson's government. Wilson had many priorities he thought more important than Rhodesia in 1965. He hoped he reach a solution in weeks rather than months, either through oil sanctions or by a negotiated solution. In fact, the Rhodesia problem smouldered on for 14 years until it was settled, or fudged, at the Lancaster House conference in 1980, well after Wilson's political career was over.

Wilson met Smith for face-to-face talks on board HMS *Tiger* off Gibraltar in December 1966. This meeting seemed to make progress but Smith then disavowed everything he had said as soon as he got back home. Wilson's frustrations continued throughout 1967. Oil sanctions were not having much effect. It was too easy for Rhodesia to get supplies through the Portuguese colony of Mozambique, and the big oil companies often openly ignored the sanctions policy. Wilson tried again, with more talks on board HMS *Fearless* in October 1968, but by then Ian Smith felt stronger rather than weaker. Smith also believed he could rely on support from the right wing of the Conservative Party and that all he had to do was wait for Britain to give in. Wilson's diplomacy got nowhere. It upset the Commonwealth countries and many on the Labour left, while making Britain look weak.

In the meantime, Wilson had to face another difficult problem in Africa over the Biafra crisis of 1967. Biafra, the northern part of Nigeria populated mostly by the Ibo people, attempted to become an independent state in its own right. There was a bitter civil war. The British government felt bound to support the official government of Nigeria and the idea of territorial integrity. This was probably the only way Britain could act but public and press opinion in Britain was strongly in favour of Biafra and its charismatic, Sandhurst-educated leader, Colonel Ojukwu. The issue gave the Wilson government a difficult time until it ended with defeat for Biafra.

By 1970, British relations with southern Africa were deteriorating badly. The South Africa cricket tour of England had to be abandoned because of the threat of disruption by anti-apartheid activists led by Peter Hain. South Africa was moving steadily towards sporting isolation. It was clear, too, that South Africa was giving support to Smith's breakaway regime in Rhodesia. Heath continued the policy of sanctions, even though they had proved ineffectual and were opposed by many on the Conservative right, such as the Monday Club and big businesses with trade interests in southern Africa. Heath sent Sir Alec Douglas-Home to Rhodesia for unofficial talks in 1971. His report was pessimistic about any solution. Ian Smith's position was strengthened by a surge in white immigration to Rhodesia in the late 1960s The Rhodesia issue stagnated.

Then, in 1972, Marxist insurgents started a guerrilla war (the so-called Bush War) modelled on the armed resistance movements fighting in Portuguese Africa. Militarily, the Smith regime could cope with this as long as there was help from South Africa but the South African regime suddenly opted for a less confrontational approach to its black African neighbours in October 1974. Portugal was going through a revolution that would end Portuguese colonial rule in Africa and the government in South Africa could read the writing on the wall. The flow of fuel and armaments into Rhodesia from South Africa was drastically reduced.

Pressure from South Africa did what British diplomacy and sanctions had failed to do. In 1976, Smith accepted the Kissinger Plan, drawn up by the United States and approved by Britain and South Africa. The plan set out the steps leading to majority rule in Rhodesia. In 1979, multiracial elections were held and the country was renamed Zimbabwe-Rhodesia. For fifteen years, successive British governments had been made to look futile by the frustrating obstinacy of Smith and his irritating ability to defy them. In the end, however, it may well be that the real failure was Smith's. Had he been willing to negotiate a reasonable settlement in 1966, the later history of Zimbabwe under Robert Mugabe might have taken a less disastrous course than it did.

Withdrawal from 'east of Suez'

The Labour government knew from the start in 1964 that there would have to be a reduction in Britain's military commitments. The Minister of Defence, Denis Healey, started a process of spending cuts designed to bring the defence budget below £2 billion by 1970. Healey's defence white paper in 1967 set a timetable for troop withdrawals from Aden,

Key chronology

Britain and southern Africa, 1963–79

1963	Dissolution of Rhodesian Federation
1964	Independence granted to Zambia and Malawi
1965	UDI for southern Rhodesia announced by Ian Smith
1966	Wilson–Smith talks on HMS *Tiger*
1968	Wilson–Smith talks on HMS *Fearless*
1971	Informal talks between Smith and the new Heath government
1974	End of South Africa's support for Smith's policies
1979	Multiracial elections in Rhodesia

Fig. 2 *Did he grow up to fight against the British? A Yemeni boy with a gun, Aden, 1936*

■ Cross-reference

Polaris missiles are introduced on page 47.

The impact of the 1967 devaluation crisis is covered in chapter 5.

■ Did you know?

The Gulf States (now the United Arab Emirates) produced nearly half of Britain's oil supplies. British troops had been stationed in the Gulf for many years. Concern for the security of the Gulf States was one of the key reasons why Britain had tried to keep control of the Suez Canal in 1956.

■ Key chronology

Britain and Europe, 1963–75

1963 First application blocked by de Gaulle's veto

1966 Second application agreed by Wilson government

1967 Application vetoed by de Gaulle

1970 Talks with 'The Six' about EEC expansion

1971 Agreement in principle for Britain's accession

1972 Treaty of Accession signed in Brussels

1973 EEC entry of Britain, Ireland and Denmark

the Middle East, Malaysia and Singapore. On the other hand, Wilson was criticised on many sides for not going far enough or fast enough. Wilson really believed in the Atlantic alliance and in Britain continuing to have a world role. There was no serious debate about giving up the expensive British nuclear deterrent. The Wilson government announced it would continue to deploy its Polaris missiles. In 1967, a commitment was made to upgrade the system to more advanced (and costly) specifications. The whole process of winding down Britain's overseas defence commitments was very slow and long-term.

All this changed in January 1968, with the drastic spending cuts introduced by Roy Jenkins after the 1967 devaluation crisis. Withdrawal from east of Suez was rapidly accelerated. Troops were to be pulled out of Aden, the Arabian Gulf, Malaysia and Singapore by the end of 1971. The development of a new high-tech warplane, the TSR2, was abandoned because it was too costly, even though Healey and Wilson wanted to keep it going.

When the Heath government came to power in 1970, there was discussion about delaying or reversing some of these withdrawals. Heath was especially reluctant to pull out of the Gulf because so much of Britain's oil came from there. The process was not complete by the end of 1971 and in some cases British troops did not come home until the late 1970s. But the old idea of a far-flung chain of British bases was finished. Britain's future military reach would be Europe and the Mediterranean. Kenneth Morgan's verdict is: *'The last pretence of a being a world power was being stripped away.'* By 1975, Britain seemed to be becoming a poorer, smaller country.

Britain and Europe, 1964–75

The rejection of Britain's application to join the EEC was a shattering blow to the Macmillan government in January 1963. Macmillan and his dogged negotiator, Edward Heath, had become convinced that British membership of the EEC was absolutely essential, for economic reasons above all. Heath in particular thought that there was no 'Plan B' to turn to: Britain would simply have to keep on trying until entry was secured.

The Labour government that came to power in 1964 was not nearly so committed to this policy. In 1962, Hugh Gaitskell had fought passionately against Britain's first application – he told the Labour Party conference that: *'it would be the end of a thousand years of history.'* Many on the Labour left and in the unions were equally hostile. On the other hand there were several enthusiastic pro-marketeers in the cabinet, especially Roy Jenkins and George Brown, who became foreign secretary in 1966. Harold Wilson was more ambivalent. He was not keen on the EEC – he much preferred relying on the Atlantic alliance and stronger links with the Commonwealth – but he could see the strength of some of the economic reasons for going in.

In October 1966, Wilson's cabinet agreed to back a new application for EEC membership. The prospects of it succeeding were not very good. This time the British bid was in danger of seeming half-hearted because of the doubts within the governing party. More importantly, the man who had torpedoed the EEC negotiations last time round, Charles de Gaulle, was still president of France and there was little sign he had changed his mind. Wilson's biographer, Ben Pimlott, has suggested that several doubters in the Labour government only ever supported the bid to join because they knew de Gaulle would block it anyway.

Wilson and George Brown went to Paris to meet de Gaulle in January 1967. They thought the meeting went quite well, in spite of some typically embarrassing behaviour by Brown at an embassy reception. They then toured the other five EEC countries tying to gain support. Then the government won a vote in parliament in favour of proceeding with the application. As everybody knew in advance, the only opinion that mattered was de Gaulle's. In June 1967, Wilson went back to Paris again. De Gaulle put him on the spot, demanding assurances that Britain would detach itself from the 'special relationship'. There was no way Wilson would go so far. In November, de Gaulle used his veto against British entry. Britain was still out in the cold.

> Was it possible for Britain at the present time (and was Britain willing?) to follow any policy that was really distinct from that of the United States, whether in Asia, the Middle East, or Europe? The whole situation would be very different if France could be convinced that Britain really was disengaging from the United States in all major matters such as defence policy and in areas such as Asia, the Middle East and Europe.

2

*From comments made to Harold Wilson by President de Gaulle at the meeting in Paris, June 1967, quoted in Pimlott, B., **Harold Wilson**, 1992*

By the time Britain's third application was being prepared in 1971, the diplomatic situation was very different. Everyone knew in advance that Britain's bid would be accepted. Instead of Harold Wilson, the British prime minister was the passionately pro-European Edward Heath. Instead of Charles de Gaulle, the French president was Georges Pompidou, a man convinced that the EEC needed Britain as much as Britain needed Europe. All the hard detailed arrangements and exceptions were already

Fig. 3 *The 'swingometer' going Edward Heath's way in the 1975 EEC referendum*

Activity

Revision exercise

Compare the evidence in this section about Britain's entry to the EEC with the evidence in Section 1. Make two lists detailing why Britain did not join the EEC until 1973:

1 the domestic political reasons

2 the foreign policy reasons

in place, as a result of the work done in 1962 by Heath's team of negotiators. The formal process of Britain's accession, along with Ireland and Denmark, took more than two years but it was mostly a foregone conclusion. In January 1973, 'The Six' became 'The Nine'.

Britain's membership had been secured, though some people some thought it was sixteen years too late and that Britain would suffer adversely from missing out on the formative years of the EEC since 1957. In 1975, British membership was confirmed when the Wilson government held a referendum. The margin of victory was decisive, by more than 2:1. This looked reassuring, proof that Britain really was 'in', but the fact that the referendum was held at all could be seen as a worrying sign of a lack of commitment.

Britain's position in the world by 1975

By 1975, Britain seemed to be in decline. Part of this was the retreat from empire abroad; part of it was the impact of economic crisis at home. Britain's major ally, the United States, was perceived as having been gravely weakened by the Vietnam War. The special relationship was under strain because the Americans felt Britain had failed to provide enough active support when it was needed both in Vietnam and in the Middle East crisis of 1973 when the Heath government was reluctant to help American support for Israel in the Yom Kippur War.

A closer look

The crisis of the special relationship

From the time the escalation of the Vietnam war began in 1964, President Lyndon Johnson wanted to gain support and approval – what forty years later might have been termed a 'coalition of the willing'. Australia sent troops to Vietnam and Johnson wanted Britain to do the same. LBJ (Johnson) had a good relationship with Harold Wilson, who was generally pro-American and a keen supporter of the Atlantic alliance, but Wilson resisted any suggestions about direct military involvement – not even a small token force that would have satisfied Johnson as a symbol.

The Vietnam War became hugely unpopular in Britain from 1966. There was a massive anti-war demonstration outside the American Embassy in London in 1968. When Edward Heath came to power in 1970, his approach was orientated towards Europe. Heath rejected attempts by the American Secretary, Henry Kissinger, to use Britain as a link with Europe. Heath insisted that the US should negotiate with all nine states, not use Britain as a go-between. Kissinger was furious. Relations became worse in October 1973 during the Yom Kippur War, when Israel seemed in danger of defeat. The US wanted to use NATO bases in Europe for an airlift of supplies to Israel. Most European states, including Britain, refused permission. Anglo-American relations were badly strained, though they did recover later.

When the Russians invade Sussex, don't expect us to come over and save you.

From comments made to an English diplomat by the US Secretary of State, Dean Rusk, 1965

Why is it that the 250 million people of Western Europe, with tremendous industrial resources and long military experience, are unable to organise an effective military coalition to defend themselves against 200 million Russians (who are themselves contending against 800 million Chinese) – but must continue, after 20 years, to depend upon 200 million Americans for their defence?

Senator Mike Mansfield, speaking in Washington, 1970, quoted in Dimbleby, D. and Reynolds, D., ***An Ocean Apart***, *1988*

In the Yom Kippur War of 1973, Israel appealed desperately to the United States for resupply. The European allies, with the single exception of Portugal, bluntly refused to let the US supply planes to use their airfields. For the first time since 1945, America was not able to persuade its allies to go along. This was a more dramatic example of Europe's strategic independence than the refusal to send troops to support America in Vietnam. This time, the Europeans, even Britain, refused to allow even the use of the American bases on their soil. Their fear of an Arab oil embargo outweighed their loyalty to American policy.

From Walker, M., ***The Cold War***, *1993*

Activity

Source analysis

Read Sources 3, 4 and 5 carefully and look at the other evidence in this chapter. How useful are these sources as evidence about strains in Anglo-American relations between 1964 and 1975?

By the mid-1970s, there was a feeling that the West was doing badly in the Cold War and that the NATO alliance was in danger of falling apart. Margaret Thatcher and the new American president from 1981, Ronald Reagan, were determined to reverse this sense of military weakness and to start 'winning the Cold War' again.

Learning outcomes

In this section, you have looked at how the 'post-war consensus' came to an end with the political and economic crises of the 1970s. The problems of high inflation and intense industrial and social unrest badly dented political unity and national self-confidence and paved the way for the rise of Thatcherism after 1975. Abroad, Britain seemed to be turning more towards Europe and away from the United States, but entry into the EEC in 1973 was not as 'final' a step as it appeared to be.

Practice question

'The record of Labour governments in the years 1964 and 1979 was one of
continuous failure'. Assess the validity of this view.

(45 marks)

Study tip Questions like this require a coherent overall argument showing the ability
to respond to a provocative interpretation, showing a grasp of alternative
perspectives and a secure sense of chronology. Before constructing an answer,
it is necessary to define what the record of the Labour governments under
Wilson and Callaghan actually was and how far, if at all, it changed over time as
circumstances and personalities changed. Then it would be useful to think through
the key quotation: is it true, or wrong, or partly true but overstated? Was there a
big difference between 1964–70, as opposed to 1974–79? A good answer would
need to be decisive in supporting or refuting the key quotation, but the answer
needs to be more than a list of reasons. There needs to be a central argument that
is balanced and shows some differentiation. Trying to be comprehensive would
lead to problems. A selective approach is vital, showing a synoptic awareness of
the whole period 1964 to 1979 but supporting the main argument with precisely
selected evidence. Historiography *could* be useful, but only if it is applied to
assessment and evaluation, not a prepared descriptive account of what historians
have written. The most important interpretation should be your own!

3 The Thatcher revolution? 1975–90

9 Politics and the economy, 1975–83

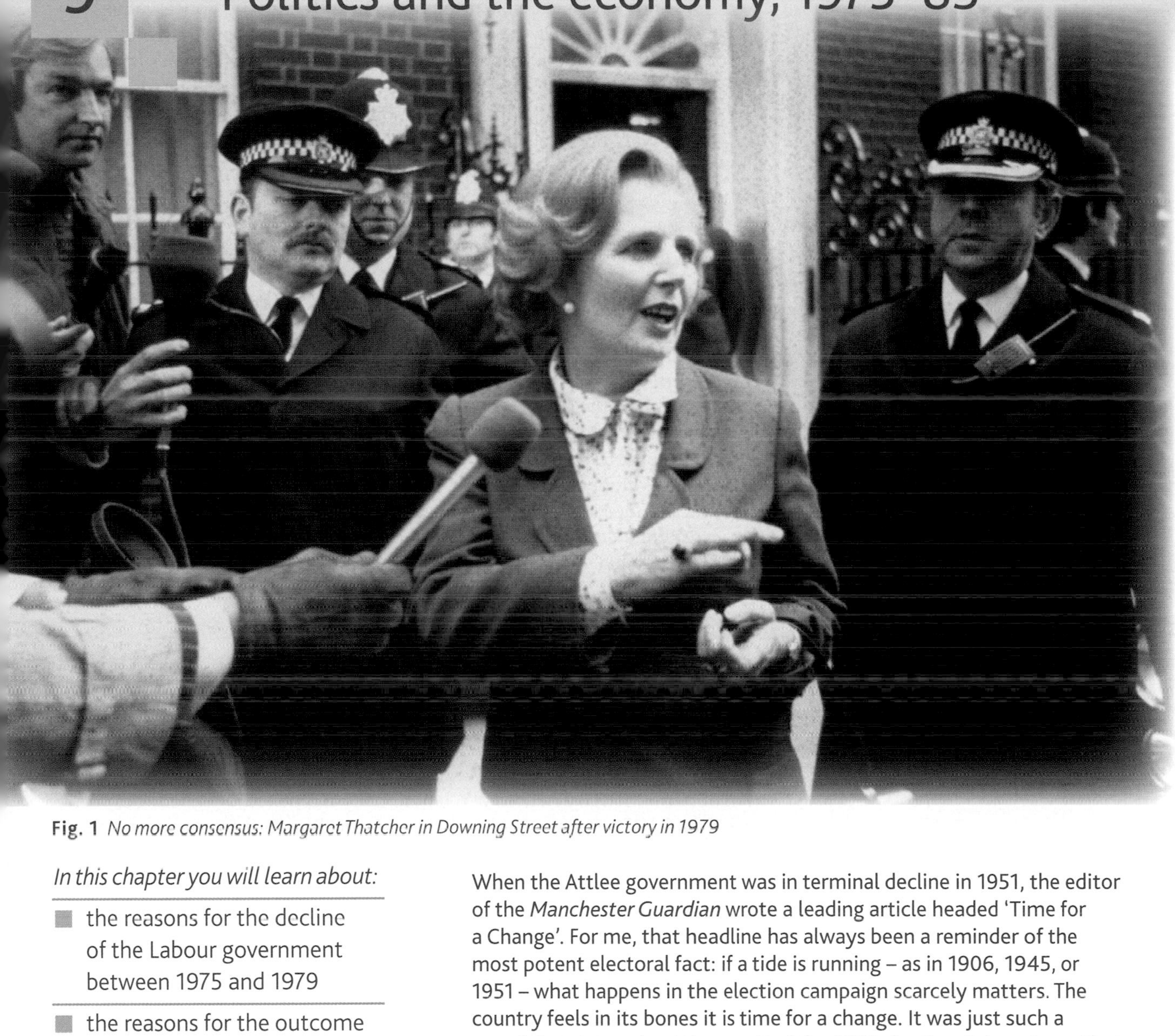

Fig. 1 *No more consensus: Margaret Thatcher in Downing Street after victory in 1979*

In this chapter you will learn about:

- the reasons for the decline of the Labour government between 1975 and 1979
- the reasons for the outcome of the 1979 general election and its political significance
- Thatcherism and its impact on the British economy
- the internal divisions in the Labour Party and the rise of the SDP
- the reasons why Labour was so badly defeated in 1983.

When the Attlee government was in terminal decline in 1951, the editor of the *Manchester Guardian* wrote a leading article headed 'Time for a Change'. For me, that headline has always been a reminder of the most potent electoral fact: if a tide is running – as in 1906, 1945, or 1951 – what happens in the election campaign scarcely matters. The country feels in its bones it is time for a change. It was just such a mood that determined the result of the 1979 election. It is an irony that the most ideological government of the century was elected less on Margaret Thatcher's plans for fundamental changes in British society than because voters decided Labour was ready for the wilderness of opposition.

1 *From the memoirs of the former BBC political editor, John Cole,* ***As It Seemed To Me****, 1995*

■ Key terms

Collectivist: an approach to government and society that stresses the importance of the general good and the necessity for state intervention.

■ **Key chronology**

The rise of Margaret Thatcher, 1975–83

1975

February Edward Heath replaced as leader by Margaret Thatcher

1978–79 Winter of discontent

1979

May Conservative general election victory

1981

February Formation of the SDP

1980

November Michael Foot elected Labour leader

1982

June Surrender of Argentine forces in the Falklands

September Unemployment above 3 million

1983

June Massive victory in general election

In retrospect, the 1979 election has been analysed as one the Conservatives were certain to win. And so, perhaps, it was, after the catastrophic winter and the draining away of Labour's claims to be uniquely fitted to rule. But only much later did it become clear quite how completely the **collectivist** epoch was drawing to a close. That was not how it seemed at the time, even though the Conservatives remained ahead in the polls throughout the campaign. Margaret Thatcher's low personal standing compared with Callaghan's (his personal lead over her stretched to 19 points by the end) alarmed many Conservative candidates. The campaign revealed a leader and a party that were uncertain about the speed at which the collectivist tide was turning.

2

From Young, H., **One Of Us: A Biography of Margaret Thatcher**, *1989*

The general election of 1979 was a landmark election, comparable to 1945 and 1997. The two elections in the crisis year of 1974 had indicated the approaching end of the long post-war consensus but did not represent a definite break with the past. Margaret Thatcher's arrival in 10 Downing Street most certainly did. As so often in history, however, the true significance of 1979 was not fully realised until after the event. Labour supporters had no inkling that their party would be in the wilderness of opposition for 18 years. Seen with the wisdom of hindsight, 1979 was indeed a watershed between the decline of the Labour governments led by Wilson and Callaghan and the radical governments of Mrs Thatcher.

■ **The Labour government, 1975–79**

When Margaret Thatcher emerged from relative obscurity to become Conservative leader, the prospects of winning back power from Labour in the near future were not promising. The party Mrs Thatcher now led was associated in the public mind with industrial unrest and the three-day week. The Wilson government seemed to be in a strong position despite its small parliamentary majority. What actually happened to Labour between 1975 and 1979, however, was a long, slow decline in the unity of the party and the authority of the government.

The first major problem was a surge in inflation due to the rush of large wage increases that were deemed necessary to get out of the industrial crisis that had brought down Heath. Some pay settlements were as high as 30 per cent; the government was in a weak position in standing up to pressure from the unions. Overall, inflation was running at 20 per cent. In January 1975, Wilson's chancellor, Denis Healey, made a speech in Leeds, giving a stern warning of the dangers: that wage inflation caused unemployment and that it was vital to control public spending. In April 1975, Healey's budget imposed steep rises in taxation. Healey's next budget, in 1976, aimed to limit wage increases to a maximum of 3 per cent.

■ **Key profile**

Denis Healey

Healey (born 1917) was from the right wing of the Labour Party. He made a good impression as defence secretary in Wilson's first government and became chancellor in 1974 when Labour came back to power. Healey was a talented politician but also very forceful; he often clashed with personalities on the Labour left. He lost to Michael Foot in the election for the party leadership after Callaghan resigned in 1980 and was elected deputy leader in 1981.

This approach intensified party divisions. Left-wingers like Michael Foot and Tony Benn did not want to put so much pressure on the unions. They also believed in more state intervention. The government decision to nationalise the failing car manufacturer, British Leyland, caused controversy about the role of government in rescuing 'lame-duck' industries. 'Stagflation' was back again.

In March 1976, the Labour government had to cope with the shock of Harold Wilson's sudden resignation. Wilson had been leader for thirteen years and prime minister for eight, more than anyone else in Labour's history before Tony Blair. Because his departure was so sudden and unexpected, all kinds of conspiracy theories were dreamed up to explain it. Wilson himself had actually encouraged some of the speculation because he kept telling people that he was being bugged by the security services, who had a plot to 'get him'; these rumours came to life again in the *Spycatcher* affair of 1986.

The truth seems to be simpler. In 1974, Harold Wilson had promised his wife that he would step down after two more years – Mary Wilson had always hated the business of politics. Wilson was also worried about his health, especially about the signs that his legendary memory was beginning to fade. In 2008, research into Wilson's speeches by a neurologist indicated that, by 1976, Wilson was suffering from the early stages of Alzheimer's disease. At the time, nobody suspected this; even one of the best-informed political commentators, Anthony Howard of the *Observer*, was 'gobsmacked' by Wilson's resignation.

Wilson's successor as prime minister was James (Jim) Callaghan, a 'safe pair of hands' with long experience and good links to the unions. Callaghan was seen as an ideal leader to maintain party unity. This was not easy because by-election defeats in 1976 reduced Labour's tiny parliamentary majority. The government faced difficult problems over the deadlock in Northern Ireland and especially over the economy. In December 1976, Denis Healey had to go to the International Monetary Fund (IMF) for an emergency loan of £3 billion. In return, the government had to make big spending cuts. Political opponents denounced this as a humiliation.

Callaghan handled the IMF crisis well and the economy recovered, but it reinforced the image of Britain in economic decline. The Conservatives claimed this was giving away Britain's economic independence; the Labour left said it was caving in to capitalism and privatisation. Although Callaghan maintained unity among Labour MPs, there was a growth of leftist militancy in some public-sector trade unions and in local councils.

In 1977, Callaghan moved to strengthen the government by making the 'Lib-Lab pact'. By this deal, the 12 Liberal MPs voted for the government in parliament and in return Callaghan promised to move ahead with devolution for Wales and Scotland. The economic situation began to improve as North Sea oil came on stream. By 1978, there were nine oilfields in production. Inflation rates fell. Economic experts were divided

■ **Cross-reference**

Stagflation is covered on page 61.

■ **Exploring the detail**

Spycatcher

The *Spycatcher* affair in 1986 concerned the efforts of the Thatcher government to suppress publication of a book by the former MI5 agent Peter Wright. One of the sensational events covered in Wright's book was a supposed plot against the Wilson government by right-wing intelligence officers.

Fig. 2 'Sunny Jim': Prime Minister, James Callaghan

■ **Exploring the detail**

December 1976

The economic crisis of December 1976 was in many ways a turning point in the history of post-war Britain. A Labour government introduced massive spending cuts. Some historians regard this as the moment when the 'post-war consensus' really ended.

■ Cross-reference

To review Britain's economic decline in the early 1970s, revisit pages 61–63.

■ Did you know?

The requirement for a minimum 40 per cent 'yes' vote had been pushed through in the House of Commons against the wishes of the government by a group of Labour MPs opposed to devolution.

■ Cross-reference

More detail on the winter of discontent can be found below, on page 87.

■ Cross-reference

Willie Whitelaw is profiled on page 61.

■ Key terms

Monetarism: an economic theory promoted by Milton Friedman and the 'Chicago School' of economists. They argued that the best way for governments to control inflation was by restraint of government spending and borrowing and, above all, by strict curbs on the money supply.

about what this recovery showed. Some saw it as proof that Britain's recent economic problems had been exaggerated; others saw only a blip in irreversible economic decline.

In 1978, the economic recovery took the heat out of the agonising about Britain's role as the 'economic sick man of Europe'. Other issues came to the fore, especially devolution, the issue that Liberals demanded to be dealt with as the price for the Lib-Lab pact. After lengthy debates in parliament, devolution acts for Scotland and Wales were passed, opening the way for referendums, but there was no decisive outcome. The vote in Wales was 4.1 against. In Scotland, more people voted for independence than against but nowhere near the required 40 per cent of those eligible to vote. When the devolution referendums took place, in the winter of 1978–79, people were distracted by the crisis of the 'winter of discontent' and the imminent collapse of the Labour government. Devolution would have to wait 20 years until the government of Tony Blair.

One important consequence of the devolution debate was that Margaret Thatcher led the Conservatives into outright opposition against devolution for Scotland and Wales, reversing the policy of Edward Heath, who had supported devolution since 1968. In the longer term, Thatcher's anti-devolution policy rebounded disastrously against the Conservatives. In 1970, the Conservative Party had held 36 seats in Scotland, half the total. By the time of the 1997 election, the party was obliterated outside England, failing to return a single MP in either Scotland or Wales. By then, of course, Margaret Thatcher was out of office.

The triumph of Margaret Thatcher

The Margaret Thatcher of the years in opposition between 1975 and 1979 was somewhat different from the dominant prime minister she was to become in the 1980s. She had not yet fully developed her ideas or her political style. Even so, many observers thought she was out of the ordinary, not just because she was a woman in the male-dominated world of British politics.

Margaret Thatcher's success as leader of the opposition was underpinned by four key factors. The first was her force of personality, the drive and confidence she showed at a time when the country, and her own party, wallowed in pessimism. She also worked hard at the skills of political presentation, using the public relations firm Saatchi & Saatchi to polish her image, a process that continued well after the 1979 election. The second factor was her deputy leader. Willie Whitelaw was very different from Mrs Thatcher in background, style and policy ideas but his main concern was party unity. His loyal support was vital in winning over the Heathites in the party.

The third factor was economic policy. Margaret Thatcher's natural instincts were against 'big government' and consensus politics. She was influenced by the ideas of Enoch Powell and Sir Keith Joseph and began to adopt policies influenced by the economic theory known as **monetarism**. These ideas, however, were not fully developed by 1979; and they did were not given prominence in the 1979 election campaign. This was due to the fourth factor: Margaret Thatcher's preference for keeping her options open. As the 1979 election approached, the Conservatives offered broad-brush themes, avoiding very detailed and specific policies such as those Edward Heath prepared before the 1970 election.

It would be wrong, however, to think of Margaret Thatcher sweeping into power on a wave of popular enthusiasm. Her standing in the opinion polls was lower than Jim Callaghan's. For all her self-confidence, Thatcher knew that a lot of people expected her to fail, either by losing the election or being out of her depth as prime minister if she won. Early in 1979, she told a colleague: *'I shall be remembered as the woman who was allowed one go – to lead the party to defeat.'* Whatever else Margaret Thatcher was going to be remembered for, that was not it.

The general election 1979

One key question about the general election of May 1979 is why it did not take place in 1978. One of the most important assets prime ministers have is the ability to choose the precise time to call an election, when the political situation is most favourable. At the 1978 Labour party conference, Jim Callaghan teased the delegates about the timing of the election. He even sang a little song about the girl who *'didn't say yes, she didn't say no.'* In the event, he decided to wait. At the time, and even more so later, it was suggested that Callaghan had made a fatal mistake. The winter of discontent had not yet begun and Mrs Thatcher was not doing well in the polls. If Callaghan had gone for it in the autumn of October 1978, the 'turning point' election of 1979 might never have happened. But Jim Callaghan chose differently and after that, events took away his power to choose.

By the spring of 1979, the political landscape had been reshaped by the winter of discontent. The economic situation deteriorated and the image of the trade unions sank to its lowest ebb since the war. Then, in March 1979, the government lost a vote of confidence in parliament, on the issue of Scottish devolution. The government was forced to resign. It was the first time since 1924 that a government was brought down by a confidence vote. It meant that the 1979 general election took place at a time Callaghan really did not want one.

■ A closer look

The winter of discontent

The industrial unrest that gripped Britain in the winter of 1978–79 was not on a massive scale. It was not as serious a challenge to the government of the day as the miners' strike that had happened in 1974, or the one that was to happen in 1984–85. But the psychological effect of the winter of discontent had a devastating impact on the public mood and thus on the fate of Jim Callaghan's government.

The wave of industrial action included disruption to transport, through strikes by lorry drivers and the train drivers' union ASLEF. There was also shock and outrage in reaction to strikes by

Fig. 3 *Ready for emergencies: army ambulances in the winter of discontent, 1979*

public sector workers, such as hospital porters and clerical staff in local councils and, above all, by dustmen and grave-diggers. People responded furiously to the sight of mountains of uncollected rubbish, of funerals being postponed, of doctors pleading with hospital staff to move sick patients from ambulances into the hospital.

These images dominated the media and the press for weeks on end. In the election campaign they were exploited to the full by the Opposition. One poster, *'Labour isn't working'*, became a symbol of Labour's vulnerability on the issues of unemployment, law and order, and the excessive power of the unions. In fact, many of the strikes in 1979 showed the weakness of the old union leaderships and their failure to control the new militancy of their workers. It was not only the Conservatives and the middle classes who reacted strongly against the winter of discontent. Many skilled and unskilled workers began to switch away from their traditional loyalty to Labour and to consider voting Conservative.

Fig. 4 *Saatchi & Saatchi election poster for the Conservatives, 1979*

Even with all these problems for Labour, the outcome of the election was not a foregone conclusion. The Conservatives were able to fight the campaign mostly by hammering away at the unpopularity of the government. Despite this, the Labour vote actually held up quite well, dipping by 3 per cent overall. However, the Conservatives benefited from a sharp drop in support for the Liberals and for the Scottish Nationalist Party. The result was by no means a landslide, but produced a comfortable working majority of 43 for the Conservatives.

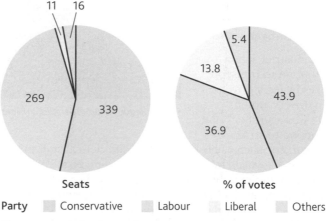

Fig. 5 *General election results, May 1979*

The first Thatcher government, 1979–83

Margaret Thatcher was not able to put her own stamp on all aspects of the new Conservative government right from the start. It took time for her to establish complete domination over the party, if in fact she ever did achieve this. Her first cabinet contained several 'wets' (Heathites who still believed in 'One Nation' politics) as well as 'dries' who were in tune with her right-wing instincts. Willie Whitelaw was appointed home secretary, with Lord Carrington as foreign secretary and Michael Heseltine minister of the environment.

Key profile

Michael Heseltine

Heseltine (born 1933) was a millionaire who became a leading Conservative politician in the 1980s. Because of his long hair and flamboyant style, he was often known in the party as 'Tarzan'. His 'One Nation' views brought him into conflict with Mrs Thatcher and he resigned from her cabinet in 1986 over the Westland affair. Many Thatcherites blamed him for the fall of Thatcher in 1990. He was later deputy prime minister to John Major.

Thatcher did, however, ensure that the key posts, especially on the economy, were held by people she regarded as 'one of us'. Geoffrey Howe became chancellor. The department of industry went to Sir Keith Joseph. Other key economic posts were given to John Biffen and Nigel Lawson, two men with a 'dry' approach to economy and finance. One exception to this trend was the Heathite Minister of Employment, Jim Prior. Many people predicted, correctly, that there were bound to be tensions between Prior and Mrs Thatcher.

Key profiles

Sir Geoffrey Howe

Howe (born 1926) was a Conservative MP with a legal background. He served as trade minister in Heath's government to 1974 and was Mrs Thatcher's first chancellor of the exchequer from 1979 to 1983. He presided over the application of monetarist principles to economic policies, resulting in very high levels of unemployment. From 1983 to 1989, he was foreign minister but his views on Europe came into conflict with Thatcher's. His resignation speech in 1990 helped to cause her fall from power.

Nigel Lawson

Lawson (born 1932) was a financial journalist and a committed Thatcherite. He served in Margaret Thatcher's first term as Geoffrey Howe's number two at the Treasury and replaced Howe as chancellor in 1983. His expansionary budgets of 1987 and 1988 are often called the 'Lawson boom'. In 1989, Lawson resigned from the government, furious about the excessive influence wielded by Thatcher's private economic adviser, Professor Alan Walters.

Key terms

Wet: a derisive nickname given to a member the Conservative Party by Mrs Thatcher and her supporters for being soft and squeamish about the social consequences of monetarist economic policies.

Dry: a nickname given to Conservatives who were firm and uncompromising in their support for monetarism.

Cross-reference

Sir Keith Joseph is profiled on page 59.

■ Cross-reference

For the miners' strike of 1984–85, see page 111.

At first, Margaret Thatcher was in no rush to have a confrontation with the unions. Later, in 1984, Thatcher chose to take on the miners in a trial of strength but she was not yet ready for this. Jim Prior was allowed to keep good relations with union leaders. Pay settlements in 1980 and 1981 were allowed to be generous. In 1981, the government intervened in a dispute between the National Coal Board (NCB) and the miners – on the side of the miners. The government pressured the NCB into withdrawing its planned pit closures, in order to ward off the danger of a strike by the NUM. Apart from the miners, workers in several industries gained index-linked pay settlements.

Despite her cautious approach to industrial relations, however, Thatcher was determined to push ahead with radical reforms in taxation and government spending. The new direction of economic policy was set according to the principles of monetarism. The impact of these policies resulted, by 1981, in steeply rising unemployment, social upheaval and massive unpopularity for Margaret Thatcher and her government.

Monetarism and its impact on the British economy, 1979–83

From his first budget in 1979, Margaret Thatcher's chancellor, Geoffrey Howe, set out to reduce government spending and to cut the high levels of taxation inherited from the outgoing Labour government. The basic rate of income tax was reduced from 33 per cent to 30. The top rate was reduced from 83 per cent to 60. Value added tax (VAT) was increased considerably, reflecting the Thatcherite vision that people should not be taxed on their incomes or property but on what they chose to spend on goods and services. These policies led to increased unemployment and a sharp contraction of industrial production. It was in the budget of March 1981, however, that monetarism was stringently applied, with very painful economic consequences, at least in the short term.

■ Cross-reference

Monetarism is outlined on page 86.

Stagflation is described on page 61.

In 1980, the economy was already gripped by a serious recession, hit both by inflation, above 15 per cent, and also by sharply rising unemployment, going above 2 million. 'Stagflation' was back. The economy would have been in an even more disastrous state but for the flow of North Sea oil and gas that saved Britain from what would otherwise have been a serious balance of payments crisis and a run on the pound. The 1981 budget applied monetarist principles, aiming to eliminate inflation by controlling the money supply. Taxes on petrol, cigarettes and alcohol went up. Government borrowing went down. Grants to local councils were cut.

In the short run, these deflationary policies made the recession worse. Ever since 1951, the key goals of the post-war consensus had been full employment and subsidised welfare. Now, unemployment was seen as 'a price worth paying' to tackle the greater evil of inflation and to force British industry to become more competitive. The impact on industry was drastic. Steel production was cut by 30 per cent, to less than 14 million tons. Many industrial plants closed down permanently. The worst hit areas were the Midlands, the North, central Scotland and South Wales. Some commentators described what was happening as the 'deindustrialisation of Britain'.

■ Cross-reference

The social impact of urban rioting in 1981 is covered in Chapter 11.

At the same time, major rioting rocked many of Britain's inner cities. The first big outbreak was in the St Paul's district of Bristol in 1980. In 1981, there were riots in Toxteth in Liverpool, Moss Side in Manchester and in Brixton and Southall in London. There was deep public anxiety about the breakdown of social cohesion.

Party divisions opened wider and several 'wets' were sacked or driven to resign. Jim Prior was moved from employment to Northern Ireland. Sir Ian Gilmour marked his departure from the government by accusing

Margaret Thatcher of *'steering the ship of state straight on to the rocks.'* The government became hugely unpopular. In April 1981, the approval rate in the opinion polls went down to 27 per cent. Some polls showed the Conservatives in third place, behind both Labour and the Alliance. These levels of unpopularity carried through into 1982 – yet in 1983 the Conservatives were able to win a massive election victory. One reason for this is that the government slackened its monetarist policies in 1982 and 1983, softening the degree of economic hardship although unemployment remained over 3 million. The key reason, however, was the 'Falklands factor'.

Cross-reference

The 'Falklands factor' is discussed in more detail below on page 94. The events of the war are covered in Chapter 12.

The divisions in the Labour Party

Between the general elections of 1979 and 1983, the Labour Party came close to political oblivion. The internal divisions that simmered through the 1970s but had been mostly kept in check by Wilson and Callaghan now boiled over as the Labour Party descended into its worst crisis since the trauma of 1931. Press coverage of Labour was almost universally hostile. Margaret Thatcher proved a stronger prime minister than Labour had predicted in the run-up to the 1979 election. The revival of the Liberals meant that Labour no longer represented the only anti-Conservative opposition. Whole sections of Labour's traditional political support leaked away.

Some Labour voters became 'Thatcher Conservatives'; some voted Liberal. Some supported the far left in attacking the Labour leadership from within. Some became apathetic: stay-at-home voters cost Labour dearly in 1983. Worst of all, key personalities broke away to found a completely new party, the Social Democratic Party (SDP) in 1981. This splintering process led to a catastrophic defeat in 1983, far worse than 1979. Labour's share of the vote plunged to 27 per cent (in 1966 it had been 48 per cent and even in 1979 Labour got 37 per cent). Only the first-past-the-post system saved Labour from a massive loss of seats. Nor was it certain that 1983 was the bottom of the slide. The Labour party seemed to have become unelectable, in terminal decline.

Cross-reference

For the 'first-past-the-post system', see page 142.

The collapse in Labour's popularity was not easy to turn around. The basic foundations of the Labour Party had crumbled as demographic change loosened the traditional loyalties of the working class. The unions were no longer such a source of strength. Many traditional Labour strongholds in local government were seen as having lost touch with the people they were supposed to serve. It seemed that the Labour Party had passed the point of no return and might cease to be a potential party of government. Pundits speculated about the 'fundamental realignment of British politics'. The clearest sign of such a realignment was the emergence of the SDP in 1981.

The emergence of the SDP

The Social Democratic Party (SDP) was born in January 1981, when a group of leading Labour politicians, the so-called 'Gang of Four', issued their 'Limehouse declaration', announcing the formation of the Council for Social Democracy. In doing so, they triggered a storm of controversy within the Labour movement. In the eyes of Labour loyalists, the four 'deserters', David Owen, Roy Jenkins, Shirley Williams and Bill Rodgers, were guilty of betrayal. Even many of their close friends believed they were wrong; that their duty was to carry on the fight within the party as Gaitskell had fought the left after 1960.

Did you know?

The 'Gang of Four' who led the SDP got their name from the original Gang of Four who led the Cultural Revolution in Communist China in the late 1960s and early 1970s.

■ Exploring the detail

The Limehouse declaration

The Limehouse declaration was so-named because it was issued from David Owen's house in Limehouse, in London's East End. The declaration proposed the formation of a Council for Social Democracy as a protest against the new system for electing Labour leaders and against the radical shift to the left in ideology and policy. Soon afterwards the name Social Democratic Party was adopted. 28 Labour MPs switched allegiance.

Fig. 6 *Strains in the Alliance: the two Davids, Owen and Steel*

The leaders of the new SDP and the MPs who left the Labour Party to join them saw things differently. In their view, they had been driven out of the party they loved by the hostility of the extremists who were now taking over. The best way to save the Labour Party was not to fight a losing battle against the Bennite left but to build a new centrist alternative capable of appealing to the middle ground. Later, after the 1997 Labour landslide, many of the SDP rebels of 1981 claimed that they had been the real architects of this victory, by 'bringing Labour to its senses' and forcing the party to reinvent itself.

At the time, the creation of the SDP came as a bombshell. The intentions of the Gang of Four were a closely guarded secret right up to the last minute. But it was not a sudden development. Looking back, historians can follow a long trail of evidence that leads back before 1979. Left-wing influence in the party increased in the 1970s, with growing support for Tony Benn and the emergence of 'hard left' pressure groups such as the Militant Tendency. Several constituencies were taken over by activists who organised the 'deselection' of their MP. One early victim of this was Dick Taverne, a Labour moderate deselected from his Lincoln seat in 1973. In response to left-wing activism, moderates formed the Manifesto Group, campaigning for more centrist policies.

In the annual BBC Dimbleby Lecture on public affairs in 1979, Roy Jenkins put forward the idea of a new centrist political party that would get away from the out-of-date politics of political polarisation and class warfare. His ideas were similar to those in the 1981 Limehouse declaration. Many in the Labour Party, not only left-wingers, had always been suspicious of Jenkins and his Dimbleby Lecture might soon have been forgotten. The real cause of the SDP breakaway was the bitter party infighting after Labour's defeat in 1979.

■ Cross-reference

Roy Jenkins is profiled on page 51.

This infighting did not start immediately. The modern trend for party leaders to resign as soon as they have lost an election had not yet taken hold. Jim Callaghan did not resign until November 1980, 18 months after losing power. This was the signal for the battle for the soul of the party to begin. The 'obvious' candidate to succeed Callaghan was Denis Healey, the candidate of the centre-right but the obvious choice was rejected. The party voted for the left-wing candidate, Michael Foot, a Bevanite and a supporter of unilateral nuclear disarmament.

This was partly due to the perception that Healey was abrasive and not a conciliator, like Wilson and Callaghan, but it also reflected a tendency to turn inwards, to focus obsessively on internal rivalries and to ignore the issue of who was most likely to win the next election. The Conservative Party was to follow a remarkably similar path after its traumatic defeat in 1997. Later, amid the poisonous atmosphere of the Blackpool party conference in September 1981, Healey narrowly defeated Tony Benn in a bitter contest for the deputy leadership.

■ Key profile

Tony Benn

Tony Benn (born 1925) was an idealistic voice on the left wing of the Labour Party. Originally Anthony Wedgwood Benn, Viscount Stansgate, he became plain Tony Benn after the 1963 Peerage Act. Benn was a minister in Harold Wilson's cabinet from 1964 but repeatedly came into conflict with the party leadership, especially during Wilson's second term from 1974. He was passionately against Britain being in the EEC. In the 1980s, there were bitter divisions between the 'Bennite Left' and mainstream Labour moderates.

By then, however, the SDP had already broken away. The snapping point came in January 1981, at a special party conference held at Wembley, dominated by the Labour left. The Wembley conference was notorious for the spitting hostility shown towards speakers by hard-left hecklers. This helped to convince moderates like Shirley Williams that it was time to give up on Labour and form a new, breakaway party.

The new SDP soon made an impact on national politics. In the summer of 1981, Roy Jenkins almost won the safe Labour seat of Warrington in a by-election. Shirley Williams did win an even more sensational by-election in the safe Conservative seat of Crosby in November. Jenkins won Glasgow Hillhead in March 1982. Many Labour activists claimed the party 'did not need' people like Owen, Jenkins and Williams. What the by-elections said was that Labour could never hope to win back power without the voters who were now switching to the SDP. In another by-election, in the safe working-class seat of Bermondsey in east London, a 'new left' candidate, the openly homosexual Australian Peter Tatchell was resoundingly defeated by the Liberals, who claimed they had 'broken the mould' of the old two-party system. Labour was widely regarded as unelectable.

The Liberal revival and the rise of the Alliance

The revival of the Liberals had already begun under the leadership of Jeremy Thorpe. The increased voting support for the Liberals in 1970 and 1974 did not result in more seats at Westminster but the monopoly of the two main parties was significantly loosened. The Liberals, along with the nationalist parties, did well in the Scottish Highlands and parts of Wales. They also gained ground in south-west England. Thorpe was forced to resign after a scandal in 1976 and was replaced by David Steel. The modest revival of the Liberals continued.

■ Exploring the detail

The 1981 Wembley Conference

The Wembley Conference was held in order to change the rules for electing the party leader. Instead of being elected just by the MPs, the leader was to be chosen by an 'electoral college' in which party activists and the block votes of the unions would have huge influence. It was also made easier to deselect sitting MPs. The Wembley conference showed the influence of the hard left at its peak.

■ **Cross-reference**

The diplomatic and military aspects of the Falklands War are covered in Chapter 12.

The origins of the conflict between Britain and Argentina over the Falkland Islands are covered on pages 118–20.

■ **Activity**

Group activity

Working in two groups, assess the political impact of the Falklands factor on the Conservative government and on the Labour Party.

The collapse of support for Labour after 1979 gave the Liberals their biggest political opportunity for 50 years. The Liberals developed extremely successful strategies for fighting by-elections and local council elections. They were especially good at 'pavement politics', tailoring their campaigning to specific local issues. The standing of the Liberals in the opinion polls shot up, matching the steep decline in support for Labour. In several areas, the Liberals replaced Labour as the main challengers to the Conservatives.

The Liberals hoped to achieve the realignment of British politics through reform of the voting system. The first-past-the-post system worked against the Liberals, whose increased share of the total vote was not matched by any increase in seats in parliament. Some form of proportional representation, what Liberals called 'fair votes', would lead to major political change. There was little chance of the two main parties going along with this. The Liberals saw an alliance with the SDP as their best way forward.

At first, there was an informal alliance. Roy Jenkins fought the Warrington by-election for the SDP 'with Liberal support'. Later, the alliance became a formal agreement. Relationships between the two parties were often tense. There were differences between the leaders, the 'Two Davids', Steel and Owen. Some elements of both parties had never wanted a merger at all. Even so, the Alliance seemed able to have overtaken Labour as the credible opposition to Margaret Thatcher's government. In mid-1982, however, the Alliance bandwagon was derailed by the 'Falklands factor'.

The Falklands factor

The political landscape was transformed in 1982 by the impact of the war in the Falklands on domestic politics. At the beginning of 1982, Margaret Thatcher was one of the most unpopular prime ministers in living memory. Unemployment was approaching 3 million. The violent disturbances in inner cities also caused concern, as did Mrs Thatcher's attacks on local councils. Although the Labour Party was in crisis, support for the SDP-Liberal Alliance was going up rapidly. There was a genuine fear among Conservative MPs that the next election might be very difficult to win. Victory in the Falklands changed all that.

The military regime in Argentina invaded the Falklands Islands in April 1982. Margaret Thatcher's immediate response was a full-scale military effort to recover the islands. This decision was a gamble that could easily have gone wrong but British forces achieved complete success. This decisive and relatively painless victory was seen as a vindication of Margaret Thatcher's bold leadership. There had been opposition to the war but, from the very beginning, the war had unleashed a wave of patriotism around the country. There was lavish approval from most of the national press, led by *The Sun*. Even most of the Labour Party supported the recovery of the Falklands.

The 'Falklands factor' galvanised the grass-roots Conservative activists. Margaret Thatcher gained in self-confidence and began to dominate the party in a way she had not been able to before. The Falklands War was a springboard for her election victory in 1983. On its own, the Falklands factor might not have been enough to bring about a landslide victory for Margaret Thatcher; she also benefited from the catastrophic weakness of the opposition.

Fig. 7 *A long way from home: HMS **Canberra** and HMS **Andromeda** supporting the Royal Navy Task Force off the Falkland Islands, June 1982*

The general election of 1983

The 1983 election witnessed the near-total collapse of the Labour Party. In October 1951, an election they lost, Labour's total vote had been nearly 14 million, a share of nearly 49 per cent. The Liberals got 2.5 per cent, with less than one million votes. In 1983, the Labour vote was almost halved – down to 8.4 million, only 27 per cent of the total vote. The Liberal–SDP Alliance was barely 2 per cent behind. The Conservative had a huge majority of 144 seats. Many people thought Labour's internal divisions were so bad that they expected the situation to carry on getting worse. Labour looked less like a party of government than at any time since the 1930s.

The 'Falklands factor' was a key element of the Conservative victory in 1983 but there is a temptation for historians to overstate its importance and for Labour sympathisers to use it as an alibi. Conservative success was not due to mass approval for Margaret Thatcher, popular though she undoubtedly was. The crucial factor was the splintering of political opposition and fact that the Labour leadership lacked credibility. Even Michael Foot's admirers thought of him as a man best suited to principled opposition to the government of the day. They could not imagine him *being* the government of the day. Another weakness in 1983 was the Labour election manifesto, a mishmash of mostly left-wing promises, including unilateral disarmament and the abolition of foxhunting. One Labour MP, Gerald Kaufman, labelled the manifesto as *'the longest suicide note in history'*.

The 1983 election saw a rise in support for the SDP–Liberal Alliance but this was much less than might have been expected in 1982. Potential support for the Alliance was taken away by the Falklands factor.

Cross-reference

Unilateral disarmament is explained on page 20.

■ Cross-reference

The first-past-the-post system is explained on page 142 and discussed further on page 91.

■ Activity

Group discussion

Working in groups, make a list of the reasons why the Conservatives became so politically dominant between 1979 and 1987 and why the Labour Party was so unsuccessful. Arrange the top three factors in each list in order of importance.

The 1983 result was also yet one more example of the distorting effect the first-past-the-post system. The Alliance got only half a million fewer votes than Labour but 186 fewer seats in parliament. Even discounting the nationalist parties, the anti-Conservative vote totalled 16 million, three million more than the pro-Conservative vote, yet Margaret Thatcher's majority was 144. This is why it is difficult for historians to answer the question: Was Conservative dominance in the 1980s more to do with a weak and divided opposition than with a wave of enthusiasm for Thatcherism?

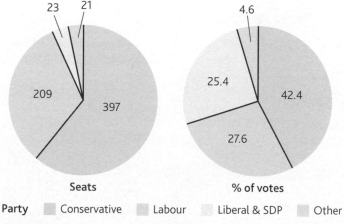

Party ■ Conservative ■ Labour ■ Liberal & SDP ■ Other

Fig. 8 *General election results, June 1983*

■ **Summary question**

Explain why the Conservative Party was defeated in 1974 but was able to secure victory in the 1979 election.

In this chapter you will learn about:

■ the reasons for the political dominance of the Thatcher government from 1983

■ the impact of Thatcherism on politics and the economy in Britain to 1990

■ the role of key personalities

■ the circumstances in which Mrs Thatcher fell from power in 1990.

Key chronology

Britain, 1983–90

1983
June Decisive election victory of Margaret Thatcher

1984
June Battle of Orgreave between police and striking miners
October IRA bomb attack on Brighton party conference

1985
March Miners vote to end strike
November Anglo-Irish Agreement signed at Hillsborough

1986
January Resignation of Michael Heseltine over Westland affair
October The 'Big Bang': deregulation of the City

1987
June Third successive Conservative election victory

1989
November Fall of the Berlin Wall and end of the Cold War

1990
March Anti-poll tax riots
November Resignation of Geoffrey Howe
Margaret Thatcher forced out by her own party

Fig. 1 *A cartoon linking Margaret Thatcher with Shakespeare's **Henry V**, **The Times**, May 1987*

I have not wasted time on the foreign secretary this afternoon, although I feel some of his colleagues must be a bit tired by now of his hobbling around with a bleeding hole in his foot and a smoking gun in his hand, telling them he did not know that it was loaded. The foreign secretary is not the villain in this case. He is the fall guy for the pig-headed bigotry of the Prime Minister herself: the Great She-Elephant, She-who-must-be-obeyed, the Catherine the Great of Finchley. The Right Honourable Lady has formidable qualities – but those qualities can turn into horrendous vices. I put it to the government front bench that to allow her to commit Britain to another four years of capricious autocracy would do fearful damage, not just to the Conservative Party, but to the state.

1   *Comments by Denis Healey in a House of Commons debate about the intelligence services, 1987, from Healey, D., **The Time of My Life**, 1989*

After the 1983 election, Margaret Thatcher achieved a total domination over society and politics in Britain. Her third election victory, in June 1987, marked the high tide of Thatcherism. By smashing the trade unions, clipping the wings of local councils, privatising industry, the sale of council houses and deregulation of the financial markets, Margaret Thatcher had, for good or bad, transformed Britain. Nor did there seem to be any prospect of the Thatcher era coming to an end. Mrs Thatcher declared that she *would go on and on*; and it was hard to see how anybody might stop her.

The opposition parties seemed incapable of challenging her government and its majority of 102. Denis Healey's taunts in Source 1 suggested that even her own cabinet had no will or ability to stand up to her.

There are no final victories in politics and most political careers end in failure. Even so, the fall of Margaret Thatcher in 1990 came as a stunning surprise at the time, not least to the Iron Lady herself. In retrospect, it is easier for historians to explain Mrs Thatcher's fall but it is still a matter of controversy and rival interpretations. Mrs Thatcher's admirers were agreed that she was indeed a transformational leader who 'had changed everything', a great prime minister who saved the nation from disaster at home and restored Britain's pride and prestige abroad. Yet for many people, including most of the nation's intellectual elite, she was the worst of prime ministers, responsible for intensifying social divisions, and also responsible for her own downfall. Getting to grips with the problems of explaining the rise and fall of Margaret Thatcher and assessing her legacy is the purpose of this chapter.

■ The triumph and decline of Margaret Thatcher

The high tide of Thatcherism, 1983–87

The 1983 general election consolidated Margaret Thatcher's position, both as prime minister and as party leader. In her first term in office, she had been an untried leader, surrounded by more experienced colleagues. Some of her policies had made her extremely unpopular. She had also been forced to make compromises with elements of the party who did not agree with her political style. The 1983 election victory liberated Mrs Thatcher. Her personal prestige was boosted by her triumph in the Falklands. Most of the 'wets' in her party had been marginalized. Mrs Thatcher was now a commanding leader at the head of a team of Thatcherites, such as the Chancellor, Nigel Lawson, the Trade Secretary, Norman Tebbit and the ever-loyal Foreign Secretary, Geoffrey Howe.

Cross-reference

Nigel Lawson and Geoffrey Howe are profiled on page 89.

■ Key profile

Norman Tebbit

Tebbit (born 1931) was an outspoken Essex MP who was appointed trade secretary in Margaret Thatcher's first cabinet and later became party chairman. His down-to-earth and abrasive style made him very popular with the new Thatcher Conservatives. He was injured in the IRA bomb attack on the 1984 party conference (in which his wife was badly hurt). In 1987, he fell out with one of Margaret Thatcher's advisers, Lord Young and left the government, though he remained loyal to Thatcherite ideals.

Margaret Thatcher had obtained an almost total mastery of the press. Her press secretary, Bernard Ingham, became hugely influential in securing favourable press coverage through informal contacts with journalists and the use of deliberate leaks to the press. Mrs Thatcher used her strong political position to act boldly. She took on, and defeated three main enemies: state controlled industries, left-wing local councils and the unions. In the economy, the key policies were the privatisation of key industries and the stimulation of free enterprise through tax cuts and deregulation.

Cross-reference

The impact of Thatcherism on the economy is covered on pages 103–104.

The Thatcher government saw left-wing local councils as enemies, both in terms of ideology and because they were blamed for wasting resources. The fiercest battles were fought with the Greater London Council (GLC) headed by a maverick left-winger, Ken Livingstone. Margaret Thatcher treated many GLC policies in education and public transport as provocations. Ken Livingstone was demonised as the face of the 'loony left'.

Key profile

Ken Livingstone

Livingstone (born 1945) made his name as a left-wing activist on Lambeth Borough Council. In 1981, he became leader of the GLC after ousting Sir Andrew MacIntosh. He remained leader until the GLC was abolished in 1986. He was the first elected mayor of London from 2001 to 2008. Livingstone was regarded as an unreliable maverick by the Labour Party leadership, who tried to block his election in 2001. After he proved popular and successful, he was allowed to rejoin the party in 2005.

In 1986, the Local Government Act abolished the big metropolitan local authorities that had been set up by the Heath government; the powers of the central government were greatly increased at the expense of local government. In the short term, this was a clear victory against the 'loony left' but, in the longer term, it created problems for central government, because central government was now in the firing line dealing with issues it previously had not needed to worry about. In *The Times* Simon Jenkins called this the *'nationalisation of blame'*.

Margaret Thatcher's most dramatic victory, however, was not against left-wing councils; it was against the power of the trade unions, in particular against the NUM and its firebrand leader, Arthur Scargill. The outcome of the miners' strike of 1984–85 is often regarded, both by her admirers and her detractors, as the defining event of Thatcher's years in power; just as the 1974 miners' strike was the defining event in bringing down Edward Heath. The strike dominated the headlines for a year. In the process, the NUM was badly split and many traditional mining communities suffered severe hardship. When the last strikers gave up the struggle in March 1985, the Thatcher's government had indeed 'smashed the unions'.

Exploring the detail

Low-spending Tory councils

The Thatcher government constantly boasted about the differences between low-spending Conservative councils compared with the high levels of public spending in Labour-controlled councils. Many council leaders argued that such comparisons were inherently unfair because Labour-controlled councils were in places with worse social problems and had to provide more expensive public services.

Cross-reference

The social consequences of the 1984–85 miners' strike are covered in Chapter 11.

Fig. 2 *Follow us, comrades! Mick McGahey and Arthur Scargill leading striking miners, 1985*

Key profile

Arthur Scargill

Scargill (born 1938) was leader of the Yorkshire miners. His HQ at Barnsley was known as 'Arthur's Castle'. Scargill played a big part in the successful strikes of 1972 and 1974. In 1981, he succeeded the moderate Joe Gormley as president of the NUM. Scargill was ideologically committed to the use of industrial action for political purposes, not just to fight for improved pay and conditions. The coal strike of 1984–85 resulted in major confrontations with the government and police; it also split the NUM. In 1993, Scargill founded a new party to promote 'real socialism' but made little impact.

■ Key terms

Mass picketing: a method by which strikers could prevent industry from operating normally during a strike. Mass pickets could put pressure on non-strikers and could blockade plants to stop transport arriving or leaving. It was used effectively in the Grunwick dispute of 1977 and was a key tactic for Arthur Scargill and the NUM in 1984.

■ Cross-reference

The Battle of Orgreave is detailed on page 112.

■ Cross-reference

Heath's actions in 1973–74 are described on pages 57–58.

For the winter of discontent, see pages 87–8.

Fig. 3 *Labour leaders old and new: The Foots and the Kinnocks, 1992*

In 1981, a previous dispute had been settled by compromise because the government had not felt ready for a rerun of 1973–74. Now, in 1984, the government was fully prepared and confident. New laws passed in 1982 made strike ballots compulsory and banned **mass picketing**. Huge stocks of coal had been built up at power stations. The flow of North Sea oil made it much less likely there would be an energy crisis like 1973. Ian McGregor, the new chairman of the National Coal Board (NCB) had government backing for taking a tough line.

Arthur Scargill was a charismatic leader but he did not gain total support for a national strike. His refusal to hold a strike ballot weakened his case and he failed to overcome the historic regional divisions among the miners. The Nottinghamshire miners formed a breakaway union, the Union of Democratic Mineworkers (UDM). Miners who disapproved of Scargill's radical tactics started drifting back to work. One key factor was the role of the police. The urban disturbances in 1981 had given the police a crash course in containing violent protests. They now had new equipment, more experience of riot control and better tactics. Margaret Thatcher's critics blamed her for the politicisation of the police, claiming they were used to defeat the miners, rather than being impartial protectors of law and order. Among many confrontations, the most famous was the 'Battle of Orgreave'.

The key factor in the defeat of the NUM was probably Arthur Scargill himself. Scargill alienated moderates; he never got the support of the Labour Party leadership. Many people felt sympathy for the mining communities and many disapproved of Margaret Thatcher's description of the strikers as *'the enemy within'* but it was easy for Mrs Thatcher and her allies in the press to demonise Scargill as a dangerous revolutionary challenging the democratically elected government. Scargill's all-or-nothing tactics almost certainly made the final defeat of the NUM worse; pit closures would have happened anyway but more pits were closed than would have been the case if the NUM had negotiated with the NCB, rather than gamble on a politically motivated strike.

The results of the miners' strike went far beyond the coal industry. The power of the unions was dramatically reduced. By 1990, total union membership was only two-thirds of what it had been in 1979. Other state industries such as British Steel and British Airways were reorganised, with massive job losses. The ability of the unions to intimidate governments was gone for good. Margaret Thatcher was quick to draw comparisons between her bold actions and the weakness of Heath in 1973–74, or Jim Callaghan in the winter of discontent. The defeat of the miners played a big part in consolidating Mrs Thatcher's popularity and authority, as was to be proved in the 1987 general election. She also continued to benefit from the weakness and divisions of the opposition parties.

The divided opposition, 1983–87

After its heavy defeat in 1983, the Labour Party's new leader, Neil Kinnock, was determined to move the party along the long road back to political credibility but this was a huge task. The parliamentary party had been weakened and left-wing activists in the unions and in local government had great influence. The hard-left Militant Tendency infiltrated several local councils. Ken Livingstone, the left-wing leader of the GLC, was engaged in running political battles against the government. Arthur Scargill's leadership of the miners' strike fuelled a lot of anti-Thatcher radicalism.

Key profile

Neil Kinnock

Kinnock (born 1942) was a left-wing Labour MP from South Wales. He succeeded Michael Foot as party leader in 1983. Kinnock changed his mind on key left-wing causes such unilateralism, nationalisation and Europe. He strongly attacked the hard left and set out to move the Labour Party back towards the political middle ground. He also started the process of modernising the party organisations and improving party discipline, helped by Patricia Hewitt, Peter Mandelson and others. Kinnock led Labour to two election defeats in 1987 and 1992 but did much to restore Labour's political credibility.

After the collapse of the miners' strike in 1985, Kinnock attempted to assert control over the parliamentary party and to regain the initiative from the hard left activists. At the 1985 party conference in Bournemouth, he made an outspoken attack on the actions of the Militant Tendency leaders of the city council in Liverpool, blasting them for taking the city to the edge of bankruptcy and for rushing out redundancy notices to 31,000 employees. Less directly, Kinnock was also distancing himself from the supporters of Tony Benn and Arthur Scargill.

By 1987, Kinnock's leadership had already done a lot to restore party discipline and to make the party organisation more efficient but, even so, Labour suffered yet another heavy defeat. From this point on, the modernisation of the party was given high priority. Labour's image became much more moderate, through the reassuring the shadow chancellor, John Smith, and a group of talented younger politicians including Peter Mandelson, Tony Blair and Gordon Brown. By 1990, the Labour revival progressed far enough for the party to have serious hopes of winning the next election.

The revival of Labour was matched by a loss of momentum for the SDP–Liberal Alliance, which found it hard to keep the levels of support gained in 1981 and 1982. This was partly due to ideological differences; opposition to Thatcher was not enough to provide unity by itself. There were also personal differences between the two Davids. The Alliance got 24 per cent of the vote in the 1987 election, nowhere near the peak of 40 per cent just before the Falklands War. In 1988, the two parties formally merged to form the Liberal Democrats.

The SDP began to shrink. The reason why the SDP existed at all was the fact that the Labour Party of 1981 was a political basket case. Moderate socialists had felt compelled to leave the Labour Party to fight against hard-left extremism. Now, as Neil Kinnock established his grip on the party, it seemed that moderate socialism was back in business and the SDP had no real identity or purpose. David Owen resigned as SDP leader in 1988. Many MPs switched their allegiance back to Labour. The Liberal Democrats remained a force in politics especially through their slick campaigning in by-elections but the hopes of 'breaking the mould' melted away.

Exploring the detail
Militant Tendency
The Militant Tendency derived its name from the *Militant* newspaper that promoted Trotskyite revolutionary socialism. Militant was an 'entryist' organisation, seeking to infiltrate the Labour Party from within. The Militant Tendency gained a foothold in Bradford and some London boroughs but its biggest success was in Liverpool, where it gained control of the city council, with Derek Hatton as deputy council leader and Tony Byrne as city treasurer.

Did you know?
There is a vivid account of Neil Kinnock's Bournemouth speech in Andrew Marr's *A History of Modern Britain*.

Cross-reference
The long-term impact of Neil Kinnock's leadership is discussed in Chapter 13.

Cross-reference
Peter Mandelson is profiled on page 138, Tony Blair on page 137, Gordon Brown on page 143; and the Two Davids on page 94.

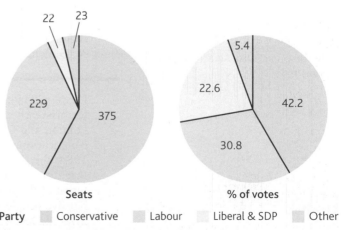

Party ▮ Conservative ▮ Labour ▮ Liberal & SDP ▮ Other

Fig. 4 *General election results, June 1987*

■ Activity

Thinking point

Analyse the general election results of 1987 and the results of 1979 and 1983 in Chapter 13, making notes on any significant fluctuations or trends. Make a list of the **three** most important factors explaining Conservative dominance.

■ A closer look

Margaret Thatcher and Northern Ireland

Another enemy Margaret Thatcher battled against in the 1980s was republicanism in Northern Ireland. Thatcher had strong unionist sympathies and was determined not to give in to terrorism. She soon faced a crisis over the campaign for 'special category' status by IRA prisoners held in the Maze prison in Belfast. Hunger strikes, led by Bobby Sands, began in 1980. The hunger strikers gained a lot of attention and support. Then a sudden by-election in Fermanagh presented Sinn Fein, the political wing of the IRA, with an opportunity. Still on hunger strike, Sands was nominated for the seat and won. A few weeks later he died. His funeral drew crowds of 100,000. Nine more hunger strikers died before the protest was called off in October 1981.

Margaret Thatcher claimed that the hunger strikes were a defeat for the IRA because their main aim, special category status, was not granted but the hunger strikes changed the political landscape. Bobby Sands and the other strikers became nationalist heroes. Sinn Fein saw the advantages of using the 'ballot box and the gun' as a twin-track strategy. In the 1983 general election, the Sinn Fein president, Gerry Adams, won the parliamentary seat of West Belfast and set out on the long road that led ultimately to the Good Friday Agreement of 1998.

■ Key profile

Gerry Adams

Adams (born 1948) became leader of Sinn Fein, the political wing of the IRA, in 1981. He was elected MP for West Belfast in 1983 but refused to attend the 'English parliament' because this would entail swearing an oath of allegiance to the Queen. Adams was one of the architects of Sinn Fein's twin-track strategy, using 'the armalite and the ballot box'. In the 1990s, he played a leading role in the IRA ceasefires and the peace process that led to the Good Friday Agreement.

■ Cross-reference

For The Good Friday Agreement, see pages 144–5.

Despite Thatcher's public stance of never negotiating with terrorists, there were secret contacts through go-betweens. The London and Dublin governments also discussed proposals for a constitutional settlement in Northern Ireland. Then, in October 1984, the IRA exploded a huge bomb in the Grand Hotel in Brighton during the Conservative party conference. The main target of the Brighton bomb, Margaret Thatcher, was unhurt, but five people were killed. There was national outrage in Britain. Despite the Brighton bomb, however, contacts with Irish government continued; the British authorities knew the IRA could not be beaten without Dublin's help on cross-border security.

In November 1985, the Anglo-Irish Agreement, setting up permanent intergovernmental cooperation, was signed at Hillsborough. There was a furious unionist and loyalist backlash. 200,000 attended a protest rally in Belfast. There was a series of atrocities on both sides. There seemed to be no way out of the cycle of violence and retaliation. In November 1989, however, the new Northern Ireland secretary, Peter Brooke, stated that the IRA could not be defeated by force and that the government would 'respond imaginatively' if the IRA offered a ceasefire. Brooke's approach provided the basis for the later 'peace process' of the 1990s.

The British economy, 1979–90

A key aim of Thatcherite economic policy was denationalisation, *'rolling back the frontiers of the state'* by the privatisation of state-controlled enterprises. A few steps were taken in this direction in the first term. BP was privatised in 1979 and British Aerospace in 1980, but the drive for privatisation gained real momentum with the successful sale of British Telecom in 1984. The British Airports Authority and the National Bus Company were also sold off, followed by British Gas and British Airways in 1986, Rolls Royce in 1987 and British Steel in 1988. The sale of British Gas, in particular, was accompanied by a high-profile advertising campaign seeking to maximise the purchase of shares by ordinary people.

Privatisation was driven by anti-socialist ideology. It was a core belief of Thatcherism that the private sector was more dynamic and efficient than the public sector. Most privatised enterprises were sold off cheaply in order to to ensure all shares were taken up. On the other hand, privatisation also brought in huge amounts of money to the government. Radical Thatcherites wanted to push ahead with further privatisations, including the coal industry and the railways, and drew up plans to privatise parts of the NHS.

These plans were not pursued until the 1990s but, even so, the privatisation of state concerns during the Thatcher years marked a significant shift in the British economy. Perhaps more than any other factor, the drive for privatisation signalled the end of the post-war consensus about economic management.

Another aspect of the 'private good; public bad' theme was the sale of council houses. Margaret Thatcher was enthusiastic about the idea of turning Britain into a 'property-owning democracy', through the widest possible private ownership of homes as well as shares. The Housing Act of 1980 gave the 'Right to Buy' to council-house tenants. In one sense, these policies were very successful. Thousands of people took advantage of the opportunity to buy their homes. On the other hand, shares in the privatised industries were mostly bought up by big commercial concerns, not by the 'little people' as government advertising had predicted.

Alongside privatisation, there was also financial **deregulation**, freeing up the City of London and the financial markets from the tight controls regulated by the Bank of England. In October 1986, the '**Big Bang**' blew away old traditions

Key terms

Deregulation: the loosening of controls on banks and financial markets. In Britain and in the United States, deregulation fitted in with political trends in favour of capitalism and free enterprise. There was a massive boom in investment banking and financial speculation. The issue of deregulation became very controversial in the Great Crash of 2008.

Big Bang: 27 October 1986, the day the London Stock Exchange was deregulated, opening the way for computer screen trading and replacing the 'old boys' network' with free competition. The Big Bang is credited with restoring London's position as a world financial centre.

Fig. 5 *The new City: the London Stock Exchange after deregulation*

Did you know?

The role of the 'City' (the London stock exchange and the financial services industry) has always been vital to the British economy. Without the 'invisible earnings' piled up by the City, Britain's balance of payments difficulties would have been much worse. The Big Bang of 1986 was intended to enable a rapid expansion of the financial sector, partly to compensate for the decline of Britain's manufacturing industry.

Cross-reference

Britain's membership of the ERM is covered on page 131.

Exploring the detail

Howe's revenge

Geoffrey Howe's resignation statement in the House of Commons did terrible damage to Margaret Thatcher's position as prime minister. Howe was furious at Thatcher's backtracking from her previous commitments on Europe. Howe took a devastating revenge. His resignation statement to parliament, broadcast on television, was quiet, polite but full of explosive criticisms of the Prime Minister's autocratic ways. The speech made a sensational impact.

Exploring the detail

The poll tax

The community charge was generally known as the 'poll tax' because the electoral register was used to identify those required to pay. It was in many ways fairer than the traditional system of charging rates according to the property value of people's home. Supporters of the poll tax claimed that the new scheme would eventually have been accepted if the government had not given in to the well-organised campaign against it.

and internationalised the stock market. A new breed of dealers and speculators in shirtsleeves and red braces took over. The City became a place where bigger risks were taken and bigger fortunes were made, faster.

The Thatcherite agenda naturally included lower taxes and more incentives for people to generate wealth. In Nigel Lawson's budget in March 1987, the basic rate of income tax was cut from 29 per cent to 27 per cent (a year later it was cut again, to 25 per cent) and personal pensions were launched, encouraging people to save for themselves rather than rely on state or company pensions.

Activity

Revision exercise

Use the evidence in this chapter to write a paragraph explaining the importance of economic factors for strength of support for the Conservative government in 1987.

The downfall of Margaret Thatcher

When her own party removed Margaret Thatcher from power in 1990, it came as a shock to the Iron Lady herself and to the world. Thatcher had become such a dominant personality that it was hard to imagine British politics without her. The TV images of the time are sharp in the memories of those who saw them: Thatcher marching down the steps of the British Embassy in Paris to tell John Sergeant of the BBC *We fight on*; a tearful Thatcher being driven away from Downing Street; Thatcher defiantly addressing parliament afterwards. The fall of Margaret Thatcher was a dramatic event. But dramatic events have many causes, not all of them sudden.

The decline of Margaret Thatcher can be traced back to 1987, the year of her third election triumph. One problem was economic. 1987 was the year of the great stock market crash that followed the 'Big Bang', the deregulation of the City in 1986. The policies of Margaret Thatcher's new chancellor, Nigel Lawson, especially his 1988 budget, led to the rapid expansion of the economy in the 'Lawson boom' but the result was a balance of payments problem. By 1990, inflation had risen to 10.9 per cent, higher than it had been in 1980. Fear of inflation was one of the main reasons why Britain entered the Exchange Rate Mechanism (ERM).

The second problem was political. From the time Michael Heseltine resigned over the Westland affair in 1986, he became a magnet for disaffected MPs. Margaret Thatcher was beginning to become isolated as many of the most loyal members of her government were pushed to the sidelines. In 1989, Thatcher's use of Professor Alan Walters as an economic adviser infuriated the Chancellor, Nigel Lawson. Lawson resigned. Thatcher alienated Geoffrey Howe by moving him from the foreign office to a lesser post. In 1990, Nicholas Ridley had to resign after making embarrassing anti-German comments in an interview in the *Spectator*.

The turbulence in the government was shown by the fact that the relatively young and inexperienced John Major filled the three great cabinet posts of home secretary, foreign secretary and chancellor in the space of 18 months. In 1990, the tensions in the government came to a head when Mrs Thatcher provoked the long-suffering Sir Geoffrey Howe into finally resigning from the government.

The third problem was self-inflicted. Margaret Thatcher wanted to replace the system of financing local government through homeowners paying rates with the idea of individuals paying a new community charge. The proposed poll tax proved bitterly unpopular with public opinion and the press. Mrs Thatcher was strongly advised to drop the scheme. She ignored the advice and pressed on. Anti-poll tax demonstrations in central London, attended by about 200,000 people, led to very serious rioting, with hundreds of rioters and policemen injured and millions of pounds worth of damage. The government's popularity in the opinion polls fell sharply.

By 1990, the Labour party recovery under Neil Kinnock and John Smith was evident. Many Conservative MPs now genuinely feared defeat at the next election. The loss of the ultra-safe seat of Eastbourne to the Liberals in a by-election was especially alarming: if the Conservatives could lose Eastbourne, they could lose anywhere. This was a key factor in Margaret Thatcher's downfall. Without the fears for their own survival among Conservative MPs, there would not have been a challenge to her leadership in the first place.

The final blows to Thatcher came from within her own cabinet. In the first ballot, held while Mrs Thatcher was in Paris for a European summit, she got 204 votes against Michael Heseltine's 152. The margin of victory was not sufficient to rule out a second ballot. At first, Mrs Thatcher intended to fight on but when she called in her ministers, one at a time, for consultation she found most of them advising her to quit. The most direct and blunt advice came from her education secretary, Ken Clarke. Mrs Thatcher resigned as prime minister two days later. Afterwards, the Conservative Party struggled to come to terms with its act of '**regicide**'.

One clever verdict on the decline and fall of Margaret Thatcher was that she was running out of enemies. Her whole premiership had been marked by battles against opponents who were first demonised and then defeated: the 'wets' in her own party, General Galtieri, Michael Foot, Arthur Scargill, Ken Livingstone. All of these were in some ways 'soft' targets. After 1987, Mrs Thatcher's main target was 'Europe' but this was not an easy battlefield to fight on, because of the risk of doing serious damage to party unity.

Another way of putting it was that Mrs Thatcher was running out of friends. By 1990, she had, in one way or another, lost almost all the key players in her years of triumph. Her ultra-loyal party chairman, Cecil Parkinson, had to resign because of a scandal in his private life in 1983. Willie Whitelaw went to the House of Lords. From 1987, Thatcher had sacked or alienated Norman Tebbit, Nigel Lawson and Geoffrey Howe. When Thatcher loyalists bitterly accused her cabinet of failing to support her during the leadership election, it was difficult to ignore the fact that she had thrown away a lot of loyalty by her own autocratic actions beforehand.

The Thatcher legacy

Assessing the legacy of Margaret Thatcher's years in power is both difficult and controversial. She polarised opinion while she was prime minister and opinion is still polarised nearly 20 years later. Part of the problem is that Thatcher's policies often seemed more divisive than they actually were. There were many continuities in the Thatcher years: welfare spending kept going up, for example, and the government held back from privatising the public services. It was often Margaret Thatcher's political style that had such a polarising effect, rather than the actual policies.

Assessing Margaret Thatcher's legacy is also difficult because she did not disappear quietly from the political scene but continued to haunt the memory of her own party for another 15 years. In 1990, she promised John Major she would be '*a good back-seat driver*'. In 1937, another outgoing Conservative prime minister, Stanley Baldwin had promised his successor: '*Once I leave, I leave. I shall not tell the new captain on the bridge how to steer the ship and I shall not spit on the deck.*' There have never been any reports of Margaret Thatcher spitting on the deck – but there were indeed plenty of times when she told the new captain how to steer the ship.

Cross-reference

The social impact of the anti-poll tax riots is covered in Chapter 11.

Key terms

Regicide: the term for the killing of a monarch, such as the beheading of King Charles I in 1649.

Fig. 6 *The end of an era? Margaret and Dennis Thatcher leaving Downing Street after her resignation, 28 November 1990*

The following 'balance sheet' provides a possible starting point for evaluation. Remember that history is not always a matter of clear choices between right and wrong and throws up many contradictions. It may well be that you judge that, sometimes, the contrasting opinions for and against may both be true.

FOR	AGAINST
• *She was Britain's first woman prime minister*	• *She alienated women voters so that the Conservatives no longer gained the majority of the female vote*
• *She enabled the Conservatives to have 18 years in power*	• *She enabled the Labour party to have eleven years in power*
• *She broke the excessive power of the unions*	• *She politicised the police and polarised society*
• *She played a key role in winning the Cold War*	• *She was not invited to the tenth anniversary of the end of the Berlin Wall*
• *She restored national pride*	• *She alienated Britain's partners in Europe*
• *She rescued Britain from economic decline and transformed the economy*	• *She caused unnecessary damage to Britain's industrial base*
• *She made Britain a property-owning democracy*	• *She encouraged private greed at the expense of the public good*

Fig. 7 *Margaret Thatcher: an assessment*

A closer look

The conflict of opinion

Margaret Thatcher was shrewd, manipulative and bold, verging on reckless. She was also extremely lucky. Had Labour not been busy disembowelling itself, and had a desperate dictatorship not taken a nationalistic gamble with some island sheep-farmers, her government would probably have been destroyed after a single term. But not until 1990 was there an end to the most extraordinary, nation-changing premiership of modern British history.

From Marr, A., A History of Modern Britain, 2007

'Maggie, Maggie, Maggie, Out, Out, Out!'

Chant of anti-poll tax protesters, 1990

In creating and touching up her image, Mrs Thatcher had an advantage over all her predecessors; no previous prime minister before her could rely on colour television pictures to tell her story. Lady Thatcher had a strange power of veto over whether any Conservative party policy fitted in with the most powerful myth in British politics. She had become a personality cult.

From Sergeant, J., Maggie: Her Fatal Legacy, 2005

'Mrs Thatcher had a very defined political philosophy – rolling back the state, curbing trade union power and putting the emphasis on the individual. It was an inevitable reaction against the welfare state and a public sector that had become very large – a vested interest that was out of touch.'

Tony Blair, 2003

'The whole situation in the Conservative Party today springs from that night when they dismissed the best prime minister Britain had had since Churchill.'

Denis Thatcher, 2005

'Because she like to create enemies, a lot of people made her the source of all the ills in their lives. So they think she destroyed manufacturing industry; she was cruel to the miners' families; she believed in no social benefits and destroyed the health service. It's all nonsense but that's the myth that has been built up around her. The rhetoric and the reality were so different. Welfare spending and health spending went up; spending on the armed forces and the police went down.'

Michael Portillo, 2004

'Margaret Thatcher was beyond argument a great prime minister.'

Sir Geoffrey Howe, 2003

'Large claims were made for Mrs Thatcher as a great prime minister but already, in 1991, they are melting before our eyes like the snows of spring. My prediction is that History will judge her just above average.'

Alan Watkins, 1991

'After 1990, I think she felt the people running the government were all in short trousers and not up to it. She probably should not have said as much as she did.'

Norman Lamont, 2005

'The price that was paid for her style of government was to wreck the Conservative Party for ten years, fifteen, whatever. She encouraged the suicidal tendencies in the party and in the media. The curiosity about Margaret is that she became more radical and fundamentalist out of office than she ever had been in.'

Chris Patten, 2004

'Margaret Thatcher carried the authority of her office always with her. It was in her handbag.'

Douglas Hurd, 2005

'Well, there's not much point being a weak and floppy thing in the chair, is there?'

Margaret Thatcher, 2001

 Activity

Revision exercise

Use the evidence of this chapter and that in Chapter 12. Assemble a range of evidence to support the views that:

1 Margaret Thatcher was a great prime minister

2 Margaret Thatcher 'wrecked the Conservative Party'.

 Summary question

Explain why political opposition to Margaret Thatcher was so ineffectual throughout the 1980s.

British society, 1975–90

Fig. 1 *Us against Them: a miner faces the police at Orgreave Colliery, June 1984*

In this chapter you will learn about:

- the social effects of Margaret Thatcher's policies such as privatisations and the sale of council houses

- the social impact of industrial disputes and the 1984–85 miners' strike

- the growth of extra-parliamentary protest movements.

The over-mighty position of the trade unions, which had been encouraged by the Labour governments, was overturned by the fiercely anti-union policies of the Conservatives in the 1980s. The long monetarist reign of Margaret Thatcher chose an authoritarian, book-keeping style to bring discipline to all spheres the government could reach. The effect, perhaps unintended, was to create an unusual degree of centralised power, which all but eliminated the voice of local government and the regions. Many British institutions had remained undisturbed for longer than anyone could remember – a succession of disgraceful or divisive episodes in the City of London, the police, the royal family and the Church of England heightened the sense of authority in decline. British society was increasingly polarised: the relative prosperity of the new 'enterprise culture' was matched by the decay of the inner cities and their despairing underclass, by falling standards of education, and by the growth of juvenile crime.

1 *From Davies, N., **Europe: A History**, 1996*

The end of the post-war consensus had a deep impact on British society. The economic rises of the 1970s and the prolonged period of high unemployment in the 1980s put a great strain on social cohesion.

Social tensions were intensified and attitudes polarised. The ideology of Thatcherism, with its emphasis on individualism and Margaret Thatcher's claim *there is no such thing as society*, seemed to be a direct attack on the ideas of the welfare state and civic responsibility. At the same time, long-term economic trends were changing Britain's industrial society. The old, labour-intensive industries were facing challenges from foreign competition and from technological innovation. The foundations of the working class and of the communities they lived in were crumbling.

This combination of political pressures from above, and social and economic changes from below resulted in recurrent social upheavals: the winter of discontent, serious urban rioting in inner cities, the great miners' strike of 1984–85, and the emergence of radical extra-parliamentary opposition. It is hard to assess how far the 'Thatcher Revolution' was the cure for or the cause of these social ills.

Key terms

North-south divide: a term frequently used to express the difference between the prosperous south of Britain and the less prosperous north. It is not a completely accurate view: many areas in the northern England look like the prosperous suburban 'south'; many areas of deprivation in London and parts of the south-west reflect the economic and social problems associated with the 'north'.

A closer look

Demographic change, 1975–90

Three key factors affected demographic trends in Britain after 1975. One, as always, was immigration. The second was the continuing shift of population from rural to urban areas. The third was the sharpening of the **north-south divide**, as old traditional industries contracted, leaving behind large tracts of dereliction in the Midlands, the north-west, the north-east, Scotland and South Wales. Far fewer people were employed in manufacturing industry. Long-term trends were shifting economic activity towards London and the south, changing the face of many towns and cities and fundamentally altering perceptions about class loyalties.

The population of Britain increased from 56 million in 1975 to 58 million by 1990. It is important to note, however, that there were periods of stagnation. In the three years from 1975 to 1978, the population actually began to fall. These fluctuations in the population reflected the economic and social background of the time. For five years running in the 1980s, for example, more than 3 million people were unemployed.

Immigration continued to be a source of social concern. There was a steady flow of immigrants from the sub-continent. Indians came mostly from an urban background and tended to assimilate more easily than those who came from rural Pakistan. There was also a sudden rush of immigrants from Bangladesh after its breakaway from Pakistan in 1974. By the late 1970s, the Brick Lane area of London was known as 'Banglatown' because so many immigrants were concentrated there. The Asian population of Bradford reached nearly 50,000.

The National Front became very active in parts of London where immigrants had settled, such as Brick Lane and Southall. Alongside the key issue of unemployment, race was also a factor in the urban violence

Table 1 *Urban population change, 1975–90*

City	Population change
Greater London	+ 600,000
Birmingham	– 112,000
Glasgow	– 77,000
Liverpool	– 118,000
Newcastle	– 61,000
Cardiff	+ 47,000
Belfast	– 44,000

Table 2 *Employment in manufacturing, 1979–92*

Year	Number employed (millions)
1979	7.1
1981	6.1
1984	5.3
1987	5.1
1990	5.0

Fig. 2 *Another riot: the Notting Hill Carnival, August 1976*

Key chronology

Social upheavals, 1975–90

1976
September Violence at Notting Hill Carnival

1980
April Rioting in St Paul's area of Bristol

1981
July Serious riots in Toxteth and Moss Side

1983
April Mass protests against Cruise missiles at Greenham

1984
June Battle of Orgreave

1985
May Fatal casualties in football riots

September Violent anti-police riots in Brixton

October Death of PC Blakelock in Broadwater Farm riots

1986
May Rioting by prisoners in 19 British gaols

1989
April 96 killed in Hillsborough football stadium disaster

1990
March Anti-poll tax riots in London

Did you know?

The teachers' dispute reflected a notable trend for the educated classes to oppose Margaret Thatcher. In 1985, Oxford University refused to award an honorary degree to her; an honour given to every one of the many previous prime ministers who had graduated from Oxford. In the 1987 election, two-thirds of those with university degrees voted for opposition parties.

that occurred in 1981 and 1985. The Thatcher government acted on the belief that immigration was a growing problem; a new Immigration Act was passed in 1981. On the other hand, it was clear that British life simply could not have carried on functioning without the migrants' contribution. The transport system, hospitals and the hotel industry were heavily dependent on recruiting workers from abroad. Many local communities would have had few if any restaurants or corner shops if it had not been for Asians from the Indian sub-continent or Hong Kong.

Social trends, 1975–90

The social impact of Thatcherism

Impact of privatisations and the sale of council houses

A key aim of the Thatcher government was to turn Britain into a property-owning democracy. This was part of 'rolling back the state' and placing the emphasis on self-reliance and the private sector.

The privatisation of previously state-controlled industries involved intensive public campaigns designed to increase share ownership by ordinary people. Between 1979 and 1990, the number of individuals owning stocks and shares went up from 3 million to 9 million. Privatisation brought a lot of revenue for the government and was popular with most of the middle classes. It did, however, make life more insecure for many employees. Some lost jobs as the privatised enterprises cut back on staff. Others found that they could no longer rely on long-term job security and reliable pension provision.

The enterprise culture aroused hostility from those working in the public sector. The unions representing public sector workers, such as COHSE and NUPE, became more militant. The teachers' unions, never previously associated with industrial unrest, carried on a lengthy dispute over working conditions in the mid-1980s.

The Housing Act of 1980, giving the 'Right to Buy' to council house tenants, was enormously successful in that huge numbers of people opted to buy their homes. By 1988, approximately 2 million new homeowners had taken advantage of the scheme to buy the homes they had previously rented. One reason the Right to Buy was so popular was that tenants were given generous discounts: the purchase price was much lower than on the open property market. The 1980 Act is regarded as one of the most successful of all Margaret Thatcher's policies, a big step towards social mobility and a 'property-owning democracy'. The Labour Party initially opposed the Right to Buy but later dropped its opposition because it was so popular with the public.

On the other hand, the Right to Buy had many negative consequences. The sale of council housing was predominantly in better-off areas and did not have a great impact in less desirable estates. Councils were ordered to use the profits from council house sales to reduce debts, not to build new council housing. The number and quality of homes available for rent was sharply reduced. With no programme to rebuild the stock of council housing, waiting lists for rented homes got longer. Many people were housed in emergency B & B accommodation which was expensive for councils to provide and not always suitable for the families involved. In 2005, such problems caused the Scottish Executive to terminate the Right to Buy in Scotland.

Impact on communities of industrial disputes

By 1975, the nature of industrial action was changing. The old traditional union bosses were beginning to lose control over their membership. Local wildcat strikes became much more common. Moderate union leaders came under pressure from younger radical activists. The rash of public sector strikes in the winter of discontent was a symbol of these changes.

These trends were intensified as the social impact of Thatcherism was felt. The role of the unions was constrained by new laws and the determination of some employers to keep the unions out of their workplaces. In 1977, strikers at the Grunwick photographic laboratories in Warrington faced a bitter struggle against their employer, who was determined to exclude union members. Newspaper proprietors, led by the Australian press baron Rupert Murdoch, went all out to reduce the power of the print unions. There was a major confrontation at Murdoch's Wapping plant in 1986. Over the next few years the old Fleet Street monopoly in newspaper production disappeared forever.

Key profile

Rupert Murdoch

Murdoch (born 1931) was already famous before the rise of Sky satellite television in the 1990s. He had made a fortune in Australian and American newspapers when he started to build up his British newspaper empire in the 1980s. He took over *The Sun* and made it the fastest-selling tabloid. He also bought *The Times*, the *Sunday Times* and the *News of the World*. The Murdoch press became very influential politically, mostly giving very strong support to Margaret Thatcher, not least against the unions. In the 1990s, support from the Murdoch press was crucial for the rise of New Labour.

Workers found their traditional skills were not in demand because they had been rendered out of date by mechanisation or by flexible working practices. The longest and most symbolic episode in the industrial struggles of this period was the miners' strike in 1984–85. The failure of the strike led to massive pit closures and job losses. The defeat of the strike reduced the influence of the whole union movement, not just the NUM. By 1990, the total trade union membership had fallen by 30 per cent since 1975.

The old certainties of the working class were being eroded; so was the way of life in their communities. In areas that had never known anything else but coalmines, shipyards and steelworks, people faced painful adjustments. There was high male unemployment; in many homes women became the main breadwinner. There were increased problems of ill health and depression, and also alcoholism and drugs. Young people could no longer expect to follow their fathers into work. Many were forced to move away.

The miners' strike, 1984–85

Arthur Scargill launched the miners' strike in a bid to prevent the downsizing of the coal industry. The strike was highly politicised and there were numerous confrontations between striking miners and the police. The biggest, pitched battle, though far from the only one was the Battle of Orgreave in the early phases of the strike.

Exploring the detail

Right to Buy

The Right to Buy was not a new idea in 1980. Councils had always had the power to sell council houses to tenants but it was rarely used. In the late 1960s, Horace Cutler, the leader of the Greater London Council (GLC), promoted the idea of large-scale council housing sell-offs. Cutler's scheme was halted in the 1970s, when the GLC was under Labour control; until Cutler returned as leader in 1977. In 1980, the Right to Buy became a key policy of Margaret Thatcher's government.

Key chronology

Industrial unrest, 1975–90

1977
July Grunwick strike: clashes between police and mass pickets

1979
February Gravediggers' strike; winter of discontent

1984
March Start of miners' strike

1985
April Final collapse of the miners' strike

1986
May Violent protests at Murdoch's Wapping print works

Cross-reference

The winter of discontent and the strikes associated with it are discussed on pages 87–88.

Did you know?

The 1996 feature film *Brassed Off* gives a vivid and sympathetic portrait of a mining community facing these strains.

The Battle of Orgreave

In June 1984, there was a mass picket of the coke plant at Orgreave in South Yorkshire by 5,000 miners. They were faced by up to 8,000 police officers assembled from all over the country. The result was a series of violent confrontations. More than 50 picketers were injured (including Arthur Scargill) and more than 70 police officers. The result of the battle was a long-lasting controversy over accusations of police brutality – in 1991, South Yorkshire police was ordered to pay compensation – but the immediate outcome was a defeat for the NUM because the lorries kept rolling in and out of Orgreave.

■ Key terms

King Coal: derived from the nursery rhyme about Old King Cole, this term reflected the historic importance of coalmining as Britain's industrial development. Since the mid-19th century, Britain had been the world's biggest producer and exporter of coal. At its peak, the coal and power industry employed 400,000. The role of the miners in the 1926 general strike and in the battle against Edward Heath's government in 1974 gave them a special status in the union movement.

■ Cross-reference

The political impact of the miners' strike is covered in Chapter 10.

■ Activity

Thinking point

Using the evidence of this chapter, list the **five** key aspects of social and industrial change that exacerbated social tensions in the years 1975 to 1990.

The outcome of Scargill's campaign to prevent pit closures was utter failure. In 1979, the coal industry employed 200,000; by 1990, the total was down to 60,000 and still falling. By the 1980s, '**King Coal**' was supplying only 20 per cent of Britain's energy needs, far less than oil and gas. The future seemed to be more about 'clean' nuclear power than 'dirty' coal. Scargill had not just been fighting against Margaret Thatcher, he was also fighting against the forces of history.

The social impact of the miners' strike, 1984–85

One of the great myths about the coal industry was the legendary solidarity of the miners and their fierce loyalty to each other. In fact, there had always been intense regional rivalries within the NUM. In the 1970s, Arthur Scargill himself had led a rebellion of more radical Yorkshire miners against the old-style moderate NUM president, Joe Gormley from Lancashire. (Gormley was once asked if he was worried that he had only won a vote of confidence by 13 votes to 12: '*Nothing to bother about*', he said, '*when I was in hospital they voted 13-12 to send me a get-well card*')

The strike launched in 1984 was never a genuinely national strike. No national strike ballot was held and the effect of the strike was to bring about a bitter split in the union. The important Nottinghamshire coalfield, with 30,000 miners, refused to join the strike and eventually formed a new, moderate breakaway union, the Union of Democratic Mineworkers (UDM). There were bitter recriminations. Scargillites accused the UDM of being 'scabs' and 'traitors'; the UDM accused Scargill of caring more about hard-left politics than the interests of the miners he was leading to defeat.

The last months of the strike were particularly demoralising. There was a steady drift back to work while the hard core of strikers determined to stick it out to the end depended on charitable handouts. The failure of the strike almost certainly made the closure programme happen quicker than it would have done otherwise.

■ A closer look

Urban crisis

The industrial changes that lay behind the miners' strike were reflected in many social trends in the 1980s. There was urban decay of many inner city areas and the intensification of social problems, including youth violence. These problems were exacerbated by high unemployment. Even before the violent confrontations of the miners strike, a series of violent urban disturbances had seemed to indicate that social cohesion was breaking down and that there was a crisis in relations between the police and the communities they served.

In 1980 and 1981, serious rioting in Bristol, Liverpool and south London led to a public enquiry headed by Lord Scarman. The Scarman Report criticised both the police and the government and highlighted the issue of race relations – according to the report, '*racial disadvantage is a fact of British life*' – and called for greater emphasis on community policing. There were further outbreaks of violent rioting and attacks on the police in 1985, in Brixton again and in Tottenham, north London. The Tottenham rioting, on the Broadwater Farm estate, led to the murder of

Fig. 3 *Rioting in the Toxteth district of Liverpool, July 1981*

a policeman, PC Blakelock. In the same year, fatal incidents in Birmingham and Brussels made football hooliganism into a major national issue in the media and calls for urgent government intervention.

The emergence of extra-parliamentary protest movements

From 1958, the most significant protest movement in Britain had been the Campaign for Nuclear Disarmament. CND continued to attract a lot of support and was given a new lease of life by Margaret Thatcher's determined backing for the policy of deterrence and stepping up the arms race against the USSR in the so-called New Cold War of the early 1980s There were, however, many other protest movements that worked outside the traditional framework of parliamentary politics and tried to involve people in direct action. Some of this reflected the polarisation of attitudes in response to Mrs Thatcher; there was also a widespread perception that the weakness of the opposition political parties had left a void that needed to be filled by direct action.

Among these movements were charities such as Shelter and Age Concern. The Church of England, so often seen as part of the Establishment, began to intervene in the public debate over social breakdown. The document *Faith and the City*, produced in 1985, caused a considerable stir as it was taken to be a criticism of the Thatcher government and was seen as 'interfering in politics'. Throughout the 1980s, the Catholic and Anglican bishops of Liverpool, Derek Worlock and David Sheppard were very active in campaigning for more action to help the poor and to maintain social cohesion.

There was also an increase in direct action. The Animal Liberation Front switched from non-violence to 'ecoterrorism' from 1982. There were arson attacks on pharmaceutical companies that tested drugs on animals and letter bombs were sent to public figures, including Mrs Thatcher. Support for environmental groups like Greenpeace and Friends of the Earth went up. Two key examples of the new trend towards direct action were the Greenham women and the anti-poll tax protesters.

Pacifism and feminism: the Greenham women

In 1979, the decision was taken to station American Cruise missiles at bases in Britain. In reaction to this, CND organised mass protest marches reminiscent of the Aldermaston marches twenty years earlier.

This time the epicentre of protest was RAF Greenham Common in Berkshire. In September 1981 a group of women protestors set up a camp outside the Greenham Common base. Other women joined them there as the camp became a focal point for feminism as well as pacifism; the camp was to remain in place for nineteen years.

In April 1983, when the Cruise missiles were due to arrive, a 14-mile human chain of protest stretched from Greenham to Aldermaston. The Greenham women attracted a lot of publicity and did much to dramatise the role of feminism in the protest movement. In 1984, the Newbury local council evicted the women and demolished the camp. The women returned after dark and rebuilt it.

Fig. 4 *'Cruise Missiles Out!' The Greenham women protesting at Greenham Common airbase, 1984*

The camp remained a powerful symbol during the 1980s and continued to exist even after it lost its original purpose. In 1989, the Cold War ended with the fall of the Berlin Wall, followed by the collapse of the Soviet Union itself. In 1991, the Cruise missiles were shipped back to the United States after a a new treaty was agreed on the limitation of intermediate nuclear weapons. Even then, the Greenham women kept their camp going. It was not finally closed until 2000. Direct action by women had become a cause in itself, bigger in the eyes of the Greenham women than the issue of nuclear disarmament.

The anti-poll tax riots

In her third term from 1987, Margaret Thatcher was determined to push through a major reform of the system of financing local government. She wished to move away from rates (paid according to the value of people's homes and businesses) to a system based on a 'community charge' paid by individuals. Who paid the charge would be decided by reference to the electoral register, hence the popular name for it was 'poll tax'. In one sense, this system would be fairer: for example, it would prevent elderly pensioners from paying high rates because they happened to live in a large house. In another sense, it could be seen as extremely unfair because everyone liable to pay would pay the same, no matter how wealthy they were. Whatever its merits, the poll tax became wildly unpopular. Mrs Thatcher's determination to push it through, in spite of being strongly advised not to by many of her ministers, was a big factor in the collapse of the Conservatives in the opinion polls in 1990.

In November 1989, the Militant Tendency set up the Anti-Poll Tax Federation. On 31 March 1990, the weekend before the community charge was to come into operation, a huge demonstration was planned to take place in Trafalgar Square. It was expected that 60,000 people would turn up. In the event, the number was more like 200,000, perhaps even 250,000, far too many to be contained within Trafalgar Square; the surrounding streets were choked by the crowds. Fighting and scuffles broke out. Some blamed anarchists and unemployed coal miners for deliberately fomenting violence; others blamed the police.

■ **Exploring the detail**

The Cruise missiles

Cruise missiles were remote-controlled rockets carrying powerful warheads and capable of hitting targets from many hundreds of miles away. They were later to play a prominent part in the first Gulf War of 1991. Stationing the missiles in Britain was part of the deliberate policy of deterrence: stoking up the pressure on the USSR and convincing the Brezhnev regime that it was impossible to keep pace with the West in the new high-technology arms race.

■ **Cross-reference**

The political significance of the poll tax is covered in Chapter 10.

Fig. 5 *A riot waiting to happen: the anti-poll tax demonstration in Trafalgar Square, just before the outbreak of violent rioting in the West End, March 1990*

The disturbances escalated into a major riot. Nearly 5,000 people were injured, mostly rioters but also numerous police officers and many bystanders who had nothing to do with the demonstration. Cars were overturned and set on fire. Many shop windows were smashed, followed by extensive looting. Over 300 arrests were made. The police were seen to have lost control. Many comparisons were made with the Battle of Orgreave in 1984 and there was criticism of the politicisation of the police. The following source comes from a hard-left viewpoint but it reflects widespread public concern about the policing of protest demonstrations:

> Obviously we understand that people generally resort to rioting because of desperation, naivety, self-defence, provocation, or because there are *agents provocateurs* in the crowd who are deliberately acting against the interests of the genuine marchers. These were probably all factors in the 31st March demo but the main reason for the riot was the police starting it. The primary role of the police is to protect the status quo (ie capitalist society) and they often provoke violence because they realise it is in the interests of the ruling class. The mass media like to report violence and they often refuse to broadcast details of peaceful demonstrations. This pushes anarchist organisations to foment violence as a way of achieving change.

2　　　　　　　　　　　　　　　　*From Wallis, S.,* **Revolution Destroyed?***, 2005*

Protest in culture and the media

The changed atmosphere of Britain in the 1980s was reflected in new, more aggressive trends in culture and the media. There was a sense that the opposition to Mrs Thatcher in parliament was so ineffectual that culture had to fill the gap instead. Playwrights like David Hare and Howard Brenton produced highly charged plays attacking what they saw as the culture of selfishness and greed engendered by Thatcherism. On television, Alan Bleasdale's *Boys From The Black Stuff* gave a sympathetic view of hard-pressed workers. *Spitting Image* and *Private Eye* kept up a barrage of satirical comment, mostly but not quite always critical of Mrs Thatcher.

■ **Exploring the detail**

Boys From The Black Stuff

The author, Alan Bleasdale, was a former Liverpool teacher turned dramatist. *Boys From The Black Stuff* was a black comedy, funny but bitter, following the adventures of casual labourers and their hand-to-mouth existence. One character, Yozzer, had a catchphrase, 'Gizzajob', that seemed to strike a chord in Thatcher's Britain.

■ **Summary question**

In what ways did class loyalties change in Britain between 1975 and 1990?

12 Britain, Europe and the world, 1975–90

Fig. 1 *The Sun and the sinking of the Argentine warship General Belgrano, 1982*

> We have ceased to be a nation in retreat. We have instead a new a newfound confidence – born in the economic battles at home and tested and found true 8,000 miles away.

1   *From a speech by Margaret Thatcher after victory in the Falklands, June 1982*

The 1975 EEC referendum seemed to confirm that Britain's destiny lay in Europe and that the days of empire were over. The wind of change had blown away Britain's colonial rule in Africa. Strategic bases east of Suez had been handed over. There were only a few imperial loose ends still to be disposed of, such as Hong Kong, Gibraltar and Rhodesia. The Falkland Islands might have been added to the list but few people gave much thought to the South Atlantic before 1982. In the event, the difficult problems of Rhodesia and Hong Kong were settled with relative ease, and Gibraltar was simply placed in the diplomatic deep freeze. It was the obscure issue of the Falkland Islands that dominated British foreign policy in the early 1980s. In the long view of history, however, the Falklands War was merely a minor episode in Britain's retreat from empire. The big issues affecting Britain's position in the world were relations with Europe and the developments in the Cold War.

Margaret Thatcher's relations with the EEC were marked by many contradictions. There were occasions when her 'handbag diplomacy' caused consternation, but also many issues on which Britain cooperated closely with Europe. Not until 1988 were there any serious doubts about Britain's place 'at the heart of Europe'. Britain's 'special relationship' with the United States was strengthened by the Thatcher–Reagan partnership that dominated the attitudes and policies of the West from 1981 to 1989. In these years, there were climactic developments in the Cold War: first, the hard-line confrontations of the so-called 'New Cold War', and then the remarkable transformation brought about by the arrival of Mikhail Gorbachev.

In 1979, it had been thought that the West was losing the Cold War. By 1990, the Berlin Wall was down, German reunification was completed and the Soviet Union was in the process of total disintegration. How much of the credit for this astonishing transformation of the world scene should be awarded to Margaret Thatcher, the Iron Lady, remains a very important question.

Foreign affairs 1975–90

Empire and Commonwealth, 1975–90

It has often been said that Margaret Thatcher was lucky in her enemies. When she came to power, she was lucky that the enemy whose stubborn persistence had frustrated British governments for fifteen years, Ian Smith, was on the point of giving up the fight. The problem of Rhodesia had bedevilled British foreign policy since 1965. By 1979, however, changing circumstances had deprived Smith of the support from Portugal and South Africa he had previously been able to rely on. Mrs Thatcher's foreign secretary, Lord Carrington, had the patience and diplomatic skills to bring about a final settlement. After tortuous negotiations at the Lancaster House conference in London in 1980, Smith was forced to accept defeat. The way was opened for black majority rule in an independent Zimbabwe-Rhodesia, led by the nationalist Robert Mugabe.

Key profile

Lord Carrington

Peter Carrington (born 1919) was a suave aristocrat and brilliant conciliator. His success over Rhodesia in 1980 did not only depend on persuading people like Smith and Mugabe into accepting a deal; it was also necessary to persuade Margaret Thatcher. There was a strong Rhodesia lobby in the Conservative Party opposed to black majority rule. As opposition leader to 1979, Margaret Thatcher had seemed sympathetic to their views.

The settling of the Rhodesia question did not remove all concerns about southern Africa. The issue of what to do about the apartheid regime in South Africa caused many rows in the Commonwealth, and Margaret Thatcher was frequently accused of failing to put enough pressure on

Cross-reference

The impact of European affairs on British domestic politics is covered in Chapters 9 and 10.

Key chronology

Britain and the world, 1975–90

1975 EEC referendum
1980 Independence granted to Zimbabwe-Rhodesia
1982 War in the Falklands
1986 Establishment of Single European Market
1989 Fall of the Berlin Wall and end of the Cold War
1990 Reunification of Germany

South Africa. Even so, resolving the issue of Rhodesia represented a big step towards finally disposing of Britain's legacy of empire. Lord Carrington was hopeful that the task of resolving the status of the Falkland Islands would be easier; but the problem of the Falklands caused the premature end of Lord Carrington's distinguished career; and Britain's biggest military action since 1945.

The Falklands War

The Falkland Islands, 300 miles east of the South American mainland, had been a British colony and naval base since 1833. Ownership of the islands, known to the Argentinians as Las Malvinas, had been claimed by Argentina since independence in 1817, based on previous Spanish claims. By the 1970s, the Falklands no longer had much strategic importance. The colony was an isolated remnant of empire, populated by a small community of mostly sheep farmers, run by the Falkland Islands Company. From 1971, the only air link to the islands was run by

Fig. 2 *Yomping to Port Stanley: British troops advancing across East Falkland, 1992*

an Argentine airline; Argentina also supplied the Falklands' energy needs. Foreign office officials were prepared to negotiate with Argentina over the future of the islands: the islanders themselves were keen to remain British.

In 1981, the Foreign Secretary, Lord Carrington, and the Defence Secretary, John Nott, approved the withdrawal of HMS *Endurance*, leaving the South Atlantic without any British naval presence. The **junta** in power in Argentina since 1976, took this as a hint that Britain was willing to let the Falklands go. Seeking popularity in the middle of an economic crisis, the leader of the junta, General Galtieri, sent an invasion force to occupy the Falklands, claiming Argentine sovereignty over Las Malvinas. Lord Carrington resigned; a very principled resignation as he had advised against pulling out *Endurance* but had been overruled.

The British government faced a dilemma. Winning back the islands by force would be very difficult and dangerous; in any case, the government had already shown it was willing to negotiate, if only the islanders could be persuaded to go along. Many governments, perhaps rightly, would have looked for a diplomatic solution. Margaret Thatcher's response was the immediate announcement that a naval task force would be sent to remove the Argentine forces and assert the right of the Falkland Islanders to self-determination.

Seen in hindsight, this decision was the making of Mrs Thatcher, sending her previously unpopular government soaring in the opinion polls. It was; however, a very risky gamble that could have ended in a disaster of Suez proportions. The sending of the task force had a remarkable impact. Rolling television coverage showed huge and enthusiastic crowds giving the fleet an emotional send-off from Portsmouth harbour. The patriotic national mood took most people, including TV reporters at the

Key chronology

Britain and the Falklands War

1976	Argentina taken over by military junta
1981	Withdrawal of HMS *Endurance* from South Atlantic
1982	
2 April	Argentine occupation of 'Las Malvinas'
5 April	Despatch of British task force
2 May	Sinking of the *General Belgrano*
4 May	Loss of HMS *Sheffield* to Exocet missile
21 May	British landings at San Carlos Water
14 June	Surrender of Argentine forces at Port Stanley

Key terms

Junta: a military group that rules a country after taking power by force.

scene, completely by surprise. The headline in the American magazine *Newsweek* was '*The Empire Strikes Back*'.

While the task force was on its long haul to the South Atlantic, there was frantic diplomatic activity. Efforts were made to get Argentina to accept UN Resolution 502 and pull her troops back. There was some hope this approach might succeed until the beginning of May. The other diplomatic urgency was to get assurances of support from the United States. It was plainly impossible to fight battles 8,000 miles from home without the use of American bases like Ascension Island. Unlike Suez in 1956, the Americans gave the green light to go ahead. The Falklands War strengthened the special relationship and the personal ties between Mrs Thatcher and Reagan.

On 2 May, the last chance of a peaceful settlement disappeared, when a British submarine sank the Argentine battleship, *General Belgrano*, causing heavy loss of life. The sinking was controversial, as the *Belgrano* was steaming away from the battle zone at the time. Many applauded the action (the headline in *The Sun* the next day was simply: '*GOTCHA!*') but many anti-war protestors claimed that the sinking had been unnecessary and was designed to finish off the chances of a peaceful outcome.

Victory did not take long but it was a close-run thing. On 4 May, an air-launched Exocet missile destroyed the British warship HMS *Sheffield*. Argentina was 400 miles away from the battle zone, not 8,000, and had far more aircraft than the British task force. Had Argentina possessed even a few more Exocets, the whole task force might have gone the same way as *Sheffield*. American diplomatic intervention was crucial in preventing the Argentine forces from obtaining more missiles. On 21 May, British troops landed at San Carlos Water, the passage between East and West Falkland, known as Bomb Alley during the dangerous phase of transferring the invasion army from ship to shore. Once the landings were secured, however, victory was certain. British troops 'yomped' their way across the mountains to Port Stanley. The Argentine forces surrendered on 14 June.

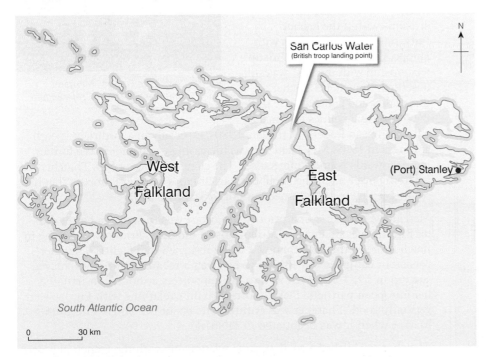

Fig. 3 *The Falkland Islands*

Victory in the Falklands boosted Margaret Thatcher in domestic politics, but the impact on Britain's foreign position was less clear-cut.

■ **Cross-reference**

The political impact of the war in the Falklands is covered in Chapter 9.

■ **Did you know?**

The distance from Britain to the Falkland Islands is more than 8,000 miles. It would have been impossible to keep the British task force supplied without support from US bases on Ascension Island and in the Caribbean.

■ **Cross-reference**

To recap on Britain's accession to the EEC and the significance of the 1975 EEC referendum for the main political parties, look back to page 65.

■ **Key chronology**

Britain and Europe, 1975–90

1975		
June	Emphatic victory for 'yes' campaign in EEC referendum	
1984		
November	British rebate obtained by Margaret Thatcher	
1986		
January	Anglo-French agreement to build Channel Tunnel	
June	Single European Act passed	
1988		
October	Margaret Thatcher's 'no, no, no' speech in Bruges	
1990		
July	British entry into the ERM	

Mrs Thatcher's critics muttered darkly that Britain would sooner or later end up negotiating a deal with Argentina over the Falklands anyway, so why fight a war now? On the other hand, the psychological impact was important. In the 1970s, Britain's international position had seemed to be in miserable decline; now there was a resurgence of national pride in Britain, comparable with the success President Reagan had had in restoring self-belief to the United States after the trauma of Vietnam.

Not everyone in Britain was filled with national pride. Some objected to the gloating of the tabloids and what they saw as Mrs Thatcher's triumphalism in celebrating victory as if it was the Second World War all over again; and in bashing the BBC and the Archbishop of Canterbury for being 'wet'. It has also been suggested that the nationalistic mood fostered by the Falklands victory indirectly weakened links to Europe.

In the wider context, the Falklands War made it even less likely that Britain would force the people of Gibraltar to accept being handed to Spain. Otherwise, the war proved to be a stand-alone event. It did not stop the continued tidying up of Britain's imperial legacy. Lengthy negotiations with China laid the foundations for the eventual handover of Hong Kong, scheduled for 1997. Diplomatic relations with Argentina reopened in 1989. Overall, the Falklands was a merely a blip in world affairs. The really significant issues for Mrs Thatcher's foreign policy were resolving Britain's position in Europe and deciding what to do about the Cold War.

Britain and Europe, 1975–90

Fig. 4 *'Say Yes to Europe': Margaret Thatcher and the EEC referendum campaign, 1975*

The confirmation of Britain's accession to the EEC in the 1975 referendum appeared to settle the European issue for the foreseeable future. It did not. The main reason the referendum took place at all was getting round the internal divisions within the Labour Party, not Britain's relations with Europe. By 1990, however, Britain's relationship with the EEC was still unsettled. Margaret Thatcher's personality and political style ruffled the consensual politics favoured by other European leaders. In the late 1980s, especially in a forthright speech at Bruges in 1988, Mrs Thatcher was increasingly reluctant to see further moves towards political integration. The circumstances of Mrs Thatcher's fall from power intensified doubts about Britain's place in Europe. What had seemed settled in 1975 turned out not to be settled at all.

Margaret Thatcher's first priority in Europe was to secure a better deal for Britain over financial contributions to the EEC. Britain was paying in much more to the EEC than was being returned in benefits. Thatcher's persistent campaign for Britain to be given a rebate eventually achieved success in 1984. It played well to her supporters at home but irritated her European partners. Despite this, Britain's relations with Europe were generally good. Thatcher was enthusiastic about the Single European Market when it was negotiated in 1985–86.

Thatcher established a good working relationship with the French president, Francois Mitterrand. They cooperated closely over the complexities of the Channel Tunnel project, which was agreed in 1986 (it finally opened in 1994). Sharing in the creation of such a symbolic link between Britain and France was hardly proof of any anti-Europeanism on Mrs Thatcher's part.

Most of her cabinet ministers were strongly pro-Europe. Thatcher was enthusiastically in favour of expanding the EEC to include the new states in Eastern Europe (though her main motive here was the idea that this would weaken the power of the European Commission in Brussels).

In her last years in power, however, Mrs Thatcher did seem to associate herself with negative perceptions of Europe. Did she change her thinking? Or was it Europe that changed? The turning point was a speech made in Bruges in 1988, setting out the Thatcher vision of the future of Europe. Most of her speech was intended to be positive but it contained numerous provocative statements that infuriated many European leaders and raised doubts about Britain's commitment to further European integration. In Britain, the Bruges speech so enthused the Eurosceptic tendency that the Bruges Group was formed to focus opposition to any European 'superstate'.

> Let me be quite clear. Britain does not dream of some cosy, isolated existence on the fringes. Our destiny is in Europe as part of the Community. But to try to suppress nationhood and concentrate power at the centre of a European conglomerate would be highly damaging. Europe will be stronger precisely because it has France as France, Spain as Spain, Britain as Britain, each with its own customs, traditions and identity. It would be folly to try to fit them into some sort of identikit European personality. Indeed it is ironic that, just when countries such as the Soviet Union are learning that success depends on dispersing power away from the centre, there are some in the EEC who seem to want to move in the opposite direction. Certainly we in Britain would fight attempts to introduce collectivism and corporatism at the European level – although what people wish to do in their own countries is a matter for them.

2

From a speech by Margaret Thatcher in Bruges, September 1988

The main thrust of Margaret Thatcher's Bruges speech was to emphasise that the EEC was a trade association between sovereign states. She was resolutely opposed to federalism and the idea of 'ever closer political union'. There were indeed elements of the European Commission, including its president, Jacques Delors, who thought that was precisely the direction in which the EEC should be going. Thatcher frequently clashed with Delors, egged on by the tabloid press; *The Sun* headline on 1 November 1990 was: *'UP YOURS DELORS!'*

Thatcher's more negative line on Europe caused tension within her government. People like Geoffrey Howe and John Major thought she was backtracking from positions she had already agreed to since 1985. On the other hand, Eurosceptics such as the Bruges group argued that it was the federalists in Brussels who were changing the EEC into something different from the Common Market that Britain had joined in 1973. It is also true that Thatcher was never openly anti-European before she left office; that was something that developed later.

One other factor driving a wedge between Margaret Thatcher and her European partners was her fractious relationship with the German chancellor, Helmut Kohl. In theory, the two should have got on well; there were many policy areas on which they were in broad agreement. Sometimes, however, personality matters more than policy: they could not stand each other. Part of this was just a matter of style and temperament but part of it was also due to Thatcher's rather anti-German view of European history and her tendency to point out too often how it had twice been necessary for Europe to be rescued from German domination by the Anglo-American alliance.

■ Did you know?

In 1990, Margaret Thatcher summoned a group of top academic historians to Chequers to discuss the lessons of German history for the future. The historians were taken aback by the openly anti-German tone of the Prime Minister; one professor suggested privately that the seminar should have been given a title 'What's wrong with the Germans?'

That man is so German!

3 *Comment about Helmut Kohl made by Mrs Thatcher to her foreign policy adviser, Charles Powell, 1990*

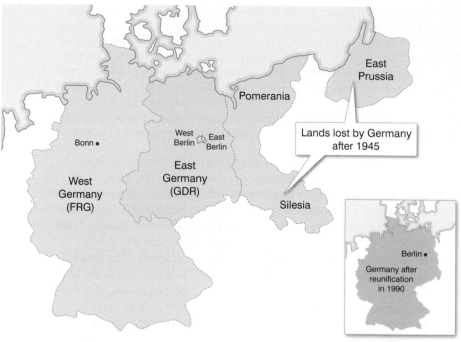

Fig. 5 *Germany before and after reunification*

As the prospect of German reunification came closer from 1988 onwards, Mrs Thatcher's fears of a united Germany dominating Europe intensified. She preferred Mikhail Gorbachev's vision of a neutral federal Germany to the idea of the old German Democratic Republic (East Germany) being swallowed up by West Germany (which is what actually happened).

Mrs Thatcher opened her handbag and took out two maps. The first one showed the borders of Europe in 1939, the second showed the borders at the end of the war. She pointed to Silesia, Pomerania and East Germany.
MRS THATCHER: Germany will take all of this.
MITTERRAND: Speeding up this process is really dangerous.
MRS THATCHER: Kohl will encourage it; he will inflame it! We have to place some limits on the Germans.
MITTERRAND: Yes, and Gorbachev cannot prevent it any more than the Americans can. We must discuss with the Germans and respect the treaties.
MRS THATCHER: First and foremost, we must respect the borders. And then, when there has been fifteen years of democracy in East Germany, then we can talk about reunification.

4 *Private talks between Margaret Thatcher and François Mitterrand of France, December 1989*

Ten years later, Germany took its revenge. There were lavish celebrations in Berlin of the tenth anniversary of the fall of the Wall in 1989. Mikhail Gorbachev and George Bush Senior were invited to take part but Margaret Thatcher, widely regarded as a heroic figure in ending the Cold War, was not. This snub was rather unfair on a distinguished elder stateswoman, but then history is often unfair.

Activity

Thinking point

Using the sources above and the other evidence in this chapter, assess the importance of Margaret Thatcher's personality and prejudices in influencing Britain's relations with her European partners.

Activity

Revision exercise

Compare the evidence in this chapter about Britain's entry to the EU with the evidence in Chapters 9 and 10. Make two lists:

1 the domestic political reasons

2 the foreign policy reasons

Britain and the end of the Cold War

In the late 1970s, after the Vietnam War, the West seemed to be losing the Cold War. When Soviet forces invaded Afghanistan in 1979, it was thought in the West that this was a dangerous threat to Western interests. In reality, it was a disastrous venture, bleeding away what was left of Soviet military might. After the opening of Soviet archives from 1991, it became obvious that the Soviet Union was on its last legs by the early 1980s, hopelessly overstretched militarily and led by a generation of old men eking out the last days of their power.

Nobody in the West knew this at the time. Between 1979 and 1981, three new 'cold warriors' emerged, a British prime minister, a Polish pope and an American president, each determined to challenge Soviet power, both militarily and ideologically. The New Cold War began. By 1990, the Berlin Wall had fallen, German reunification was a fact and the supposed Soviet superpower was disintegrating. The West had won the Cold War. Margaret Thatcher, the Iron Lady, was widely praised for her part in this success. In the early 1980s, Thatcher's strong support for deterrence and winning the arms race was an important factor, admired by cold warriors and detested by those who believed in peaceful coexistence and *detente*.

Fig. 6 *A very special relationship: Margaret Thatcher and Ronald Reagan, Camp David, 1984*

■ **Key chronology**

Britain and the Cold War, 1975–90

1977 SALT I (Strategic Arms Limitations Talks)

1981 Election of Ronald Reagan

1983 Cruise missiles based at Greenham Common

1984 First meeting between Thatcher and Gorbachev

1989 Fall of the Berlin Wall and end of the Cold War

1990 German reunification settled by 'Two-plus-Four' talks

■ **Key profiles**

Pope John Paul II

Karel Wojtyła (1920–2005), Archbishop of Cracow, was elected pope in 1979. John Paul II was a staunch anti-communist and his influence was greatly feared by the communist leaderships in Poland and the USSR. His official visit to Poland in 1980 drew enormous crowds and greatly strengthened the demands for reform from the Polish Solidarity movement.

Mikhail Gorbachev

Gorbachev (born 1931) was the man who tried to reform the Soviet communist system in order to save it. He emerged as leader of the USSR in 1985 and from 1987 he promoted his key ideas of *perestroika* (restructuring and modernisation) and *glasnost* (openness). In trying to reform the USSR, Gorbachev was willing to end the Cold War and let the Soviet satellite states in east Central Europe go their own way. Gorbachev succeeded in ending the Cold War, but could not prevent the total collapse of communism.

Margaret Thatcher's contribution to ending the Cold War rested on two pillars: her combative style and determination to confront the USSR in the early 1980s, and her willingness to negotiate with the new reformist Soviet leader, Mikhail Gorbachev. Above all, Thatcher's foreign policy was founded on reviving the special relationship with the United States. In the 1970s, relations were strained because the Americans felt Britain had failed to provide enough active support either in Vietnam or in the Middle East crisis of 1973, when the Heath government was reluctant to help American support for Israel in the Yom Kippur War. The mood changed from the moment of Ronald Reagan's inauguration as president in January 1981.

■ **Cross-reference**

The impact of the Yom Kippur war on Anglo-American relations is discussed in Chapter 8.

Reviving the special relationship

There was a strong bond between Margaret Thatcher and Ronald Reagan, both personal and ideological. Both were from the generation whose lives had been shaped by the Second World War. Mrs Thatcher was particularly influenced by her wartime memories. Her special hero was Winston Churchill. Her view of twentieth century history revolved around the idea that American armies had twice ridden to the rescue after 'those Europeans' had made a mess of things.

In Margaret Thatcher, Reagan found a triple ally. First, she shared his belief in free markets as the path to prosperity and as the buttress against socialism at home and abroad. Second, Mrs Thatcher's strategic loyalty was rooted in the Atlantic Alliance and the old 1940s perception of the world. Third, Mrs Thatcher shared a key aspect of Reagan's temperament – a belief in the importance of morale in public life and in the bracing effect of freedom on the moral fibre of the nation.

5   *From Walker, M., **The Cold War**, 1993*

Through the 1980s, on issues like the Falklands War, deploying Cruise missiles and being tough with the USSR, the Thatcher–Reagan link was a powerful factor in how the West won the Cold War. The Thatcher–Reagan bond (the 'Ronnie and Maggie show') lasted long after they were out of politics. At Ronald Reagan's funeral in 2004, Lady Thatcher's eulogy was played on videotape: *'We have lost a great president, a great American and a great man. And I have lost a dear friend. We here still move in twilight. But we have one beacon to guide us that Ronald Reagan never had – his example.''*

The New Cold War was marked by tough rhetoric and many confrontations. In 1983, there was a major war scare over NATO military exercises in the North Atlantic. Then Soviet jets shot down a Korean passenger airliner, KAL 007, when it strayed off course into Soviet airspace; everyone on board was killed. Cruise missiles were stationed in Europe. The Reagan administration stepped up plans for its 'Star Wars' anti-missile shield. All this caused serious tensions between the Soviet Bloc and the West. It has been suggested that the outcome of the Cold War was ultimately decided by this Western firmness, especially by the high levels of defence spending that the USSR simply could not match. If so, Margaret Thatcher must be credited with an important contribution.

Another view is that it was not military pressure from the West that ended the Cold War but Mikhail Gorbachev. Margaret Thatcher can claim some of the credit for this, too. Gorbachev established his authority between 1985 and 1987. He was thirty years younger than the elderly relics who had led the USSR until 1985. He was a realist who knew things could not go on as they were. His favourite saying as he promoted reform of the USSR was: *'If not us, who? If not now, when?'*

Gorbachev made a remarkable impression on the hard-line conservatives, Thatcher and Reagan. Mrs Thatcher met Gorbachev for the first time in 1984 and declared herself to be impressed. *'I like Mr Gorbachev'*, she said, *'He and I can do business together'*. Ronald Reagan surprised his own advisers by his willingness to move fast and to gamble on

Gorbachev's ability to carry through negotiations and bring the Cold War to an end. In so far as success in ending the Cold War was due to Gorbachev, Mrs Thatcher deserves some of the credit for that, too.

The final end of the Cold War was not quite how Gorbachev, or Thatcher, wanted it. There was no big peace settlement to negotiate a shared future for the two Germanies. The peoples of Eastern Europe voted with their feet. 1989, the 'year of miracles', saw a sudden rush to unity in Germany, not by a merger but by the instant take-over of the East by the West. Helmut Kohl became the hero of the hour, at the head of the new unified Germany, now with a population of 80 million.

Ronald Reagan had left the scene in 1988. Mikhail Gorbachev was overtaken by events as the Soviet Union and the whole communist system fell apart in 1991. Margaret Thatcher fell from power in November 1990. Her legacy and reputation within Britain remained controversial and divisive. In the new Europe, however, there were no such divided opinions. For the newly independent states of Eastern and Central Europe, Margaret Thatcher, the Iron Lady, deserved nothing but admiration.

Learning outcomes

In this section, you have looked at the years of 'Thatcherism', from Mrs Thatcher's emergence as Conservative leader in 1975 to her dramatic downfall in 1990. In this 'Thatcher revolution', the Conservatives established a new period of political dominance over a divided and ineffectual opposition, replacing the post-war consensus with radical economic policies and an assault on the power and influence of the trade unions. Abroad, Mrs Thatcher renewed Britain's commitments to the special relationship with the United States, redefined Britain's relationship with Europe and played a leading role in ending the Cold War.

> ### Activity
> **Source analysis**
>
> Read carefully sources 4 and 5 and look at the other evidence in this chapter. Working in two groups, construct an argument that Britain's contribution to ending the Cold War:
>
> **1** was extremely significant
>
> **2** was insignificant compared with that of Mikhail Gorbachev.

Practice question

'Margaret Thatcher's legacy was deep divisions in British society.' With reference to the years 1975–90, assess the validity of this view.   *(45 marks)*

Study tip Questions like this require a coherent overall argument showing the ability to respond to a provocative interpretation, showing a grasp of alternative perspectives and a secure sense of chronology. Before constructing an answer, it is necessary to define in what ways society could be seen as having 'deep divisions' (the miners' strike? The north-south divide? Cultural attitudes? The politicisation of the police?) and the extent to which the claim is justified. Is it true, or wrong, or partly true but overstated? (Some people would argue that the real cause of divisions in Britain was not Thatcherism but the inevitable consequences of industrial and social change). A good answer would need to be decisive in supporting or refuting the key quotation, but the answer needs to be more than a list of reasons. There needs to be a central argument that is balanced and shows some differentiation. Trying to be comprehensive would lead to problems. A selective approach is vital, showing a synoptic awareness of the whole period 1975 to 1990 but supporting the main argument with precisely selected evidence. Historiography could be useful but only if it is applied to assessment and evaluation, not a prepared descriptive account of what historians have written. The most important interpretation should be your own!

Fig. 1 *John Major and Neil Kinnock according to* **Spitting Image***, 1992*

In this chapter you will learn about:

- the internal divisions weakening the Conservative Party

- the leadership of John Major and the difficulties facing him

- the role of economic developments and of key personalities in the rise of New Labour

- the reasons why the Labour Party achieved a landslide victory in the 1997 general election.

What defeated the Tories in 1997? The 'feelgood factor', or the lack of one, was part of the story. New Labour, shamelessly wooing the middle class, was another part of it. But there was more to it than that. Under John Major something had collapsed within the structure of the Conservative Party as we knew it. The post-Thatcher Conservative Party took refuge in the form of group therapy that Tories have always understood, based on nostalgia, mythology and selective memory. Ironically, it was Labour who chose (or were bullied by Tony Blair into choosing) to enter a serious debate about post-Thatcherism. By contrast, the Conservatives after Thatcher seemed too often to be engaged in the kind of political posturing that comes naturally to professional politicians but puzzles ordinary voters. It was still puzzling to them when they went to the polls in 1997.

1 *From Critchley, J. and Halcrow, M.* **Collapse of Stout Party***, 1998*

Our politics and performance have not lived up to our principles. We are unpopular above all because the middle classes – and all those who aspire to join the middle classes – feel that they no longer have the incentives and opportunities they expect from a Conservative government. Our party should still be following the policies pursued in the 1980s – small government, a property-owning democracy, tax cuts, deregulation and national sovereignty.

| 2 | *From a speech by Margaret Thatcher, January 1996* |

Key chronology
The Conservative Party, 1990–97
1990 Fall of Mrs Thatcher
1992 Election victory of John Major
Black Wednesday and exit from the ERM
1993 Rebellion against Maastricht treaty by Conservative MPs
1994 Tony Blair elected Labour leader after death of John Smith
1995 Major re-elected party leader
1997 Landslide election victory for New Labour

At the time, the 1997 general election seemed like a political earthquake. Many commentators argued that the Conservative Party had been torn apart by 'civil war' after the 'betrayal' of Mrs Thatcher. Further defeats in 2001 and 2005 suggested they might lose forever their traditional place in British politics as the 'natural party of government'. The resurgence of the Liberal Democrats, like the success of New Labour, seemed to reflect fundamental changes in British society, 'breaking the mould of British politics'.

In reality, the Conservative collapse in 1997 should not have been a shock. The revival of the Labour Party had been gaining momentum since 1992. The rise of New Labour was a powerful challenge to a deeply-divided Conservative Party. As a result, Tony Blair came to power in exceptionally favourable circumstances. Labour had a massive majority in parliament. Most of the nation was ready to give the new government a chance.

Several important questions arise from 1997. Was the Labour landslide due to negative factors, to the inward collapse of the Conservative Party? Or was 1997 a mark of positive approval for the rebranded Labour Party under a new and popular leader? Was 1997 the rejection of Thatcherism? Or was it proof that Thatcherism had actually triumphed, that Blair and New Labour were continuing the Thatcher legacy in their policies? Was Conservative decline in the 1990s just a swing in the electoral cycle? Or was Britain now ready for a new form of politics for a new society?

The Conservative government under John Major

The emergence of John Major as Margaret Thatcher's successor in 1990 was the culmination of an astonishingly rapid rise. It was a surprise to most of the Conservative Party and to the Majors themselves. On the day John Major entered Downing Street, his wife Norma said wonderingly: *'Things like this just don't happen to people like us'*. Major had been little known before he became foreign secretary in 1989 after Geoffrey Howe resigned.

The party Major now led was in a state of shock. There was especial hostility to Michael Heseltine and a fierce determination among right-wingers (actively encouraged by Thatcher herself) to take revenge against those who had 'betrayed Maggie'. One key reason for Major's rise to the leadership was that Thatcherites saw him as 'one of them': the leader most likely to be loyal to the Thatcher legacy. In fact, this view of John Major was not especially accurate. His natural instincts were to unify the party.

Major's main assets appeared to be his calm temperament and the capacity to avoid making enemies. The Conservatives jumped ahead in the opinion polls and the tone of the national press was very positive. Some of this was the 'honeymoon effect' experienced by new

■ Exploring the detail

The First Gulf War

The First Gulf War broke out in 1990 when Saddam Hussein of Iraq sent forces to conquer the oil-rich state of Kuwait in the Arabian Gulf. In 1991, an American-led coalition, backed by a UN resolution, expelled Iraqi forces from Kuwait in a short military campaign. Saddam suffered a terrible defeat but did not fall from power. The invasion of Iraq in 2003 was in many ways a sequel to the First Gulf War.

■ Cross-reference

A profile of Saddam Hussein can be found on page 170.

governments; but it also reflected the intensity of feeling about Mrs Thatcher by 1990. Major showed his desire for party unity by keeping a careful balance in his cabinet. Douglas Hurd and Kenneth Clarke kept their jobs, at the foreign office and in education. Norman Lamont, who had managed Major's leadership campaign, became the new chancellor. Michael Heseltine came back as environment secretary, with Chris Patten as party chairman.

John Major's first big tasks involved foreign affairs and Europe. Britain was already fighting the First Gulf War, which reached a successful conclusion in March 1991. Major then turned his attention to Europe and made a big speech in Bonn, setting out his aim to see Britain take a place 'at the very heart of Europe'. This speech was well received, especially by pro-Europeans. Major and his aides hoped that it would be possible to follow a middle way on Europe, avoiding conflict between the poles of opinion in Britain. Such hopes did not last long.

Fig. 2 *The First Gulf War: oilfields burning in Kuwait, 1991*

■ Exploring the detail

The Maastricht Treaty

The Maastricht Treaty turned the EEC into the European Union. The treaty was intended to deepen European integration and to modernise the structures of the EU. A single currency (the euro) was planned to come into operation by 1999. The clauses in the Social Chapter were intended to strengthen workers' rights. Right-wing opponents regarded the Social Chapter as 'too socialist'.

■ Cross-reference

The foreign policy aspects of Britain's relations with Europe at this time, including the Maastricht Treaty, are covered in Chapter 16.

The poll tax is introduced on page 104.

John Major faced an uphill task in negotiating the Maastricht Treaty, designed to reform the structures of the European Community. Bargaining with other European member states at Maastricht was difficult enough. Selling the deal to sceptical political and public opinion at home was much harder. The Maastricht Treaty was agreed in December 1991 and signed in February 1992. Major's skilful diplomacy secured opt-outs for Britain from plans for a single currency and from the Social Chapter. These opt-outs won over most doubters in the Conservative Party but opposition to Europe had not gone away. Maastricht was one of the reasons Major delayed calling an election until 1992; he had wanted to call one as soon as possible after coming to power.

In domestic politics, the first big issue was the poll tax, which had played such a big part in Mrs Thatcher's downfall. Many wanted Major to scrap the proposed tax immediately but this risked splitting the party. Only in November 1991, after very lengthy discussions, was the poll tax finally abandoned in favour of the new council tax. This was a costly move, because it admitted that £1.5 billion had been wasted on the attempts to implement the poll tax, but it allowed Major to get away from an unpopular policy that could be blamed on his predecessor.

The British economy, 1990–92

John Major's government inherited a difficult economic situation at the end of 1990, as Major himself well knew, because in 1990 he was Margaret Thatcher's chancellor, trying to deal with the problems of the recession that had followed the 'Lawson boom' of the late 1980s. The recession was marked by declining manufacturing output, high interest rates, a steep rise in unemployment and a serious slump in house prices.

In Britain, unemployment and the collapse of the housing market were the most painful aspects of the recession. From mid-1991 to early 1992, unemployment rose from 1.6 million to 2.6 million. Many homeowners were trapped in 'negative equity' (having to repay mortgages that were higher than the current value of their homes). Many had their homes repossessed. Conservative policy advisers were worried that this 1990s recession seemed to affect the Tory middle classes, especially in the south, whereas earlier recessions had hit the industrial north.

With an election imminent, Major's government resorted to high public spending. Half of this spending was forced, as a result of rising unemployment, but huge government borrowing was used for subsidies on transport and increased spending on the NHS. Most governments are tempted into lavish spending on the eve of an election, especially as in Major's situation in 1991–92, when there was a high possibility of being defeated. The revival of the Labour Party meant that, unlike 1983 and 1987, the 1992 election was going to be very close.

The Conservative election victory of 1992

In 1990, many Conservatives had feared defeat in the next election; that was the overriding reason for displacing Mrs Thatcher. The political momentum was with Labour. Neil Kinnock's leadership had restored party discipline and curbed the hard left. Kinnock's shadow chancellor, John Smith, gave Labour a reassuring image of moderation and competence. The party organisation had been overhauled and was more professional in policy presentation. The beginnings of a Labour revival had been visible even in 1987. By 1992, Labour was winning back many of the voters who had deserted them in the 1980s.

The decision to call an election was left until March 1992, almost the last possible moment before the end of the five-year parliamentary term. Michael White of the *Guardian* wrote that: *'these are the least favourable circumstances for re-electing a sitting government since 1964.'* The opinion polls placed the Conservatives on an average 29 per cent, with Labour ahead on 41 per cent and the Liberals at 15 per cent. Most observers predicted a Labour victory.

John Major himself, however, was surprisingly upbeat. He said later: *'I did not believe what the polls were telling us. I had this instinct we wouldn't lose. It was also a bit of blind faith. I couldn't actually believe that I had come from where I came from, up to where I was now, to be cut off after just eighteen months'*. Major's optimism was vindicated. Towards the end of the longer-than-usual election campaign, opinion swung back towards the Conservatives. On the eve of the election, the polls were predicting victory by 303–298 over Labour. The actual margin of victory was more decisive: 336 seats for the Conservatives and 271 for Labour.

Elections are always lost as well as won. In 1992, Labour's weaknesses mattered as much as the strengths of the Conservative campaign. Labour expectations had been high; at a lavishly-staged election party rally in Sheffield, Neil Kinnock was greeted almost as a conquering

Exploring the detail

The recession of the early 1990s

The recession of the early 1990s did not only apply to Britain. Many other countries were affected, especially Japan. World trade was badly damaged by the collapse of the Japanese financial system in 1990 and the long recession that dogged the Japanese economy throughout the 1990s.

Did you know?

Labour loyalists blamed the right-wing press for wrecking Labour's chances. The right-wing press seemed happy to agree – a headline in *The Sun* boasted that *'It Was The Sun Wot Won It!'*

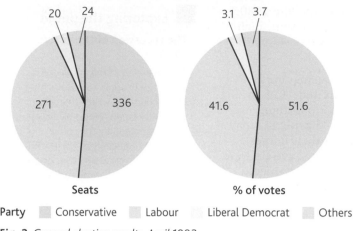

Party ■ Conservative ■ Labour ■ Liberal Democrat ■ Others

Fig. 3 *General election results, April 1992*

hero. Afterwards, Kinnock was accused of over-confidence. John Smith was blamed for making commitments on taxation that allowed the Conservatives to scare off middle class voters.

The Conservatives ran a good campaign. Chris Patten was an effective party chairman, even though he lost his own seat in Bath. John Major won a lot of respect for his old-fashioned 'soapbox' politics, making impromptu speeches on the street in towns like Luton, standing on his soapbox. Although people blamed the Conservatives for the economic recession, they were still seen as the party best able to get the country out of the mess. Many voters just did not feel Labour had reformed enough; memories of the 1980s were still too strong.

The two party leaders who fought each other in the 1992 election, Mr Major and Mr Kinnock, are both convinced Mrs Thatcher would not have won. Mr Kinnock argued that Mr Major was able to defuse the row over the poll tax, which she would not have been able to do, and was above all able to present himself as the candidate for change. After eleven years of Mrs Thatcher the country was longing for new leadership and Mr Major was able to capitalise on that feeling. On the day Thatcher resigned, Kinnock is convinced, Labour lost its biggest electoral asset. Mr Major is equally dismissive of the idea his predecessor could have achieved the result he did.

But the argument that Mrs Thatcher could have won has at least one important advocate in the Labour Party – Tony Blair. In the summer of 2002 I asked him, *'Could she have won?'* He replied, *'I am one of the few people who would unhesitatingly say yes. Although Neil Kinnock made absolutely heroic efforts to change the Labour Party, by 1992 we were not sufficiently, fundamentally changed'.*

 3

From Sergeant, J., *Maggie: Her Fatal Legacy*, 2005

'Black Wednesday' and its impact

The glow of John Major's election victory lasted only a few months. In September 1992, his premiership was thrown badly off course by a toxic mixture of financial crisis and internal party divisions over Europe. In his remaining years in office, Major never really recovered.

The turning point was 'Black Wednesday', the crisis of 16 September 1992 that forced Major's government into panic measures to prevent the devaluation of the pound and ended in a humiliating defeat as Britain was forced to withdraw from the Exchange Rate Mechanism (ERM) less than two years after joining it. John Major's popularity took a hammering from the right-wing press who had done so much to get him re-elected a few months earlier. Divisions within the party, about personalities and about Europe, widened. Public opinion turned against the Conservatives, just when the Labour Party was reinventing itself as a party of moderation and economic competence.

A closer look

Black Wednesday, 16 September 1992

Britain had joined the ERM in October 1990. Margaret Thatcher had resisted doing so since the creation of the ERM in 1979 but was eventually persuaded into the decision to join by pressure from her foreign secretary, Douglas Hurd, and her new chancellor, John Major. The ERM required Britain to maintain a fixed rate of exchange (2.95 German marks to the pound) with a narrow band allowed for fluctuations. By September 1992, the British currency (together with several other ERM currencies) was coming under pressure from foreign exchange speculators. The pound was trading at a low level, close to its minimum allowable rate of 2.77 marks. This led to the crisis of 16 September.

The day began with a wave of speculative selling of the pound on financial markets. John Major's government was determined to avoid any devaluation of the pound and to remain within the ERM. The Chancellor, Norman Lamont, announced an increase in interest rates (already high at 10 per cent) to 12 per cent. Dealers continued to sell pounds. Later in the day, Lamont pushed interest rates up to 15 per cent, hoping to persuade foreign investors to buy pounds again. The Bank of England spent huge amounts from its reserves in buying up pounds.

These increasingly desperate attempts to prop up the pound all failed; the pound continued to sink. Major and Lamont summoned key members of the cabinet, Douglas Hurd, Kenneth Clarke and Michael Heseltine, to an emergency meeting at Admiralty House. This inner circle accepted the decision to give up the struggle and withdraw from the ERM. Hurd later described the Admiralty House meeting as *'dipping hands in the blood'*. At 19.00, Norman Lamont announced the decision live on TV. Standing at his side was a young policy adviser called David Cameron. Interest rates were fixed at 12 per cent, down from the temporary peak of 15 per cent earlier in the day.

The day caused an immediate sensation and also had dramatic long-term effects. The Conservative reputation for economic competence was destroyed and Major's government was savagely criticised by opposition leaders, Gordon Brown for Labour and Paddy Ashdown for the Liberals, and in the national press. There was a steep drop in support for the Conservatives in opinion polls. Lamont's position as chancellor was badly weakened, even though he did not actually lose his post until seven months later. The Eurosceptic wing of the Conservative Party was strengthened, happy to see moves towards European integration suffer such a setback. Some of them preferred to speak and write about 'White Wednesday'. Many observers, including John Major himself, looked back at the events of 16 September 1992 as 'the beginning of the end'.

The effects of Black Wednesday on the British economy proved to much less catastrophic than was feared at the time. Within a relatively short time, the economy stabilised and it could be seen that coming out of the ERM had as many beneficial effects as negative ones. The political consequences, however, were disastrous for the Conservative government, both at the time and for years afterwards.

The long-standing Conservative electoral asset of being trusted on the economy was thrown away. John Major's personal authority was badly weakened. He was fiercely criticised by newspapers that had previously supported him. The Labour Party shot ahead in the polls. For the rest of 1992, Labour's average lead was 17 per cent.

The British economy, 1992–97

Britain's economic situation started to improve almost immediately after Black Wednesday in 1992. Many people, including Norman Lamont, regarded having to leave the ERM as beneficial. It prevented Britain from having to keep high interest rates to protect the stability of sterling. It allowed exchange rates to float downwards, which helped British exporters. General economic conditions were also beginning to improve in 1993. Unemployment rates slowed down and the housing market began to pick up. From 1993 to 1997, economic recovery accelerated. Government borrowing was reduced as inflation came under control.

Why the economy improved so markedly is a matter of debate. One factor was Kenneth Clarke, who replaced Norman Lamont as chancellor in 1993. Clarke was a good communicator, giving out a breezy air of confidence. He was also a lucky chancellor. He took over when the American economy was coming out of recession and world trade was expanding. The British economy seemed to be doing better than foreign competitors, partly because of the benefits from financial deregulation and flexible working practices. In comparison, the German economy was struggling with the huge costs of unification and had sluggish growth rates compared with Britain.

A prominent theme of economic policy in the mid-1990s was privatisation. The coal industry was privatised in 1994. The complex and controversial privatisation of the railways was carried through in 1996. The government set about privatising the Post Office but ran into opposition and eventually abandoned the scheme. Many people acquired shares in the new privatised industries and the stock market was buoyed up.

By 1997, most economic indicators were positive. Unemployment was down. Productivity was up, though not by much. Consumer spending went up. Car ownership increased. House prices rose sharply and negative equity was a thing of the past. Business was supportive of government policies. In many ways, the British economic situation by 1997 was as promising for the government in power as in any election year since 1959. Yet people were surprisingly reluctant to give Major's government credit for this. The 'feelgood factor' was missing.

Growing internal divisions in the Conservative Party after 1992

Despite his election success in 1992, John Major came under fire from sections of his own party. Many right-wingers pushed for more radical social policies. Politicians with leadership ambitions saw a chance to advance their claims. Eurosceptics saw an opening to push the government to the edges of Europe, if not out of the EU altogether. For the rest of his time in office, exhausting battles against his own party dominated everything about Major's premiership, drowning out his positive achievements in a sea of party infighting and political setbacks. John Major's significant achievements after 1992, including a sustained economic recovery and substantial progress on Northern Ireland, did not win popularity or political support. It is typical of Major's fate as an unlucky prime minister that his successor, Tony Blair was able to claim the credit for what Major had begun.

A closer look

John Major and the issue of Northern Ireland

One undoubted success for John Major was a political breakthrough in Northern Ireland. From 1993, the government received secret messages hinting that Sinn Fein was ready to discuss a peace agreement. Talks between the Sinn Fein leader, Gerry Adams, and John Hume of the moderate SDLP produced a plan for a resolution of the conflict that had seemed insoluble. Major was traditional Conservative, instinctively on the side of the Ulster Unionists. He had only a small parliamentary majority and knew he might need voting support from the unionists at Westminster. Major was also sceptical about the sincerity of the IRA. Even so, he went ahead.

There were big obstacles to be overcome. Major and his Northern Ireland secretary, Patrick Mayhew, were often regarded with suspicion by the political leaders in Belfast. Unionists were fearful of being 'sold out by the British'. On the republican side, there was deep-rooted hostility to the 'perfidious British'. On many occasions, progress stalled. On the other hand, the fact that the first steps in the peace process were taken by a Conservative prime minister was helpful. A Labour leader might have found it easier to get the trust of the republicans, but any agreement would almost certainly have been brought down by a Conservative and unionist backlash.

Progress in the peace process was helped by John Major's good working relationship with the Irish taoiseach, Albert Reynolds, and by the prosperity and social change that Ireland was experiencing after accession to the European Union. The new American president, Bill Clinton, also made a constructive contribution, encouraging Sinn Fein away from armed struggle. Major and Reynolds went public in 1993 with their joint Downing Street Declaration. In 1994, the IRA announced a ceasefire. Loyalist paramilitaries matched this with a ceasefire of their own. There was a strong sense of war-weariness on both sides of the conflict. A former IRA gunman, Eamon Collins wrote in his memoirs in 1997: *'I like to think that both sides looked down into a Bosnia-style abyss; gulped and then stepped back.'*

Getting a final agreement was very difficult. Unionists did not believe in the IRA's commitment to peace. The negative influence of Ian Paisley and his DUP hard-liners was a hindrance. The IRA got impatient and went back to violent methods. An IRA rocket was fired at 10 Downing Street during a cabinet meeting; massive bombs damaged the financial district at Canary Wharf and the centre of Manchester in 1996. But the peace process continued. When Tony Blair took over from Major in 1997, the framework was in place for the Good Friday Agreement that brought the 'Troubles' to an end in 1998.

Key chronology

The peace process in Northern Ireland

1993 The Hume–Adams Plan
      Downing Street Declaration
1994 IRA ceasefire
1995 Bomb attack on Downing Street
1996 Renewal of IRA ceasefire
1997 Arrival of Senator Mitchell as mediator
      Election of Tony Blair
1998 The Good Friday Agreement

Cross-reference

The impact of international relations on the peace process in Northern Ireland is discussed in Chapter 16.

Exploring the detail

Ian Paisley and the DUP

Ian Paisley was known in Northern Ireland politics as 'Dr No'. The Democratic Unionist Party (DUP) was made up of his personal followers, always opposed to any attempts at compromise by the 'official' Ulster Unionists. During and after the negotiations for the Good Friday Agreement, it was feared the DUP could cause a breakdown. Eventually, in 2007, Paisley accepted the peace process and became first minister of Northern Ireland, sharing power with Sinn Fein.

Between Black Wednesday and the 1997 election, John Major suffered a slow political death. At times, he might appear to be on the road to recovery, but political disasters kept occurring. Some of these setbacks were trivial in themselves but the cumulative effect was devastating. Major's tribulations might be summed up as satire, sabotage and sleaze.

Satire

John Major was an easy target for cartoonists and satirists. *Private Eye* ran series of episodes of an Adrian Mole spoof, *The Secret Diary of John Major aged 47 and three-quarters*. On television, Major was the butt of brilliantly funny impersonations by Rory Bremner and by the puppeteers of *Spitting Image,* who presented him as the Grey Man. None of this satire was vicious and Major remained personally more popular than his party; but the image of Major as a well-meaning but bumbling and inadequate leader stuck to him.

Sabotage

The negative perceptions of Major made it harder for him to face down the increasingly blatant actions by anti-Europe elements in his own party. In July 1993, rebel MPs blocked Major's attempt to get parliament to ratify the Maastricht Treaty. Major won the vote in the end but his authority was damaged. ITN's Michael Brunson asked Major why he did not sack the rebels. Thinking the microphone was switched off, Major replied: *'Think from my perspective, a prime minister with a majority of eighteen. Where do you think the poison is coming from? From the dispossessed and the never-possessed. Do we want three more of the bastards out there?'* The quote leaked to the Daily Mirror and became headline news.

There was no leadership challenge against John Major in 1993 but the speculation about a challenge further undermined him. Major reshuffled his cabinet in 1994 but this had little impact. Eurosceptics such as Bill Cash and Iain Duncan Smith felt free to express active opposition. Rebel backbenchers like Teresa Gorman continued to make provocative statements. Press speculation continued about possible challengers for the leadership from disaffected cabinet ministers. The names of Michael Portillo and John Redwood were frequently mentioned.

By the summer of 1995, Major felt so insecure that he called for a leadership election so that he could be re-elected to his own job. It was a case of 'back me or sack me'. Some observers saw the move as a bold gamble; others saw it as a sign of weakness and desperation. At Prime Minister's Questions, Major was mocked by Tony Blair: *'I lead my party. You follow yours.'*

A closer look

The re-election of John Major as Conservative leader

On 22 June 1995, at a press conference in the rose garden at 10 Downing Street, John Major caused a political sensation by initiating a Conservative leadership election. Such a thing had never happened before, a sitting prime minister inviting rivals within his party to run against him in a secret ballot. Major was driven into taking this extreme step by the extent of negative speculation against his leadership. Comment in the *Daily Mail*, the *Daily Telegraph* and *The Sun* was relentlessly hostile, openly calling for a strong leader, such as Michael Portillo, to replace Major and 'save the party'.

In the end, Portillo decided not to run. The main challenger was John Redwood, backed by a disparate collection of Thatcherites and Eurosceptics including Tony Marlow and Teresa Gorman. The first ballot was to take place on 4 July. On that day, John Major had a private meeting with Michael Heseltine; it was agreed Heseltine would become deputy prime minister. Heseltine made sure everyone in the party knew he had voted for Major. The result of the first ballot was decisive: 218 for Major, 89 for Redwood. There was no need for a second ballot. Major had won his gamble.

How much this strengthened Major's position is debatable. Michael Heseltine, who proved to be loyal and effective ally, especially good at defending the government in media interviews. Major had won in spite of the national press: even the *Daily Telegraph* wrote that Major had *'inflicted a spell of humility on the scribblers'*. But 89 Conservative MPS had voted against him, when his government only had a small majority. The attitude of the press was as hostile as ever. The verdict of *The Times* was: *'Yesterday Conservative MPs threw away their last best opportunity to win the next election.'* Opposition to Major within the party, especially on Europe, continued almost as intensely as before his re election.

Key profile

John Redwood

John Redwood (born 1951), known to his detractors as 'the Vulcan', was secretary for Wales in John Major's cabinet. Redwood was a brilliant economic theorist, strongly in favour of monetarism, who had been a policy adviser to Mrs Thatcher. He was also a leading Eurosceptic. In 1995, he ran against Major for the Conservative leadership. In 1997, Redwood surprisingly launched a joint leadership bid with the pro-European Ken Clarke; but the party opted for William Hague instead.

One deadly cause of John Major's weakness was the 'back seat driving' of Margaret Thatcher. She encouraged the Maastricht rebels by demanding a referendum to approve the treaty. Her memoirs, published, just after the party conference in 1993, were lukewarm about Major. She gave her support to John Redwood in his challenge to Major in 1995. She did little to discourage her admirers from reminding everyone what a dynamic leader she had been compared to Major. In the run up to the 1997 election, her comments seemed to show more approval of Tony Blair than of her chosen successor as prime minister.

Fig. 4 *The Redwood rebellion: John Redwood and his supporters launching his leadership challenge in the House of Commons committee room, June 1995*

Sleaze

Scandals and accusations of 'Tory sleaze' dogged John Major's final years in office. Press coverage became even more intrusive and sensationalist. Much was made of the contrast between these scandals and John Major's 'Back to Basics' campaign, launched in 1993.

Cross-reference

Mrs Thatcher's 'back-seat driving' is covered on page 105.

■ Cross-reference

The role of the 'Bennites' (supporters of Tony Benn) is covered on pages 92–3.

All kinds of incidents, important and trivial, were lumped together as 'Tory sleaze'. Many were about sex, such as the scandals that caused the resignation of two cabinet ministers, David Mellor and Tim Yeo, and some minor backbenchers. Other scandals centred on corruption. In 1994, the Scott enquiry, set up by Major to investigate illegal arms dealing, proved that government ministers had broken the rules and been 'economical with the truth'. Two leading Conservatives, the novelist Jeffrey Archer and the former minister Jonathan Aitken, were convicted of perjury. The so-called 'Cash for questions' affair was very damaging to the Major government because it lasted such a long time and kept 'Tory sleaze' in the news right through the 1997 election campaign.

Most governments run into problems of this kind but the impact on John Major's government was much worse than usual. Although many of the scandals were minor, the sensational press coverage inflicted severe damage on a government that was already weakened and was being targeted by newspapers that had deserted the Conservatives. To make matters worse, every setback was exploited with ruthless efficiency by the opposition. It was typical of John Major's bad luck in politics that the Labour Party led by Tony Blair was more united, better organised and more kindly treated by the media than at any time since 1945.

■ The revival of the Labour Party, 1990–97

The revival of the Labour Party in the 1990s seemed to be dominated by the ideas and personality of Tony Blair, who became leader of the party in 1994 and had three years in which to prepare for power. Blair set out with great skill to remodel the Labour 'brand'. The promotion of 'New Labour' was intended to live down his party's extremism in the 1980s, when Labour had seemed unelectable. Blair wanted to convince Middle England that Labour Party had fundamentally changed, both ideologically and in party unity. The 'Blair Project' achieved dramatic success between 1994 and 1997 but transformation of Labour's fortunes was not only due to Blair. His predecessors, Neil Kinnock and John Smith, also made major contributions.

The rise of New Labour, 1992–97

When Neil Kinnock replaced Michael Foot as Labour leader in 1983, Labour was in danger of being marginalised by Thatcherism and by the rise of the SDP. Kinnock played a big part in dragging Labour back into the political mainstream. He took on the extreme left, represented by the Militant Tendency and the 'Bennites'. After heavy defeat in 1987, Kinnock further reorganised the party and moved its policies towards the centre ground. Some party activists blamed

Fig. 5 *Team of the future? The Labour leadership in 1992 (left to right: John Smith, Margaret Beckett, Gordon Brown, Tony Blair)*

him for losing the 1992 election after Labour had been ahead in the polls; but the Labour Party Kinnock left behind was infinitely stronger than it had been in 1983.

Kinnock's successor was John Smith, his shadow chancellor. As the Conservative Party sank into its sea of troubles after Black Wednesday, Smith seemed ideally suited to lead Labour towards victory. John Smith's death from a heart attack in 1994, at the age of 51, was a shock to the whole nation. Smith's unexpected death presents historians with an important question, to which there can never be a final answer: how would Labour have fared after 1994 with Smith in charge rather than Blair? Many people have argued that Smith might have achieved all that Blair did, perhaps more. Others have speculated that Smith was innately too cautious and would not have acted as boldly and decisively as Blair did in dumping the socialist traditions of 'Old Labour'. Either way, when Blair became Labour leader in 1994 he benefited enormously from the legacy Smith, and Kinnock, left behind.

Key profiles

Tony Blair

Tony Blair (born 1953) did not look or sound like a traditional Labour politician. Educated at a Scottish private school, Fettes College, Blair was much more typical of the Middle England he wanted to win over than he was of Labour loyalists. That explains why he placed so much emphasis on the label 'New Labour'. Blair had few hang-ups about political ideology; what drove him was the desire to win power. To do this, he focused on policy, party discipline and political presentation. He was prime minister from 1997 until he stepped down in 2007.

John Smith

John Smith (1938–94) was MP for Monklands East, a Labour stronghold in the west of Scotland. He was popular and respected at Westminster, with a political style that was calm and reassuring; he was a skilful performer in parliament and on television. Smith became Labour leader in 1992, succeeding Neil Kinnock. Why Kinnock's Welshness should have been a political disadvantage while Smith's Scottishness proved to be an asset might seem puzzling but opinion polls showed this to be true. Smith might well have become prime minister but for his sudden death from a heart attack in 1994.

From the beginning, Tony Blair wanted a dramatic shift in policy to show how Labour was breaking with its past. John Smith had already prepared the way for this by moving to abolish the trade union block vote by introducing 'One Member One Vote' (OMOV) in 1993. Many Labour traditionalists regarded OMOV as surrendering to the anti-union ideology of Mrs Thatcher, but Blair wanted to get the party as far away as possible from trade union power and from the memories of the winter of discontent in 1979.

The second big reform was the abolition of clause four. This wiped out one of the iconic socialist principles enshrined in Labour's constitution: the commitment to state ownership of key industries. Blair's aim was to move Labour forwards, dropping outdated socialist ideas and embracing

Key chronology

Political developments, 1990–97

1990	
October	Resignation of Mrs Thatcher
1992	
May	Narrow Labour defeat in the general election
June	Resignation of Neil Kinnock as Labour leader
September	Tory reputation for economic competence ruined by Black Wednesday
1994	
February	Sudden death of John Smith
March	'Granita' meeting between Gordon Brown and Tony Blair
October	Clause Four abandoned by Labour
1996	
October	Commitment by *The Sun* to support Labour
1997	
May	Landslide victory in the general election

Did you know?

The trade union block vote gave great power to the unions at Labour Party conferences. Union leaders were able to cast many thousands of votes (in accordance with the size of the union membership) as they wished.

Cross-reference

Clause four is explained on page 21.

the modern capitalist economy. The SPD in West Germany had done this at its party conference in Bad Godesberg in 1959, now it was time for Britain to catch up. Securing the abolition of clause four gave Blair the modernising image he wanted.

Party unity and discipline was given a high priority. After John Smith's death in 1994, the danger of a divisive leadership contest had been avoided by a deal between Blair and his main rival, Gordon Brown. In later years, this deal was to cause friction, but the Blair–Brown partnership was hugely effective. Behind them, the party's organisation was slick and controlled. Philip Gould closely monitored public opinion through focus groups. Peter Mandelson ran the efficient machinery coordinating public statements and keeping all elements of the party 'on message'. The notoriously error-prone Labour Party stopped making errors.

In the past, the Conservatives had always outmatched Labour in campaign funds and in support from the national press; negative press coverage of Neil Kinnock in the 1992 election campaign was just one example of this. Overcoming this problem was perhaps the most important factor in the success of New Labour by 1997. Blair's press secretary, Alastair Campbell, used his experience as a former journalist to change Labour's relationships with the press and media. Journalists and newspaper owners, many of them unenthusiastic about John Major anyway, were won over. One of the Conservative Party's most powerful weapons had been neutralised.

Key profiles

Peter Mandelson

Peter Mandelson (born 1953) became famous as the 'Prince of Darkness', the clever spin doctor who was behind the slick presentation of New Labour. Mandelson was Neil Kinnock's director of communications from 1985 and masterminded Labour's election campaign in 1987. He entered parliament in 1992 and became a close adviser to Tony Blair. He was twice a cabinet minister but on each occasion had to resign after a scandal; as industry minister in 1998 and as Northern Ireland secretary in 2001. He then left British politics to become an EU commissioner but made a sensational return to join Gordon Brown's cabinet in 2008.

Alastair Campbell

Alastair Campbell (born 1957) was Tony Blair's press secretary from 1994 to 2003. He had worked as a journalist for several newspapers including the *Daily Mirror*. Campbell had great success in improving Labour's press coverage through well-organised briefing to journalists. He was particularly effective in rebutting hostile news stories as soon as they appeared.

The general election of 1997: reasons for Labour's victory

In one sense, explaining the terrible Conservative defeat in 1997 is easy. In a democracy, no government lasts forever. Sooner or later the pendulum of party politics always swings and the voters decide it is 'time for a change'. This happened to the Conservatives in 1964 and to Labour in 1979. But 1997 seemed to be more significant than that.

The Conservative Party seemed to be undergoing a fundamental crisis of identity.

Although opinion polls during the campaign showed a large Labour lead, many Labour supporters genuinely feared the power of the Tory electoral machine might cause yet another disappointment like 1992. (Political journalists knew full well Labour would win easily.) In the event, Labour won by a landslide. Many Labour candidates were visibly amazed by their victories in 'safe' Conservative seats. Even the safest seats, in places like Harrogate and Hove, proved not to be safe at all. For many people, the symbolic image of election night came from Enfield, where a previously unheard-of Labour candidate, Stephen Twigg, ousted one of the Conservative 'big beasts', Michael Portillo.

Most Conservatives, including John Major and Michael Heseltine, had expected defeat. Major himself said years later: *'Winning four consecutive election victories was a miracle – winning for a fifth time was an absolute impossibility.'* Election night was a grim experience for Conservatives. Half of all Conservative MPs lost their seats. Many of the casualties were high-profile personalities: Michael Portillo, David Mellor, Norman Lamont, Malcom Rifkind. The Conservatives got 31 per cent of the vote, the lowest figure since 1823. They now had only 165 seats in the Commons, with not a single seat in Scotland. It was a bigger disaster than 1945.

There were many reasons for Conservative pessimism before the campaign:

- The traditional Conservative image of party unity had been shattered by the Eurosceptic rebellions.
- The accusations of 'Tory sleaze' were damaging. Martin Bell's campaign against Neil Hamilton dominated evening news bulletins and had adverse effects on the wider Conservative campaign.
- The Referendum Party, lavishly financed by Sir James Goldsmith, won no seats but attracted enough voters to cause Conservative defeats in some marginal seats, as in the defeat of David Mellor in Putney.
- The economic situation had improved by 1997, but there was no 'feelgood factor' or approval for Conservative economic policies. The blame for Black Wednesday still loomed over Major's government.
- Many national newspapers that had always strongly supported the Conservatives were now lukewarm or had even gone over to support for Labour.
- The Labour Party was no longer an easy target for attack but was a formidable fighting force. The usual Tory tactics of frightening voters away from Labour's 'socialist extremism' simply did not work anymore.
- Tony Blair was a skilful communicator, particularly effective in presenting an air of moderation and winning over 'Middle England'. Blair did especially well with women and young voters.
- Labour was no longer the party of 'tax-and-spend' economic policies. Gordon Brown had done a lot to convince people that Labour was the party of prudence and economic competence.
- The Labour campaign was run by a disciplined 'spin machine' that was very effective in dealing with the media and the press, both in refuting Conservative attacks and in selling Labour policies. Labour spokesmen were always 'on message' with access to up-to-date information.

Exploring the detail

The downfall of Conservatism?

In 1995, the philosopher John Gray argued that the Conservative Party was causing its own downfall because Mrs Thatcher's governments since 1979 had eroded the institutions and cultural traditions that had always underpinned Conservatism. Thatcherism had moved away from the old Tory party values and from traditional supporters in rural and suburban areas. There was a new breed of Conservative MPs appealing to a new breed of Conservative voters.

Cross-reference

To recap on Black Wednesday and its impact, look back to page 130.

■ There was widespread tactical voting, with Labour supporters voting Liberal (and vice-versa) according to how the anti-Conservative vote could be maximised. This resulted in the election of several new Liberal MPs. It also secured the defeat of many Conservative candidates by their Labour opponents.

Fig. 6 *Things can only get better? Tony and Cherie Blair in Downing Street, May 1997*

The Labour landslide of 1997 ended eighteen years in opposition. A Labour government had a strong parliamentary majority for the first time since 1966. Many people thought of 1945 and the hopes of a 'new Jerusalem'. The fact that so many new Labour MPs were youthful or female was in tune with the ideas of a new beginning. The Conservative Party was left in a black hole of unpopularity, destined for years in the wilderness. John Major did not hang around to take part in this experience. On the day Tony Blair moved into 10 Downing Street, Major made it clear he was resigning as party leader and then went to the Oval to watch cricket.

> The Major Years produced a strong economic record. After the 1990–92 recession, there was low inflation (below 4 per cent); steady economic growth (2–3 per cent) and repeated praise from international organisations such as the OECD. There was a renaissance of culture and sport through National Lottery funding and unsung improvements to public services through the Citizen's Charter. In foreign policy, the Major government adapted smoothly to the post-Cold War world, with a clear appraisal of priorities and capabilities. It was a better legacy than many governments leave.
>
> 4   *From Seldon, A.,* **Major: A Political Life**, *1997*

■ **Summary question**

To what extent was the decline of the Conservative Party in the 1990s due to economic factors?

14   New Labour in power, 1997–2007

In this chapter you will learn about:

- the personalities and policies that shaped Blair's first government after 1997

- the reasons for Labour's continued electoral success in 2001 and 2005

- the development of the British economy from 1997 to 2007

- the attempts to revive the Conservative Party during its years in opposition.

Fig. 1 *Still the prime minister for Middle England? Tony Blair, 2007*

We have been elected because we represent the whole of this nation and we will govern for the whole of this nation. We have won support from all walks of life, from all classes of people, every corner of the country. We are now today the people's party. The party of all the people, of the many not the few, the party that belongs to every part of Britain.

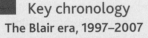

From a speech by Tony Blair, May 1997

Blair's coalition was wide but shallow. This twisted a knot of tension around the heart of the new government from the beginning. The scale of his parliamentary majority was bound to arouse great expectations about the rapidity with which Blair could deliver change. The qualified nature of his true support was guaranteed to aggravate New Labour's apprehension about taking any risks with its popularity. The previous terror of losing would soon morph into an anxiety about the consequences of victory.

2   *From Rawnsley, A., Servants of the People: The Inside Story of New Labour, 2000*

Key chronology

The Blair era, 1997–2007

1997   Labour landslide
1998   Good Friday Agreement
1999   NATO intervention in Kosovo
2001   Re-election of Labour government
2003   Invasion of Iraq
2004   Expansion of the EU
2005   Third successive election victory
2005   7/7 terrorist attacks in London
2007   Blair succeeded as prime minister by Gordon Brown

■ Key terms

Third Way: a New Labour term promising to get away from the divisive and out-of-date ideas of the old Labour left, dominated by the trade unions and Marxism, and from the old right, dominated by selfish capitalism.

First-past-the-post: a description of Britain's electoral system. MPs are elected in single-member constituencies by winning the most votes, i.e. being first past the post. This might be by a huge majority of 20,000, or by a handful of votes. Thus a small electoral swing towards one party can decide the result in many marginal seats. Equally, a party can win a big share of the vote but very few seats.

With the 1997 landslide, Labour began a decade in power, winning an unprecedented three consecutive election victories. Political commentators talked once again about a 'fundamental realignment of British politics'. Tony Blair claimed his government would be a '*big tent*', incorporating talents from other parties and offering Britain a new consensus that he called the **Third Way**.

When Blair stepped down in 2007, it was difficult to measure the extent to which he had achieved his goals. No Labour leader in history had achieved such sustained electoral success. Blair had also forced the Conservatives to change: in 2005, the party chose David Cameron, who looked and sounded rather like a new Tony Blair. Yet many of Blair's promises and policies remained unfulfilled. Reform of the public services was patchy and aroused opposition. Constitutional reform stuttered and stalled. Blair's hopes of building a new consensus were badly damaged by an unpopular war in Iraq and by his close links to the even more unpopular George W. Bush.

By 2007, Blair's 'big tent' no longer seemed so attractive or inclusive. The Conservatives were starting to come back from the political dead. Many Labour supporters were demanding a return to traditional Labour values. So, as with most political careers, Tony Blair's ended with a sense of anti-climax. Yet his impact on politics and society in Britain was significant and wide-ranging. Coming to a decisive historical judgement on his career is a difficult and complicated task.

■ The first Blair government, 1997–2001

Few governments have arrived in office in more favourable circumstances than New Labour in 1997. Tony Blair could rely on a huge majority in parliament. The Labour Party appeared more united than at any time since 1945. Blair led a group of talented politicians, who had spent three years preparing for power and had a clear sense of direction in carrying through what they called the 'Blair Project'. The Conservative opposition was demoralised. The economic situation was favourable. Press coverage, even from traditionally Conservative newspapers, was positive. The new government basked in the glow of almost universal public goodwill.

In many ways, however, the extent of support for Labour was deceptive. The massive parliamentary majority did not reflect a massive surge in the Labour vote. Although 43 per cent of votes were cast for Labour, this was a share of a low turnout. Fewer people voted for Labour in 1997 than in any of the elections between 1945 and 1966; the Labour vote in 1997 was 500,00 less than John Major's Conservatives had received in 1992. The 1997 'landslide' was based on factors such as Tory voters staying at home, tactical voting for Liberal candidates and the peculiar distortions that can arise from Britain's winner-takes-all, **first-past-the-post** electoral system.

Expectations of the new Labour government were very high, perhaps unrealistically so. There was optimism about a fresh start, with the hope that politics would become less cynical, more relevant to young people. The media made much of 'Blair's Babes', the many young women among the new Labour MPs arriving at Westminster. Blair's cabinet was also full of confident and capable politicians: Robin Cook at the foreign office, Jack Straw as home secretary and David Blunkett at education. Above all, there was the powerful partnership between Tony Blair and Gordon Brown. This partnership did not always run smoothly – sometimes it was compared to a stormy marriage – but it was to dominate British politics for more than a decade.

Key profile

Gordon Brown

Gordon Brown (born 1951) was elected MP for Dunfermline in 1983 and was a protégé of John Smith. He was considered a strong candidate for the party leadership before he made a deal with Tony Blair in 1994. He had a key role in election planning in 1997. After Labour came to power, he was chancellor of the exchequer for ten years, longer than any other chancellor in modern times. His relationship with Blair was often tense but they made a powerful and effective team. Brown succeeded Blair as prime minister in 2007.

A closer look

The 'politcal marriage' between Blair and Brown

For thirteen years, the key relationship in British politics was the Blair–Brown partnership at the heart of New Labour. Blair became party leader, won power and remained prime minister for ten years. Brown played a dominant role in preparing Labour policies up to 1997 and then held the post of chancellor for an unbroken ten years. The two men had entered parliament at the same time, in 1983, and shared an office together. Yet it was also a famously stormy relationship, marked by frequent rows that were often in the public eye because 'Brownites' and 'Blairites' gave rival briefings to the press. In 2001, the BBC journalist, James Naughtie, analysed the relationship in his book, *The Rivals: The Intimate Story of a Political Marriage*. Since then, other journalists have described the relationship as a 'feud', or as 'Labour's civil war'.

According to legend, the marriage was arranged at a private meeting over dinner at the Granita restaurant in Islington in 1994. After the sudden death of John Smith, it was essential for the reformers and modernisers in the Labour Party to make plans for the upcoming leadership election. At that time, Brown would have been regarded as the more experienced of the two prospective leaders but it was agreed at the Granita dinner that Blair would become leader, working in close partnership with Brown as strategist and policy expert. Afterwards, it was widely said that Blair had agreed to step down at some point in the future to allow Brown to have his turn as leader. This question, exactly *when* Brown would take over, caused tensions between 'Blairites' and 'Brownites' within the Labour government, especially after 2001.

Blair's government itself did a lot to whip up the high expectations. The Foreign Secretary, Robin Cook, spoke eloquently about a '*foreign policy with an ethical dimension*'. The government promised to be '*tough on crime, tough on the causes of crime*'. They promised to push through reforms in education: the slogan 'Education, education, education' became almost the signature tune of the government. Tony Blair promised to make his government a 'big tent' that would have room for people from outside the Labour Party. It was rumoured that Blair might give a cabinet post to the Liberal leader, Paddy Ashdown. There was a commitment to work with the Liberal Democrats on a fairer voting system, with Roy Jenkins at the head of a Commission for Electoral Reform.

Blair's first Labour government was very well prepared for power but did not achieve nearly as much as had been promised. Later in his career, Blair admitted his own sense of frustration at the unfulfilled hopes of 1997. One explanation is that there were simply too many promises, not enough delivery. A second explanation, favoured by Blair himself, is that the government acted too cautiously, with too much fear of the popular press. Many Labour MPs had been in opposition so long they still *thought* like the opposition, even now they were in government. A third explanation might be the obsession with focus groups, opinion polls and 'spin'. Blair has been accused of reacting to events with instant soundbites, rather than following a consistent long-term strategy.

On the other hand, the Blair government's first term of office did have its successes. Blair aimed to be the first Labour prime minister ever to win a second full term in office; at no time did he look like failing to achieve this. Even Blair's enemies agreed that he was extremely skilful in massaging public opinion, always persuasive in his appearances on television. In August 1997, when the nation was in shock after the death of Diana, Princess of Wales in Paris, the Prime Minister's statements about *'the People's Princess'* showed a typically sure grasp of the public mood. Cabinet ministers like Robin Cook and David Blunkett were also skilful media performers. Few governments have overshadowed the opposition as completely as New Labour did throughout its first term.

Fig. 2 *Mourning for the People's Princess: the funeral of Diana, Princess of Wales, 1997*

Blair's government could also claim three substantial achievements: in the economy, in Northern Ireland and in foreign policy. Labour succeeded in its aim to be trusted on the economy. Gordon Brown's decision to hand over decisions on interest rates and inflation targets to the Bank of England was regarded by many as a masterstroke. Inflation was coming down and employment was going up. The living standards of the middle classes were rising, partly because of the housing boom.

The successful outcome of the peace process in Northern Ireland in 1998 was a personal triumph for the Prime Minister, who devoted most of his first year in power to a detailed, hands-on involvement in the negotiations. The peace process had been pushed forward a long way before Blair arrived on the scene; there were many important factors behind

Cross-reference

The foreign relations aspect of the peace process in Northern Ireland is covered in Chapter 16.

the Good Friday Agreement signed in Belfast in April 1998 apart from Tony Blair's contribution. His personal commitment was, however, vital.

John Hume of the SDLP had already persuaded the Sinn Fein leader, Gerry Adams, to commit to a peace plan. The Northern Ireland Secretary, Mo Mowlam, had much success bringing together the loyalist and republican paramilitaries. President Clinton's special envoy, Senator George Mitchell, was a superb mediator. Blair himself developed a close working relationship with the Irish taoiseach, Bertie Ahern, a vital factor in keeping the republicans on track. Perhaps most important of all, Blair proved capable of reassuring David Trimble and the Ulster Unionists during the tense final negotiations.

Even after the Good Friday Agreement was made, it was still possible it might come unstuck, for example when thirty people were killed in a terrible bomb attack on Omagh. Throughout his first term and all the way to 2007, Blair remained closely involved in the difficult task of moving the two sides closer towards implementing a final peace settlement. Many people regarded Northern Ireland as his greatest single achievement. In 1999, Blair was also widely praised for his part in persuading the United States to support NATO intervention in Kosovo.

Constitutional change

The movement towards peace and a power-sharing government in Northern Ireland was part of a wide range of constitutional changes, including devolution in Scotland and Wales. A new Scottish Assembly was established at Edinburgh, based on a system of proportional representation. A Welsh Assembly was set up in Cardiff though without tax-raising powers. Another reform was the introduction of an elected mayor for London in 1999. The government made a major political effort to reform the House of Lords; it ended with a rather messy compromise in which hereditary peers were not abolished but cut to 92. A Freedom of Information Act was passed and the European Human Rights Act was incorporated into British law.

Fig. 3 *The new Welsh Assembly in Cardiff, 2006*

This rush of activity had mixed results. In Scotland, the Scottish Nationalists (SNP) continued to gain support when it had been hoped devolution would take away their momentum. House of Lords reform was

∎ **Exploring the detail**

Opposition to the Good Friday Agreement

This opposition came from both sides. The leaders of Sinn Fein, Gerry Adams and Martin McGuinness, were very nervous of a republican backlash against them 'selling out'. The Omagh bombing in 1998 was carried out by just such dissident republicans in the so-called Continuity IRA. David Trimble and the Ulster Unionists feared the powerful negative influence of Dr Ian Paisley, the leader of the hard-line Democratic Unionist Party (DUP).

∎ **Cross-reference**

Britain's role in the Balkans is covered in Chapter 16

∎ **Key chronology**

Constitutional changes, 1997–2000

1997	Freedom of Information Act
	Devolution referendum in Scotland
	Devolution referendum in Wales
1998	Scotland Act
	Government of Wales Act
	Human Rights Act
1999	House of Lords Act
2000	First election for mayor of London

seen as unsatisfactory by almost everyone. Schemes to reform the electoral system got nowhere and were shelved. The mayor of London proved to be very successful, but the mayor who won the election was Ken Livingstone, the left-wing maverick who had led the GLC in the 1980s and just about the last person Tony Blair wanted to get the job. The way judges interpreted the Human Rights Act created unexpected difficulties for the government.

Blair himself was disappointed by the failures to implement his ambitious policy programme, including the slow progress of reforms to the public services. In January 2001, he showed this frustration by promising a massive increase in public spending, especially on health, and a more urgent approach to forcing reforms through. The fact that he set up a special delivery unit in July 2001 to ensure this showed that he was unhappy with the delivery of policies since 1997. He intended to be much more radical once the 2001 election was safely won.

> Blair was a 'late developer' as prime minister. Most successful prime ministers, including Clement Attlee and Margaret Thatcher, achieve a lot early on and fade towards the end. Blair's youth (the youngest prime minister since 1812) and his slowness in developing his own political agenda made the Blair premiership the mirror image of the norm. He began with a whimper and finished with a bang.

3   *From Seldon, A., Blair Unbound, 2007*

■ The Labour government, 2001–07

Labour's continuing electoral success in 2001 and 2005

Many people believed that New Labour had achieved less than it should have done by 2001. Yet Labour was able to remain in power, with a strong parliamentary majority, through consecutive election victories in 2001 and 2005. Victory was achieved in 2005 even though the Prime Minister's personal popularity had taken a hammering after the invasion of Iraq in 2003. When Blair handed over to Gordon Brown in 2007, there was little prospect of Labour losing power before 2010. No Labour government had even come close to achieving such dominance. Why was Tony Blair able to secure this run of electoral success?

Table 1 *General election results, 1997–2005*

Year	1997	2001	2005
Labour	419	413	355
Conservative	165	166	198
Liberal Democrat	46	52	62
Others (SNP, DUP, PC, etc)	29	28	30
Labour majority	179	166	71

Success in 2001 came relatively easily. Blair's personal standing in the country was high. Labour was still able to rely on the support of sections of the national press that had traditionally been pro-Conservative. The continuing high levels of support for the Liberal Democrats (who gained their highest number of seats in parliament any third party had had since the 1930s) damaged the prospects of the Conservatives more than Labour. The economic situation remained good, especially for the middle classes.

The Conservative Party was still struggling to overcome its internal problems, with a young and inexperienced leader in William Hague.

Blair's second term in office was more problematic and the Labour success in 2005 is harder to explain. By then, the government had lost several leading performers. Peter Mandelson and David Blunkett had been forced to resign by scandals; Robin Cook resigned in protest against the Iraq war; Charles Clarke had to resign as home secretary because of the embarrassment when prisoners awaiting deportation escaped from custody and could not be traced. The rivalry between Blairites and Brownites was starting to arouse intense press speculation. The Labour government might well have been in deep trouble but for the fact that the Conservative opposition was still desperately weak and ineffective.

The Conservative Party – continuing internal divisions

After his defeat in 1997, John Major instantly resigned as Conservative leader. He had been badly bruised by the experience of leading such a divided and rebellious party and no wish to carry on. Unlike Edward Heath and Margaret Thatcher, Major was happy to leave the field clear for his successors. Life was going to be difficult enough for them anyway. Conservative divisions on Europe remained. So did the bitter recriminations against those who had 'betrayed Maggie'.

From 1997 until 2005, through two more election defeats and no less than four changes of party leader, the Conservative Party continued to fight its 'civil war'. The party had apparently completely lost what the historian John Ramsden calls its *appetite for power*. So many Conservative MPs had lost their seats or retired at the 1997 election that William Hague's party was only half the size of the party that had chosen John Major in 1990. The party was also more Eurosceptic than before, and two prime candidates, Michael Heseltine and Ken Clarke, faced hostility from the Right. Another possible candidate, Michael Portillo, was temporarily no longer an MP

There was more negative campaigning to 'stop Heseltine' or to 'stop Clarke' than any desire to rally round a candidate with the potential to win a future election. The new leader was William Hague, a 36-year-old with limited political experience and no power base in the party. Hague won because he had fewer enemies than his better-known rivals and because he was Mrs Thatcher's preferred choice. Mrs Thatcher's high-profile support did Hague little good, as it highlighted his inexperience and lessened his authority.

■ Key chronology

The Conservative Party leadership, 1990–2007

1990	
November	Fall of Mrs Thatcher
December	Election of John Major
1995	
June	Re-election of John Major
1997	
June	Election of William Hague
2001	
June	Election of Iain Duncan-Smith
2003	
May	Duncan-Smith replaced by Michael Howard
2005	
June	Election of David Cameron

■ Key profile

William Hague

Hague (born 1961) was first noticed at the age of 16, making an assured speech at the 1981 Conservative Party conference. He became a popular and effective MP for Richmond, known for his Eurosceptic views and for his skill as a debater. As party leader, Hague attempted, at least at first, to make Conservative policies more socially inclusive. He was not able to carry this through, however, because right-wingers were obsessed with infighting and with promoting policies that had already proved unpopular with voters.

By 2001, Hague had retreated to right-wing policy positions designed to shore up the Conservative core vote: 'the fight to save the pound' and a hard line against immigration. This may have prevented some Conservative voters from right drifting to UKIP or the British National Party (BNP) but did nothing to appeal to the middle ground. The outcome was another crushing defeat. Many observers pointed out that the average age of the party membership was 63. The Conservative Party faced a steep decline unless it underwent drastic change but the party was not yet ready to change.

After Hague's resignation in 2001, the strongest candidates were Ken Clarke, still highly popular with voters, and Michael Portillo, who had returned to parliament as a social liberal, promising to make the party more modern and inclusive. The party chose instead the little-known Iain Duncan Smith.

■ **Key profile**

Iain Duncan Smith

Duncan Smith (born 1954) came from a military background, educated at HMS Conway and the army college at Sandhurst. He was one of the original Maastricht rebels against John Major. He won in 2001 because of negative voting against Clarke and Portillo, not because of any belief in his ability to lead the Conservatives back into power. Duncan Smith had little charisma and made little impact in the opinion polls. Within a few months of his emergence as leader, Conservative MPs were plotting to get rid of him. In 2003, Duncan Smith was ousted and Michael Howard was installed as leader, unopposed.

Whether choosing a different leader in 2001 would have brought the Conservatives greater success in the next election, it is impossible to know; but the choice of Iain Duncan Smith seemed to demonstrate the fact that the Conservatives had a death wish similar to that in the Labour Party between 1979 and 1983. To reject Clarke and Portillo was to reject the voters the Conservatives needed if they were ever to get back to power. The fact that the party removed Duncan Smith in 2003 and replaced him with Michael Howard seemed to show that they had woken up to this fact.

■ **Key profile**

Michael Howard

Howard (born 1941) was an experienced and able politician but had become something of a hate figure as an extremely unpopular home secretary in the 1990s. In 1997, he had come last in the race to succeed John Major. As leader, Howard performed strongly against Tony Blair in the Commons and improved party organisation and morale. The party that Howard led, however, was still obsessed with Europe and went down to defeat again in 2005.

■ **Activity**

Debating interpretations

Assemble the arguments for and against the proposition that: 'Between 1997 and 2005, the Conservative Party made itself unelectable.'

Conservative recovery

In 2005, the Conservatives suffered a third successive defeat, though probably by a lesser margin than if Iain Duncan Smith had remained as leader. What made the 2005 defeat different from 1997 and 2001 was that, at last, the Conservatives decided to learn the lessons of defeat and to make the changes necessary to win over the voters. This time, the party's choice was David Cameron, who promoted the image of the Conservatives as a rejuvenated, united party, more representative of the country as a whole and longer obsessed with the past.

Key profile

David Cameron

David Cameron (born 1966) came from a wealthy background and was educated at Eton and Oxford. His early career was in public relations; he was also a policy adviser to Norman Lamont at the time of Black Wednesday in 1992 and later to Michael Howard. Cameron was elected MP for Witney in 2001, only four years before he became party leader. He played a key role in drafting the Conservative election manifesto in 2005.

The Labour Party found it more difficult to attack Cameron than his predecessors. Accusing him of being 'smooth but superficial' was a problem because of his apparent similarities to Tony Blair. Dismissing Cameron as a 'Tory toff' seemed out-of-tune with New Labour claims to have made Britain a classless society. Labour attacked Cameron for making vague promises without spelling out the costs and policy details, but that was exactly the method New Labour had used from 1994. For the first time since 1997, the Conservatives seemed to offer a credible alternative.

By the time Tony Blair left office in 2007, Cameron's Conservative Party had recovered much of the ground lost since 1992. Restless right-wingers were reluctant to follow the more socially liberal line set by Cameron but many traditional Conservative supporters seemed ready to switch back to the party, turning away from fringe parties like UKIP. Opinion polls suggested many seats lost to the Liberals in 1997 were likely to be won back next time. Whether Cameron would be a Conservative Neil Kinnock (recovery but not victory) or a Conservative Tony Blair (outright success) could only be guessed at.

The political impact of the war in Iraq

The defining issue of Blair's second term, however, was the invasion of Iraq in 2003 and Blair's perceived closeness to George W. Bush, the most unpopular American president of modern times. The Iraq War aroused bitter opposition to Tony Blair, often from those who had previously been enthusiastic supporters. The whole pattern of domestic politics was shaped by the controversies over Iraq and the so-called 'war on terror'.

The shocking events of 11 September 2001 had a huge impact on Tony Blair's thinking. He was convinced that global terrorism was a deadly danger and that special measures were needed to provide people with greater security. Increasingly, this brought him into conflict with people concerned to protect civil liberties. Blair's close links to George W. Bush became a domestic policy issue because of the intense hostility to Bush in Britain and Europe. Thus, Blair had to fight two wars over Iraq, one against Saddam Hussein and the other to win over political and public opinion at home. Both these wars went badly.

Exploring the detail

Changing the public perception

'Decontaminating the Conservative brand' was a term reflecting the PR background of the new Conservative leadership. David Cameron and his closest advisers (nicknamed the 'Cameroons') knew that the Conservatives were seen as 'the nasty party', badly out-of-touch with modern British society. For them, it was essential to 'decontaminate the brand', to reach out beyond the narrow 'core' support for the Conservatives to make the party more tolerant and inclusive, no longer hostile to all kinds of social groups including ethnic minorities, single mothers, homosexuals and young people.

Cross-reference

The foreign policy issues concerning the Iraq war and the special relationship with the US are covered in Chapter 16.

The events of 11 September 2001 are also explained on page 169.

Fig. 4 *The Sun*, WMD and Saddam
Hussein, 2003

Fig. 5 The *Daily Mirror* and the
invasion of Iraq, 2003

Fig. 6 *The Sun* on the threats from Iraq's
WMD, 2003

Cross-reference

Saddam Hussein and weapons of
mass destruction are covered on
pages 170–71.

Exploring the detail

The case of Dr David Kelly

Dr Kelly was a weapons expert at
the Ministry of Defence. He came
to public notice through two BBC
journalists, Andrew Gilligan and
Susan Watts, who gave conflicting
reports of his statements to them
about the search for WMD, especially
Gilligan's sensationalist claim that
the intelligence dossier had been
'sexed up' to exaggerate the urgency
of the threat from Saddam. Dr Kelly
committed suicide after being grilled
by a parliamentary committee and
pursued by the press. When his body
was discovered near his home in
Oxfordshire in July 2003, the case
dominated the national news and
rocked the government.

Opposition in Britain had many different elements. Robin Cook, the
Foreign Secretary, resigned in protest, followed after some hesitation, by the
Overseas Development Minister, Clare Short. Many people were opposed
in principle to the war and argued that it would be an illegal war without
full backing from the United Nations. Public opinion polls showed most
people in support of Blair but with a large and vocal minority who did
not believe war was either necessary or morally justified. What did most
damage to the Prime Minister's credibility was not so much the war itself
as the reaction against his methods of winning support for the war.

In September 2002, an intelligence dossier was published to show the
urgent danger from Saddam's weapons of mass destruction (WMD),
including nuclear and biological weapons. The dossier backfired.
It failed to convince those who thought the threat from WMD
was overrated. People questioned why Alastair Campbell, Blair's
press secretary, had a key role in drafting the dossier. There were
accusations that the dossier was about political presentation than hard
intelligence In May 2003, claims by the journalist Andrew Gilligan
that the dossier had been 'sexed up' for political purposes caused a
sensation.

If WMD had been discovered in Iraq after the fall of Saddam, none of this
would have mattered much. But there were no WMD. Blair's opponents
claimed that this proved deliberate deception, that 'Bliar' had consistently
lied in pursuit of his warmongering policies. This was not really true:
Blair genuinely believed in the WMD evidence and so did many of the
intelligence community, but it was widely asserted. The tragic death by
suicide of the scientist David Kelly further damaged the government's
reputation. An enquiry chaired by Lord Hutton eventually absolved the
government from blame and criticised the BBC but this did little to alter
the public mood of cynicism and condemnation.

Meanwhile, the course of the war led to further difficulties. Saddam was
quickly overthrown but the war did not end neatly. British and American
forces became bogged down in a war of occupation. The government
was blamed by its many critics for human rights abuses by British and
American soldiers. The security situation eventually began to improve in
2006 and there were hopes that troops could start coming home; but the
unpopularity of the war remained a powerful political factor right to the
end of Blair's time in office.

The 'wobble', 2004

There was a brief 'wobble' in Tony Blair's authority in 2004. The Hutton Inquiry into the circumstances around David Kelly's death reported its findings in January. There was a backbench revolt against the introduction of top-up fees for university students. The relationship with Gordon Brown was going badly. Newspaper columnists speculated that Blair might resign before the next election. In the end the 'wobble' was no more than that. The general election of May 2005 was won relatively easily, though with a reduced majority. This election victory showed the underlying strengths of the Labour government but, if the Conservatives had been able to mount a strong challenge in 2004 and 2005, Labour might have been vulnerable. In 2005, however, the Conservative Party was still a long way from political recovery.

The British economy: Labour's economic policies and their impact

In the first few years of the Labour government, the economic policies directed by Gordon Brown were mostly cautious. The priorities were to keep inflation low, to keep government spending under control and to prove to Middle England that Labour was pro-business. All this was achieved, partly because Labour had inherited very favourable economic circumstances. During Tony Blair's first term, Labour's handling of the economy proved immensely reassuring to industrialists and financiers and to the middle classes. Gordon Brown's tax policies enabled Labour to get away from its previous image as a 'tax-and-spend' party. Meanwhile, the Conservative Party had, at least temporarily, completely lost its former reputation as the 'party of economic competence'.

From the 2001 election on, however, Brown's policies became more adventurous, with a massive injection of money into the public services. The big increases in investment were reflected in new schools and hospitals and pay rises for doctors, nurses and teachers. Labour claimed credit for catching up after years of neglect. Critics argued that public spending and government borrowing were too high. There was also criticism of the funding of new projects through the Private Finance Initiative (PFI) using the private sector. The buildings usually got completed quickly but large debts were stored up for the future.

By 2007, Gordon Brown had completed an unprecedented ten years as chancellor. Throughout this time, inflation was kept under control and record numbers of people were in work. Living standards remained high and the consumer economy boomed. On the other hand, economists such as Will Hutton warned that the consumer boom was based on ever-rising house prices and on high levels of credit card spending and personal debt. There was a danger that the 'bubble' of middle class prosperity might not last.

> The verdict on Labour's economic record is certainly positive. Some credit for this must go to Brown and some, less directly, to Blair. The main achievement of the Blair–Brown partnership was to retain key features of Thatcher's reforms (particularly lower income tax rates and restrictions on trade unions) that allowed the economy to grow. And the fact that inequalities and poverty have declined somewhat, and not worsened as they quite often tended to do under Thatcher, reflects the impact of Brown's measures to provide more support for low-income families in work.

4   *From Sinclair, P. 'The Treasury and Economic Policy' in ed. Seldon, A.,*
***Blair's Britain 1997–2007**, 2007*

Activity

Source analysis

Look at Source 4 and the statistics on growth, inflation and unemployment in Figures 7 and 8.

Outline the arguments for and against the claim that the British economy was performing well between 1997 and 2007.

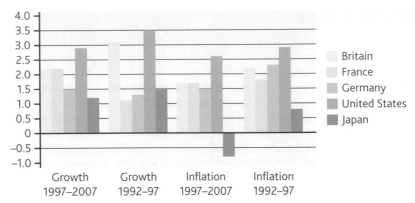

Fig. 7 *Average annual growth and inflation rates (%), 1992–2007*

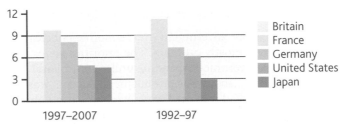

Fig. 8 *Average annual unemployment rates (%), 1992–2007*

Exploring the detail

Cash for honours

The 'cash for honours' scandal involved accusations that Labour fund-raisers had promised the award of honours to people making large donations to the Labour Party. A heavy-handed police investigation led to the senior party figures such as Lord Levy (known as 'Lord Cashpoint' for his flair in fund-raising), Tony Blair's policy adviser, Ruth Turner, and the Prime Minister himself being taken in for questioning under oath. No charges were ever brought but a cloud of suspicion hung over Blair's last months in office.

The departure of Tony Blair

Tony Blair had always promised to leave 10 Downing Street at a time of his own choosing, with Gordon Brown as his successor. By the middle of 2006, there was mounting pressure for him to go sooner rather than later. Brown and his supporters were becoming impatient. Opposition to Blair over Iraq was still strong. Blair's long honeymoon with the national press was beginning to lose its glow. The 'cash for honours' scandal was looming. Many elements within the Labour Party were yearning for a return to traditional 'Old Labour' values. There was increasing speculation that, if Blair did not choose to go soon, his own party would mount a coup against him.

Blairite loyalists pressured the Prime Minister to hang on, in order to give time for his reform agenda to work through and to protect New Labour's legacy. Blair himself wanted to stay longer, not just for the sake of being in power but because he felt he had only just got going after a slow start. *'My final two years have probably been the most productive'*, he said after stepping down. This idea provides the theme of Anthony Seldon's second Blair biography: *Blair Unbound*. But Blair's position had weakened. By 2007, many leading Labour politicians such as Robin Cook, Peter Mandelson and David Blunkett had left the government. The previously effective political partnership between Blair and Brown was breaking down.

In September 2006, there was frenzied speculation that Brown would lend his support to a coup against Blair. He did not; but the civil war within the government did not stop. Although, the so-called 'September coup' against Blair never happened, the speculation prompted him to state at the party conference a few weeks later that he would step down within a year. Perhaps feeling liberated from all the uncertainty, Tony Blair started out on a furious round of activity, both at home and abroad, determined to make the most of the Blair legacy. He finally resigned as prime minister in June 2007 and made it clear he would also be resigning as an MP. Gordon Brown was elected unopposed as Blair's successor, Britain's twelfth prime minister since 1945.

The Blair legacy

Making judgements about contemporary history is always difficult. In 2007, it was still too early to know how the wars in Iraq and Afghanistan would end; or how the economic situation would develop; or how united and successful the Labour Party would be after Blair. Any assessment given this soon after events can only be provisional. (Some historians would say that this is not only true of contemporary history. In the 1960s, Communist Chinese leader Zhou Enlai was asked to assess the significance of the French revolution 200 years before. He said: *'It's too early to tell.'*)

One damning verdict, by Simon Jenkins in *The Times*, claimed: *'Blairism won power with a smile and a platitude – but in office never found the levers to put policy into practice. Blair made government more centralised but less effective. In the end, he left the voters dissatisfied.'* Naturally, Tony Blair saw it differently. In his last-ever Prime Minister's Question Time, he made a robust defence of his record:

> DAVID CAMERON: The Prime Minister has told us who is going to wear the crown; can he tell us who wielded the knife?
>
> TONY BLAIR: Consider the ten years of achievements by this government: economic stability through the independence of the Bank of England; record investment in our public services; better maternity leave and maternity pay; support for pensioners; repeal of Section 28; a ban on tobacco advertising; and, of course, the minimum wage. What do all these things have in common? The right honourable gentleman's party voted against them.

4   *From Tony Blair's final appearance at Prime Minister's Questions, June 2007*

Cross-reference

Evidence about Blair's achievements in foreign policy is to be found in Chapter 16.

Activity

Talking point

Figure 9 might provide a starting point for an evaluation of Tony Blair's achievements.

FOR	AGAINST
• He won three elections, the greatest success ever by a Labour prime minister	• He achieved less in power than he could have done. Attlee's legacy in 1951 was greater
• There was sustained economic prosperity and economic stability	• Blair and Brown were lucky to inherit a favourable siuation in 1997; and government debt was high by 2007
• He dominated British politics and forced the Conservative Party to undergo radical change	• He alienated many traditional Labour voters by moving away from Labour principles and being too pro-business
• He achieved a historic peace settlement in Northern Ireland	• His later attempts to mediate peace in the Middle East failed
• He played an important leadership role in Europe	• He failed to secure British entry to the euro by ceding to influence from Gordon Brown and the national press
• He gave a strong lead in the 'war against terror', especially after 7/7/2005	• His drive for identity cards and greater powers for the police undermined civil liberties
• He was a world statesman, giving a strong lead on issues like Africa and climate change	• His strengths were in presentation - the practical results did not match up
• His policy of 'liberal interventionism' helped bring stability to the Balkans	• The invasion of Iraq was a disastrous error

Fig. 9 *Tony Blair: an assessment*

Cross-reference

Look back at how the Conservative party conference delegates were asked to play 'Place the face' in 2008.

Activity

Group activity

Place the face

Arrange 11 separate photographs of Britain's prime ministers between 1945 and 2007 (Attlee, Churchill, Eden, Macmillan, Douglas-Home, Wilson, Heath, Callaghan, Thatcher, Major and Blair) on a display board. Working as individuals or in pairs, place the faces in rank order according to their achievements. Tabulate the results to arrive at an average score. This activity can be extended to involve people outside the class.

Summary question

Explain why the Conservative Party spent so many years in the political wilderness after 1997.

15

British society, 1990–2007

Fig. 1 *No riots here: Notting Hill Carnival, 2007*

In this chapter you will learn about:

- social issues and the impact on society of population trends

- changing attitudes towards 'multiculturalism'

- developments affecting women, youth and relations between the classes

- developments in popular culture and the media.

In 1990, Britain's population was 3 million fewer than in 2007. The ethnic mix of the country was simpler. Of the 3 million non-white British, the largest groups were Indian (848,000) black Caribbean (500,000) and Pakistani (476,000). No serious concern was expressed politically about whether Muslims could fully integrate. The largest white migrant group was from Ireland, which was then still relatively poor. Any Poles or Russians in Britain were diplomats or refugees from communism. The term 'bogus asylum seeker' would have been met with a puzzled frown. Britain was far less penetrated by overseas culture and people than she would later become.

1   *From Marr, A., **A History of Modern Britain**, 2007*

This snapshot picture of Britain in 1990 hints at the speed and scale of the social and cultural changes that transformed British society between the departure of Mrs Thatcher in 1990 and the departure of Tony Blair in 2007. These changes affected the size and shape of the population, social attitudes, culture and the media.

■ Population change and social issues, 1990–2007

Demographic change

By 2007, immigration had risen to the top of the public agenda. Pressure groups, internet blogs and sections of the national press claimed that the swelling of Britain's population through immigration was as a problem requiring urgent attention in order to maintain social cohesion and to protect the 'British way of life'. In the 2001 election, opinion polls found that immigration was regarded as a vital issue by only 3 per cent of voters; similar polls in 2007 put the figure at nearly 30 per cent. There were worries that Britain's population was growing too fast, that the country was 'full up' and there would be rising community tensions as a result.

Demographic change in Britain, however, involved more than immigration. People were living longer, due to improvements in medical care and living standards. There were accelerating changes in where people lived and shopped, such as the rapid expansion in the number and size of out-of-town shopping centres and the massive increase in 'single-occupiers' (people living alone). Economic factors meant that London and the south-east grew rapidly, with housing, transport and social services stretched. In Scotland and parts of the old industrial north, the population was declining, with depressed house prices and urban decay.

Governments attempted to counter this by granting funds for regeneration and by relocating government departments out of London. Regeneration projects had considerable success as towns and cities such as Glasgow, Birmingham, Leeds and Gateshead benefited from new museums, art galleries and concert halls and extensive property development. But London and the south-east continued to attract the lion's share of economic growth during the years of prosperity from the early 1990s to 2007.

The greying of Britain

One fundamental population trend was the changing age profile of the population as a whole, above all the vast increase in life expectancy. Britain's population was becoming older with every passing year. By 2007, the average age was 39 years; in 1997, only ten years earlier, it had been 37. In 2007, for the first time in history, there were more people of retirement age in Britain than young people under 16. There was a surge in the over-60s generation because those born in the 'baby boom' after 1945 were reaching retirement age. The percentage of the population over 80 years of age had doubled in 20 years and seemed set to continue growing.

By 2007, this 'greying of Britain' was having important social consequences. There was a surge in demand for medical treatments for the elderly, such as hip replacements, eye surgery and relief for arthritis. NHS hospitals and local authority nursing homes struggled to cope with rising demand for long-term care and the steep rise in cases of dementia. As the proportion of the population over 65 rose, pensions became a major political issue. More and more people were depending for longer and longer on their pensions; the costs of both state and private pension schemes skyrocketed. Pundits predicted the retirement age would have to go up to 70.

■ Exploring the detail

Policy Exchange report

In 2008, Dr Tim Leunig of the centre-right think-tank Policy Exchange issued a report stating that regenerating the post-industrial cities in the north could not succeed. He suggested people in places like Sunderland and Liverpool would be better off if they moved to London or Oxford. The report drew a storm of criticism (many people, including David Cameron, described it as 'barmy') but it raised an important issue about the consequences of demographic change as a result of market forces.

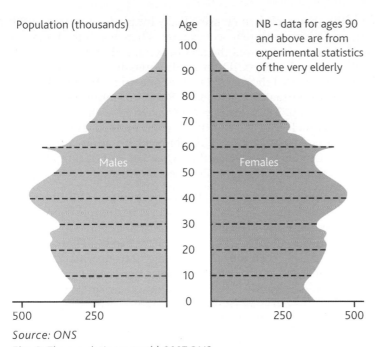

Population (thousands)   Age   NB - data for ages 90 and above are from experimental statistics of the very elderly

Males   Females

500   250   250   500

Source: ONS

Fig. 2 *The population pyramid, 2007 ONS*

The 'grey pound' was also a big factor in social and economic change. A new generation of active retired people (many having retired well before the state retirement age of 65 for men, 60 for women) had more disposable income than previous generations. They went on long-haul holidays, bought second homes, surfed the internet, joined voluntary organisations such as the University of the Third Age, and provided important new markets in property, shopping and leisure. The advertising industry was quick to target these new consumers.

On the other hand, the millions of pensioners who had not been lucky enough to retire early because of private or occupational pension schemes, or had not benefited from the huge rises house prices, the ones dependent wholly on the state pension, were less fortunate. Many pensioners struggled to cope with 'fuel poverty' (defined as needing more than 10 per cent of their income to pay for energy costs, especially heating). It was clear that the effects of the greying of Britain would continue to have a big impact on British society far into the future.

The end of the countryside?

Another demographic shift, from the countryside into towns and cities, could be traced back well before 1945. It was in the 1990s, however, that its impact on society became an urgent public concern. In 1951, almost half the population had lived in rural or semi-rural areas; by about 2000 only about 3 per cent of the workforce was employed in agriculture. Intensive farming methods changed the landscape. Many small farmers went out of business. Many farmers also 'set aside' land to cut down food production in return for EU grants.

Country life was hollowed out. In thousands of villages, there was no school, no shop, no post office, perhaps even no pub. Younger people were forced to move out because they could not afford the house prices being paid by commuters and owners of second homes. Urbanisation swallowed up large slices of the countryside through housing estates, road building, and out-of-town shopping centres. Most of these trends had been happening for a long time but a number of factors came together to make them noticed.

In the 1990s, livestock farmers were badly hit by the outbreak of BSE in cattle and a ban on British beef exports. There was a fresh scare in 1996, when scientists proved the link between BSE in livestock and the terrifying human disease vCJD. In 2001, a massive outbreak of foot-and-mouth disease caused the mass slaughter of cattle. Much of Britain's countryside was virtually closed down. Rural communities faced severe economic hardship. These feelings contributed to a sort of countryside rebellion, over fuel costs and hunting. Farmers joined forces with road hauliers in a fuel blockade that briefly brought Britain to a standstill in 2002. When Labour MPs pushed through a ban on hunting, the ban stirred deep opposition from the Countryside Alliance.

Many people felt the Blair government was unsympathetic and urban-oriented, although there were efforts to help and promote country life. There were subsidies for diversification, for rural public transport and schemes to provide affordable housing for local people. There were attempts to get away from the stranglehold of the supermarkets through farmers' markets and organic farming. These measures made only a marginal difference. By 2007, Britain was a more urban country than ever.

Migration

Britain has always been a nation of immigrants. In all phases of the period from 1951 to 1990, waves of incomers had been changing communities. Between 1989 and 2007, however, immigration became a central social and political issue. Globalisation accelerated the movement of people. So did the consequences of famines and regional conflicts. The rapid expansion of the European Union opened the way for people from Central and Eastern Europe to move to Britain. The numbers of new arrivals increased rapidly, sometimes placing strain on local authorities and on community relations.

Inward migration included many immigrants in the traditional sense, people from New Commonwealth countries such as India, Pakistan and Bangladesh, often relatives of people already living here. But, in the 1990s, there was a sharp increase in the numbers of asylum-seekers, fleeing from violent upheavals in places like Somalia, Afghanistan and Iraq. Associated with asylum-seekers were economic migrants using the asylum system as a means of entry. The issue of so-called 'bogus' asylum-seekers aroused massive public controversy; and the sheer weight of numbers made it very difficult for the authorities to process so many claims.

Exploring the detail

The Countryside Alliance

In September 2000, a loose alliance of farmers and lorry drivers launched a fuel protest that blockaded oil refineries and temporarily interrupted fuel supplies. Soon afterwards, there were protests from the Country Landowners' Association against the ban on hunting. This led to the formation of the Countryside Alliance, part of a surge in extra-parliamentary protest against the Labour government. Labour was seen by many in the countryside as a 'townies party', lacking concern about issues such as transport costs, rural school closures, or the long traditions of foxhunting.

Other migrants were skilled workers and professionals, coming to fill skills shortages; the families of immigrants already living in Britain; foreign students at British universities; people from the new states who acceded to the EU in 2004 and 2007. There was also increased outward migration, as British people went abroad for employment opportunities or bought retirement homes in sunnier locations.

After 2004, many 'guest workers' entered Britain from the A8 countries (those who had just joined the EU), especially

Fig. 3 *A multicultural Britain, Whitechapel in East London*

from Poland. People in this last category were not, strictly speaking, immigrants at all, since they were moving within the EU and because many of them came intending to work for a period of time before returning home. But the popular press lumped all incomers together under the label 'immigrants'.

It was hard to separate myths from realities about migration. Newspapers like the *Daily Express* focused on problems, associating migrants with criminal behaviour and with taking jobs away from local people, or driving down wage levels by accepting low pay. The pressure group Migrationwatch headed by a retired diplomat, Sir Andrew Green, focused on the dangers of large numbers of immigrants arriving so quickly that public services such as health and education were overstretched and social cohesion might break down. Some of the adverse reaction was sensational and alarmist but there was also genuine concern.

Most economists argued that the nation benefited economically from migrants: they filled labour shortages, brought valuable skills, set up useful small businesses and were a net gain to the economy. They argued that most migrants were young, active and healthy, so they did not make heavy demands on social services. Migrant families tended to have more children at a younger age, with a beneficial impact on overall birth rates. It was also pointed out that migration did not flow only one way. Many migrants returned home; about one-third of migrants from Poland did so. Many British people were leaving to work abroad or to buy retirement homes in Spain. Such reassurances did not convince everybody.

One of the problems in analysing migration patterns is keeping track of numbers. For many categories of migrants, there were only rough estimates available. Working out accurate numbers of illegal workers or failed asylum seekers was very difficult. Another problem was predicting possible long-term trends. The flow of migrants fluctuated according to circumstances and economic conditions. One expert predicted in 2007 that Britain's population would increase to 71 million by 2050, but this prediction was based on economic trends that would almost certainly change over time.

Was Britain an integrated, multicultural society in 2007?

Issues of migration and demographic change were interwoven with the development of Britain as a multicultural society. Ethnic diversity had been a fact of life for a long time; by 2007, its effects were more noticeable. Mosques were a familiar feature of most towns and cities. Schools, local government and corporate organisations launched initiatives to celebrate the cultural background of people from ethnic minorities, many of whom had been born in Britain. Some people took pride in the progress made towards a genuinely multicultural society; others were critical at the failure to move faster. There were continued complaints that police forces were 'institutionally racist'. The BBC chairman, Greg Dyke, called his workforce 'hideously white'.

Such comments showed the concerns from one side of the debate about multiculturalism, that 'white Britain' was failing to do enough to ensure equality of respect and opportunities for ethnic minorities. From the other side came complaints that not enough emphasis was being placed on the responsibilities of immigrants to adapt to the British way of life, and that the identity of traditional working class communities was being unfairly neglected. Two explosive incidents seemed to show the urgency of these concerns. The first was the murder of a black teenager, Stephen Lawrence, in 1993; the second was the terrorist attack on London on 7 July 2005.

Did you know?

In 1993, a black student, Stephen Lawrence was murdered by a gang of racist white youths at a bus stop in east London. The identity of the youths was known but there was not sufficient evidence to convict them. The actions of the police were widely criticised. The murder became a national issue and a landmark in race relations. A high court judge, Lord MacPherson chaired a public enquiry; the MacPherson Report concluded that the Metropolitan Police was 'institutionally racist'.

■ A closer look

The terror attacks on London, 7 July 2005

Fig. 4 *Terror comes to Britain: Tavistock Square, London, 7 July 2005*

'7/7' was the day, nearly five years after '9/11' in the United Sates, that **jihadist** terror came to London. In four separate suicide bombings, on a bus in Tavistock Square and on three underground trains, 52 civilians were killed. In the confused response to the attacks, an innocent young Brazilian was mistaken for another suicide bomber and was controversially shot dead by armed police. The attacks caused much soul-searching about security issues and about community relations.

The most alarming fact about the attacks was that the bombers were not foreign imports but British-born citizens who had seemed to be assimilated into society. The leader of the group, Mohammed Siddique Khan, had been a well-respected community worker in West Yorkshire. It was suggested that it was urgently necessary to find out why men like Khan had become so alienated and how to improve community relations to make ethnic minorities feel more British. One common perception was that Britain's foreign policy, especially the war in Iraq, had dangerously alienated British Muslims.

Others argued that the essential need was for greater security through better border controls, identity cards and other restrictive measures. Others pointed to the defeat of IRA bomb attacks between the 1970s and the 1990s and emphasised the importance of carrying on normally without overreacting and cutting back civil liberties.

Which statement is closest to your view?	General	Muslims
Multiculuralism makes Britain a better place.	*62%*	*82%*
Multculturalism threatens Britain's way of life.	*32%*	*13%*
People who come to Britain should adopt the values and traditions of British culture.	*58%*	*29%*
Britain should deport foreigners who encourage terrorism.	*91%*	*74%*
I feel proud when British sports teams do well.	*90%*	*88%*

2

From a MORI opinion poll for the BBC, August 2005

Media and culture

Technological change has been occurring at ever-increasing speed throughout the twentieth century. Between 1990 and 2007, it appeared to be happening faster than ever, partly because it had such a direct and personal effect on individual people. This was the age of the information revolution, the age of the gadget.

This revolution had already begun by 1990. Portable radios, video recorders, personal computers and mobile telephones were already widely used. By the standards of 2007, however, these technologies might have come from the Dark Ages. Mobile phones were the size and weight of a brick. Nobody would have had a clue what the word 'laptop' meant. The computer games industry was in its infancy. Surfing was something people did on a beach. Tourists everywhere carried lots of film for their cameras. Many people even wrote letters to each other.

Less than two decades later, the chief forms of personal communication were by texting, emailing and mobile phone. CD sales were plummeting because it was so easy to download music to a PC or an MP3 player. The video recorder was already a relic of the past, overtaken by the DVD. Laptop computers became easily affordable. The internet became the way to buy tickets, book holidays or go shopping. The first stop for most people searching for information was Google or Wikipedia. GCSE and A level examiners were beginning to do their marking online. Politicians began to use texting for their polling and election campaigning. Television had entered the digital age, with a vast proliferation of channels available and the facility to watch programmes at any convenient time, not just when they were broadcast.

In 2007, it was difficult to realise how recent many of these changes were. Nor was there any sign of the pace of change slowing down. Not just in Britain but all over the world the impact of globalisation was transforming culture and leisure, just as it was transforming the world economy.

Summary question

Why did levels of migration into Britain increase between 1990 and 2007?

16

Britain, Europe and the world, 1990–2007

Fig. 1 *Victory in the Cold War: celebrating the end of the Berlin Wall, 10 November 1989*

In this chapter you will learn about:

- the factors influencing Britain's relations with Europe

- Britain's role in NATO and interventions in the Balkans, 1991–99

- the extent to which Britain was affected by the special relationship with the United States

- Britain's position in the world by 2007.

The true division in foreign policy today is between those who want the shop 'open' against those who want it 'closed'; between those who believe that the long-term interests of a country lie in its being out there, engaged and interactive, as opposed to those who think the short-term pain of such a policy is too great. In the era of globalisation, where nations depend on each other and our security is held in common or not at all, the outcome of the struggle between extremism and progress will be what determines our future here in Britain. We can no more opt out of this struggle than we can opt out of the climate changing around us. Inaction, pushing the responsibility onto America, deluding ourselves that the problem would go away, this too is a policy, and it's a policy that is profoundly, fundamentally wrong.

> **1** *From a lecture to the Foreign Policy Centre by Tony Blair in 2006, on the third anniversary of the invasion of Iraq*

Britain's place in the world was radically changed after 1990. Europe's centre of gravity was shifting eastwards as states in Eastern Europe broke free from Soviet domination and moved towards the EU. The end of the Cold War meant that NATO had to find a new role. Post-Soviet Russia was weak, both economically and politically. The dominance of the United States seemed to be unchallenged. Britain, its special relationship with the United States apparently stronger than ever, expected to play a role in the new order of democracy and freedom.

Between 1990 and 2007, British foreign policy had to forge new relationships. These relationships included those with the Irish Republic, the governments of the expanding European Union and the United Nations. One key aim of British policymakers, especially Tony Blair, was to use Britain's special relationship to build a diplomatic bridge between the Europeans and the Americans. The attempts to achieve this had only partial success and relations between Britain, the United States and Europe were placed under great strain by post-Cold War conflicts in the Balkans and in the Middle East.

Post-Cold War Britain

Britain and Europe, 1990–2007

When Margaret Thatcher was removed from power in 1990, the problem of Europe was causing deep divisions within the Conservative government. How her successor, John Major, would handle Britain's relationships with her European partners was a key issue, both in terms of party politics and of British foreign policy. This was especially important because European integration was moving towards major organisational changes, together with the plans for the accession of many new member states. In 1990, the European Economic Community had 12 member states. By 2007, now renamed the European Union, it had expanded to 27 states and was involved in negotiations with numerous new applicants for membership, including Turkey, Croatia, Serbia and the Ukraine.

This rapid enlargement forced many changes in the nature of the EU and its methods of reaching decisions. It also presented new and difficult challenges for British foreign policy. What had started out as 'The Six', an economic community dominated by the partnership between France and West Germany, was now becoming a much more political organisation in which the states of the 'New Europe' were bound to play a prominent role. British policymakers had to decide how much Britain would actually be 'at the heart of Europe', or whether to continue the ambivalent relationships that had been characteristic of Mrs Thatcher's Britain in the 1980s.

John Major's European colleagues regarded him as much less confrontational than Mrs Thatcher. It was widely believed that Britain's relationships with Europe would

Fig. 2 *The Good European? John Major with the German chancellor, Helmut Kohl, Maastricht, 1992*

Key chronology

Britain and the post-Cold War world, 1990–2007

- **1990** Reunification of Germany
- **1991** End of the USSR

  Coalition victory in the First Gulf War

  Outbreak of war in Yugoslavia
- **1994** End of apartheid in South Africa
- **1995** Srebrenica massacre

  Dayton agreement ends Second Balkan War
- **1999** NATO bombing campaign against Serbia
- **2000** British intervention in Sierra Leone
- **2001** 9/11 terror attacks

  NATO forces conquer Afghanistan
- **2003** Start of Iraq War
- **2005** G8 conference at Gleneagles
- **2007** Tony Blair appointed Middle East special envoy

rapidly improve. Major's first test was how to handle the treaty on European Union, eventually signed at Maastricht in February 1992, coming into force in November 1993. The negotiations leading up to the Maastricht treaty were tense and difficult. Major's style enabled him to establish good personal links with other heads of government, particularly with the German chancellor, Helmut Kohl, but Major was determined to prevent the treaty from becoming too 'federalist'. He also wanted to secure a number of 'opt-outs' for Britain.

> ■ **Key chronology**
>
> **The European Union, 1990–2007**
>
> 1992 Treaty on European Union, Maastricht, extending inter-government cooperation
> 1995 Expansion of EU from 12 states to 15: accession of Austria, Finland and Sweden
> 1997 Treaty of Amsterdam: amendment and consolidation of existing treaties
> 1999 Launch of the euro
> 2001 Treaty of Nice: reform of institutions to cope with expansion to 25 member states
> 2002 The euro confirmed as the sole legal currency in the 12 eurozone states
> 2004 Expansion of EU from 15 to 25 states: accession of Czech Republic, Cyprus, Estonia, Hungary, Latvia, Lithuania, Malta, Poland, Slovakia and Slovenia
>   Treaty establishing a constitution, Rome (this treaty was never ratified)
> 2007 Enlargement of the EU to 27 states: accession of Bulgaria and Romania
>   Treaty of Lisbon: to increase efficiency and democracy (replacing the 2004 constitution treaty)

■ **Cross-reference**

The impact of Europe, including the Maastricht Treaty, on the internal politics of the Conservative Party is covered in Chapter 13.

Maastricht was something of a personal triumph for John Major. Many in Europe had expected him to be a soft touch but he proved very effective both in winning allies and in driving hard bargains. His biographer, Anthony Seldon, claimed that Major achieved more than Mrs Thatcher would have been able to do, both in terms of the negotiations with Europe and in selling the deal to the Conservative Party at home. Later in 1992, however, Europe threw up difficult challenges to British foreign policy, especially the disintegration of Yugoslavia.

Although John Major maintained good personal relations with European leaders, he was handicapped by the anti-European attitudes within the Conservative Party. There was little or no prospect of Britain joining the single currency. It was difficult to see how Major could fulfil his promise of 1991 to *'place Britain at the very heart of Europe'*.

■ **Cross-reference**

To recap on Black Wednesday and Britain's withdrawal from the ERM, look back to pages 130–131.

Many people hoped that the election success of Tony Blair and New Labour in 1997 would transform Britain's role within the EU. Blair had already made many eloquent statements about the need for a 'new relationship' with Britain's European partners. His political style seemed to fit well with other new European leaders, like Gerhard Schroeder, the German chancellor, and with the aspirations of the 'New Europe'.

Throughout his ten years as prime minister, Blair played a prominent role in European affairs. He had a high personal standing and considerable powers of persuasion. Britain took a leading role in negotiations for EU enlargement and for the Treaty of Nice, extending the organisations of the EU. Blair was especially enthusiastic about strengthening the role of the EU in the wider world. Britain was at the centre of efforts to develop a common European strategy against the threat of global terrorism after the events of 11 September 2001. Blair tried his utmost to make Britain a bridge between Europe and the United States, above all in action against Iraq in 2002 and 2003, but also towards the peace process between Israel and the Palestinians and towards Iran.

Tony Blair took the lead in European initiatives on issues such as climate change, world trade and aid for Africa at meetings of the G7 countries (later the G8, involving Russia). The G8 summit at Gleneagles in 2005 was a personal triumph for Blair's diplomacy. Support from the German chancellor, Angela Merkel, ensured that the initiatives begun at Gleneagles were carried forward at the G8 summit at Heiligendamm in 2006. Overall, however, Britain's position in Europe remained ambivalent. Britain did not join the euro on its launch in 1999 and seemed as far away from joining as ever in 2007. The national press remained hostile to all things 'Europe'. Deep divisions between some European countries and Britain were opened up by the war in Iraq.

Fig. 3 *The world statesman: Tony Blair with UN Secretary-General Kofi Annan and the German chancellor, Angela Merkel, at the G8 summit, Heiligendamm, 2006*

By the time Blair left the scene in 2007, his personal prestige in Europe was still high and he had excellent relationships with the new French president, Nicolas Sarkozy, as well as with the German chancellor, Angela Merkel, and with the 'new Europe'. But there were few concrete achievements to match. Progress on climate change and 'making poverty history' was frustratingly slow. Attempts to reform the workings of the EU ended in the rejection of a proposed new constitution. A new, diluted scheme for reform was presented in the form of an amending treaty, finally signed at Lisbon at the end of 2007, but this aroused considerable controversy and there was no certainty that all 27 states would ratify the treaty.

A closer look

International diplomacy and the peace process in Northern Ireland

The question of Northern Ireland was the responsibility of the British government and the political parties at Westminster and in Northern Ireland itself. Even Sinn Fein and the IRA were legally British citizens, however fervently they wished not to be. Yet there was always an international dimension. By the early 1990s, it was recognised that cooperation between London and Dublin was vital to the peace process. This cooperation was greatly strengthened by the involvement of the United States, after the inauguration of President Clinton in 1993. The prosperity that Ireland experienced in the 1990s due to the benefits of EU membership also had an important effect; so did regular contacts between British and Irish officials at EU meetings.

Relations between London and Dublin had already moved closer in the 1980s. In the 1990s, the prospects for peace were improved by the breakthrough of democracy in Eastern Europe and in South Africa. A surprisingly close personal link between John Major and the Irish taoiseach, Albert Reynolds, improved inter-governmental cooperation. Major held very traditional Conservative views, instinctively supportive of the Ulster Unionists. The new taoiseach,

Exploring the detail

Reynolds and Major

The links between Reynolds and Major proved resilient in the face of many disagreements. At one tense private meeting from which all advisers were excluded, there was a real shouting match. Albert Reynolds was asked by one of his aides how the meeting had gone: *'He chewed the bollocks off me'*, said the Taoiseach, *'but I took a few lumps out of him'*. After Reynolds lost power in 1994, Major continued to work closely with his successor, John Bruton. Anglo-Irish diplomacy was crucial in preventing the fragile peace process from breaking down.

■ Cross-reference

The internal political history of the peace process in Northern Ireland is covered in Chapters 13 and 14.

■ Activity

Group activity

Use the evidence in this chapter and in Chapters 13 and 14. Working in small groups, make a list of the three most significant factors for the success of the peace process in Northern Ireland and place them in order of importance.

Albert Reynolds, was a committed nationalist. Yet these two very different personalities got to know and like each other from frequent contacts at European finance meetings. The Major–Reynolds partnership opened the way for cooperation between Tony Blair and Bertie Ahern from 1997.

As a result, Tony Blair inherited a great political opportunity when Labour came to power in 1997. A lot of the vital work in building confidence between the unionists and nationalists had been done. Blair also developed an excellent personal relationship with Bertie Ahern, Irish taoiseach from 1997 to 2008. This relationship remained strong throughout the tense negotiations leading up to the Good Friday Agreement of 1998 and the difficult problems of implementing it in the years that followed. One of Blair's advisers said later: *'You could never slide a cigarette paper between Blair and Ahern. They consulted on absolutely everything – and neither of them ever took his eye off the ball.'* The personal commitment shown by both leaders did much to advance the peace process. By the time Blair resigned from office in 2007, Anglo-Irish relations represented one of the most important and durable successes of British foreign policy.

■ Key chronology

Britain and the wars in the Balkans, 1991–99

1991
July Secession of Slovenia
September War between Serbs and Croats in Slavonia
1992
April Start of war in Bosnia
1995
July Massacre at Srebrenica
November Peace agreement at Dayton, Ohio
1998
November Ethnic cleansing of Albanians from Kosovo
1999
March–June NATO bombing campaign against Serbia
August Peace terms accepted by Milošević
2000
June Overthrow and capture of Milošević

Britain, NATO and the Balkans, 1991–99

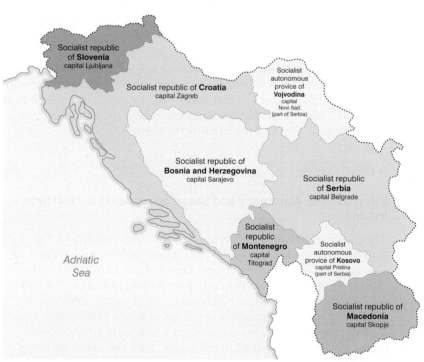

Fig. 4 *Yugoslavia before disintegration*

The end of the Cold War led to optimism that the expanding European Union would have a big part to play in world affairs, setting up new arrangements for collective security and in the peaceful resolution of disputes, such as the conflicts between Greeks and Turks over Cyprus, or the issues between Israel and the Palestinians. This optimism was shattered by the problems of the Balkans as Yugoslavia disintegrated.

The crisis in Yugoslavia was not a sudden one. From 1989, the Yugoslav president, Slobodan Milošević, was changing from Communist Party boss to extreme Serbian nationalist, threatening violent action against the

Albanian population in the province of Kosovo. In 1991, the prosperous northern republic of Slovenia declared independence and the Yugoslav state began to break up. Violent clashes between the two largest republics, Serbia and Croatia, culminated in war and atrocities, particularly in the town of Vukovar in November 1991.

Both the EU and the UN began urgent diplomatic efforts to maintain the peace but made little progress. The British former foreign minister, Lord Carrington, was appointed EU intermediary in September 1991, to supervise talks on new constitutional arrangements. The UN appointed an American diplomat, Cyrus Vance, to set up a United Nations Protection Force. The British foreign secretary, Douglas Hurd, was optimistic that international mediation would be effective and Britain could make a major contribution.

Cross-reference

Lord Carrington is profiled on page 117.

Key profile

Douglas Hurd

In 1991 Hurd (born 1930) became foreign secretary, a job for which he seemed perfectly suited, in John Major's government. He was an experienced Conservative politician from the pro-Europe wing of he party, loyal to Mrs Thatcher in many respects but very different in his approach to Britain's role in Europe. He was closely involved with European attempts to mediate in the Balkan conflicts between 1992 and 1995 but these efforts met with little success as Slobodan Milošević consistently went back on the agreements reached after lengthy negotiations.

The efforts of European diplomats failed. There was confusion of aims, between trying to maintain a multi-ethnic Yugoslavia, or allowing it to break up altogether. By 1992, Croatia had declared independence and it was already obvious that the multi-ethnic republic of Bosnia was in great danger of being attacked by both Serbia and Croatia. War began in Bosnia in April 1992. The Muslim population of eastern Bosnia was driven out by violent 'ethnic cleansing', carried out by Bosnian Serb paramilitaries backed by Milošević's government.

In August 1992, John Major hosted a joint EU and UN conference in London and a UN peacekeeping force was put in place. In October 1992, the Vance–Owen plan, by Cyrus Vance and the former British foreign secretary, David Owen, set out a framework for a lasting settlement. At the time, Major was widely praised for his actions but there was no concerted European pressure. The United States was reluctant to intervene in Europe. Serb aggression continued. The war in Bosnia carried on for three more years, with Sarajevo under constant siege. British and European mediation was seen as ineffectual, especially after the massacre of Srebrenica in July 1995.

Fig. 5 *The price of the failure of diplomacy in the Balkans: UN forces removing dead bodies after ethnic violence, Vitez in Bosnia, 1993*

A closer look

The massacre at Srebrenica

In 1995, Bosnian Serb forces under the command of General Ratko Mladić were advancing through central Bosnia and seemed likely to overrun the town of Srebrenica, populated mostly by Bosniaks. The

UN had declared Srebrenica to be a 'safe haven' and many Bosnian refugees had moved there. A small force of Dutch UN peacekeepers was stationed at Srebrenica but had orders not to get involved in any fighting. The Serb forces entered Srebrinica and began arresting all males and marching them out into the nearby countryside. Shootings began. The Dutch peacekeepers urgently asked for instructions by radio but were ordered not to intervene. More than 7,000 Bosnian men and boys were massacred in one of the worst atrocities to occur in Europe since the end of the Second World War.

Srebrenica was not just an atrocity. There were many atrocities in the Balkan wars, committed by all sides. But Srebrenica had particularly important consequences. Ratko Mladić, together with his political boss, Radovan Karadžić, was later indicted as a war criminal. After the Balkan wars ended in 1999, the fact that the two men escaped arrest and were protected by Serbia became a barrier to Serbia's entry into the EU. Guilt about allowing the Srebrenica massacre to take place caused recriminations in the Netherlands and much soul-searching about the failure of UN peacekeeping missions. But the most significant impact was on British, European and American foreign policy.

Events in the Balkans, 1995–99

After the horrors of the siege of Sarajevo and the Srebrenica massacre, reliance on EU diplomacy and UN peacekeeping was perceived to have failed badly. British foreign policy turned to the United States and NATO. President Clinton was persuaded to intervene; the central command and the military power of NATO was essential to force the warring Balkan political leaders to negotiate. American air strikes on Serb forces led to a peace conference at Dayton, Ohio. A peace treaty was signed in Paris in December 1995. This guaranteed Bosnian independence, protected by a UN force and with substantial economic support from the international community.

From 1997, Tony Blair continued John Major's policy of involving NATO and the United States. When the final phase of the Balkan wars began as a result of Serbian attacks on Kosovo, Blair devoted his main diplomatic efforts to persuading a reluctant President Clinton to back military action against Serbia. In 1999, a prolonged NATO bombing campaign against Serbia forced Milošević into pulling his forces out of Kosovo. Not long afterwards, Milošević was overthrown and sent to The Hague to be tried as a war criminal. The collapse of Yugoslavia was now complete and the way was open for new states such as Slovenia and Croatia to join the EU.

For Tony Blair, the military intervention of 1999 was a big success. It strengthened his belief in 'liberal interventionism'. It convinced him of the vital importance of Britain's special relationship with the United States and of Britain's key role in bringing closer together American and European policy. The success in the Balkans in 1999 moulded Blair's thinking and did much to shape his later policies, above all on Iraq.

The impact of the special relationship on Britain's position in the world

Blair and the special relationship

For Tony Blair, the lessons of the interventions by the West in the former Yugoslavia were clear. Reliance on the United Nations and Europe to resolve conflicts in the Balkans had clearly failed. Blair was utterly convinced he had been right in persuading a reluctant Bill Clinton to back military intervention against Milošević, and that it was essential

■ **Exploring the detail**

NATO

The North Atlantic Treaty Organisation (NATO) was formed in 1949 to defend the Western Alliance in the Cold War. When the Cold War ended between 1989 and 1991, NATO needed to find a new role. Involving NATO in peacekeeping in the Balkans was far more effective than the using the United Nations, because the UN depended on member states to provide troops, whereas NATO had a unified central command under American leadership.

■ **Activity**

Creative thinking

Prepare a brief report to the British foreign secretary in 2000 from a policy adviser. You can either emphasise the need for an interventionist approach or emphasise the dangers involved in such interventions.

Fig. 6 *Another very special relationship: Tony Blair and George W. Bush, 2006*

to keep the United States involved in European affairs and to make full use of NATO to defend the new world order. Blair firmly believed in liberal interventionism to prevent the recurrence of massacres and ethnic cleansing. From 1999, Blair's ideas could be summed up as: 'No more Srebrenicas'.

The 'war on terror'

The terror attacks carried out by al-Qaeda against the United States on 11 September 2001 led to the so-called 'war on terror', a struggle that widened divisions between the Muslim world and the West, and within the West itself. By 2001, Tony Blair had already established a good working relationship with George W. Bush; they were in complete agreement about the threat from international terrorism. At the time, most European governments agreed with them. It was only later that differences began to show.

Fig. 7 *The Middle East*

Before 9/11, the United States had felt invulnerable from outside attack. The collapse of the Twin Towers and the simultaneous attack on Washington came as a shock. The American response was the invasion of Afghanistan, then ruled by the Taliban and providing a base of operations for Al Qaeda. A United States-led coalition invaded Afghanistan and expelled the Taliban. This seemed to show the benefits of liberal interventionism. The Taliban was deservedly hated and many rejoiced at its downfall. It was hoped that the new Afghanistan might quickly develop into a modern democratic state; but there was no instant pacification of the country. Despite strenuous efforts to capture them, Osama bin Laden and the Taliban leader, Mohammed Omar, escaped. A new democratic regime, led by Hamid Karzai, was established at Kabul but progress towards economic and political development was slow.

■ **Exploring the detail**

Al-Qaeda and global terrorism

Al-Qaeda first attacked the World Trade Center in New York in 1993 and also carried out bomb attacks on US embassies in Africa in 1996. By 2001, al-Qaeda had a base of operations in Afghanistan, where there were training camps for jihadists to plan actions against the West. Al-Qaeda was a loose conglomeration of fighting cells with no clear chain of command. Osama bin Laden's role was to provide charismatic leadership and vast sums of money. After the invasion of Iraq in 2003, a new organisation, al-Qaeda in Iraq, became prominent in the insurgency against the US-led coalition forces.

■ **Cross-reference**

The term 'jihadist' is explained on page 160.

■ **Key chronology**

Britain, the United States and wars in Afghanistan and Iraq

2001	
October	Invasion of Afghanistan and overthrow of the Taliban
December	Formation of democratic Afghan government
2002	
July	UN resolution directed against WMD in Iraq
October	Failure to agree second UN resolution
2003	
March	Invasion of Iraq by American-led coalition
April	Overthrow of Saddam Hussein
2005	
August	Renewed threat from Taliban in Afghanistan
2007	
January	US Army 'surge' against insurgents in Iraq
December	British withdrawal from Iraq announced by Gordon Brown

It is difficult to know whether or not the reconstruction of Afghanistan would have succeeded if it had remained the main focus of Western attention. As it was, that attention was drawn towards Iraq, first the huge diplomatic effort during 2002 and then the invasion of Iraq and the overthrow of Saddam Hussein in 2003. For years, Iraq took centre stage and Afghanistan was neglected. In that time, the Afghan government struggled to cope with the complex political situation in Kabul; and the Taliban regrouped. In 2006 and 2007, the security situation deteriorated badly. It became necessary to send large contingents of troops to shore up Karzai's regime.

■ **Key profile**

Saddam Hussein

Saddam (1937–2006) was a member of the Ba'ath Party, based on revolutionary socialism and pan-Arab nationalism, which seized power in Iraq in 1968. From 1979, Saddam ruled as a dictator. His regime crushed opposition within Iraq and built up a large army. Saddam repeatedly clashed with the West. He nationalised the western-owned Iraq Petroleum Company, fought a long war against Iran in the 1980s and invaded Kuwait in 1990, provoking the First Gulf War. He was overthrown in April 2003 during the Second Gulf War. He was executed by the new government of Iraq in 2006.

The invasion of Afghanistan also led to the detention of numerous foreign fighters and to the introduction of special measures to deal with these 'enemy combatants'. It was considered impossible to try them by normal judicial process and yet impossible to set free men who were dangerous terrorists. A special holding facility, Camp Delta, was set up near the American base at Guantanamo Bay on the island of Cuba. Men were intensively interrogated by methods that many lawyers considered to be torture. Several were transported to countries like Egypt and Morocco by secret flights known as 'extraordinary renditions' and subjected to 'special interrogations'.

As news about these procedures leaked out over the next few years, criticism intensified. George W. Bush and his closest ally, Tony Blair, became massively unpopular at home and abroad. The ideals of liberal interventionism were discredited. From 2003, the invasion of Iraq caused bitter divisions among

Western nations and intense criticism of Tony Blair because of his links to President Bush. By 2007, 'Blair's war' in Iraq would become the defining issue of his political career; and of Britain's position in the world.

The Iraq War

The First Gulf War of 1990–91 had defeated Saddam Hussein but not removed him from power. Through the 1990s, Saddam had been 'contained' by economic sanctions and by 'no-fly zones' enforced by NATO air patrols. From the time he came to power, George W. Bush and his **neo-conservative** advisers were keen to deal with the 'unfinished business' of Iraq. They considered that 'containing' Saddam had failed and more drastic action was essential. Iraqi exiles encouraged the belief that there would be an enthusiastic welcome from the people if Saddam were to be overthrown.

Information from Iraqi exiles also encouraged fears of the threat Saddam might represent to the West. The first fear was that Iraq might link up with al-Qaeda and provide a new base for terrorism, like Afghanistan before 2001. The second was that Iraq might develop atomic or biological weapons, universally labelled 'WMD' (weapons of mass destruction). This second fear was genuine, even though later events proved it did not really exist. Saddam had expelled UN weapons inspection teams in 1997 and seemed to be hiding something.

Tony Blair was convinced that the threat of Iraq's WMD was real. He was desperate to ensure that no breach opened up between Europe and the United States. British policy was designed to prevent this by using diplomacy at the United Nations. Blair's critics claimed that he knew Bush was going to invade Iraq anyway, that he agreed with Bush's aim of regime change and was simply using UN resolutions as a way of bringing Europe round. It was argued that Blair's efforts to be a bridge between Europe and the Americans was fatally flawed because he was so closely identified with Bush that he had no power to influence American policy at all.

Blair's defenders argue that he was genuinely convinced about the dangers of WMD and that he was correct in his analysis of the need for the United States to be part of the international world order and not retreat to unilateral action or isolationism. For Blair, those who said: 'Leave it to the UN' or 'The Europeans are right' had forgotten the disasters like Srebrenica in the 1990s.

Blair made strenuous efforts to win over his European allies by pushing for a second UN resolution. Bush and the Neo-Conservative 'hawks' in Washington allowed these efforts to continue but were set on invading Iraq anyway. The invasion of Iraq was launched by American forces backed by a 'coalition of the willing' including Britain, Poland and Italy among others. Military victory and the overthrow of Saddam Hussein came quickly but there was no neat or decisive end to the war. The occupying forces found themselves bogged down in a long struggle against insurgents, a struggle that soaked up thousands of troops and billions of dollars.

There was intense opposition from many in Europe and in the United States who regarded it as an illegal, unnecessary war. There were no signs of atomic or biological weapons programmes. Establishing a new democratic government was an immensely difficult process as the war brought all the internal divisions of Iraq into the open. Violence became endemic, with suicide bombings and horrific reprisals by local militias; the violence undermined plans for economic reconstruction.

For a time, the British forces in Basra and southern Iraq seemed to be successful but the situation steadily deteriorated as Shia militias became more powerful. Eventually, it became too dangerous for British troops to go out on regular patrols. In 2006 and 2007, there were improvements in

Fig. 8 *Military victory? Iraq, 2003*

the security situation and in the training of Iraqi troops. Several provinces were handed over to Iraqi forces and the government in Baghdad, headed by Nouri al-Maliki, became more stable but few of the expectations when the war was launched in 2003 had been proved right. Even the small improvements in Iraq had to be weighed against the need to send more troops to Afghanistan rather than bring them home.

When Tony Blair left Downing Street in 2007, it was still too early to make a definitive judgement on the degree to which the Iraq War had been a failure. The war had damaged Blair's reputation, and that of Britain, very badly. On the other hand, a democratic government existed in Iraq instead of Saddam Hussein's terrible dictatorship and it could still be hoped that this government might have a stable and successful future in the long term. In judging the success or otherwise of British foreign policy to 2007, it was clear that much would depend on the future of Iraq and on the outcome of the continuing war in Afghanistan.

Britain's position in the world by 2007

By the end of 2007, Britain had achieved only very limited and partial success in Iraq, well short of the ambitious goals set out in 2003. In any case, troop reductions in Iraq were countered by the need to reinforce the British war effort in Afghanistan; there was no 'bringing the boys home'. It was still possible to hope that future developments would eventually lead to a new, secure Iraqi state, but it seemed there was little to justify the immense cost in lives, expense and diplomatic effort, not to mention Tony Blair's reputation.

Disappointed hopes and expectations did not only apply to the outcome of the wars in Afghanistan and Iraq. Britain had given strong support to efforts to mediate peace between the Palestinians and the state of Israel. The general outline of a two-state peace settlement was clearly established from 1993 and President Clinton twice seemed close to bringing the two sides together, in 1993 and again in 2000, but deadlock remained.

Under the Bush administration, the peace process seemed to be going nowhere. Israel blamed the Palestinians, especially the radical Hamas movement, for preferring terrorism to peace. The Palestinians blamed Israel for being intransigent and for continuing to build illegal settlements on Palestinian territory, against international agreements. Many on all sides blamed the United States for failing to give the peace process a high priority and for seeming to give unconditional support to Israel, a key ally in the war on terror.

The years since 9/11 revealed an old historical truth: problems are not usually solved – they are just overtaken by other problems. By contrast with the 1990s, when it was hoped to replace the Cold War with a 'new world order', the prospects of achieving it no longer look so good. Liberty is no longer on the forward march. The French refer to their 30 years of economic growth after the Second World War as the *trentes glorieuses*, the Thirty Glorious Years. Future historians may look back at the three decades from Portugal's Carnation revolution in 1974 to Ukraine's Orange revolution of 2004 as the Thirty Glorious Years for the spread of liberty, not only in Europe, but across the world.

2   *From Garton Ash, T., 'We friends of liberal international order face a new global disorder', in the **Guardian**, 11 September 2008*

Tony Blair made notable efforts to mediate in the Middle East, both through direct diplomacy and working with the EU, especially in providing economic assistance to the Palestinian territories. He had a genuine commitment to the peace process but the Iraq War and his close relationship with George W. Bush made it difficult for Blair to be seen as even-handed. In 1997, the 'Quartet' (UN, EU, US and Russia) gave Blair the role of special envoy to the Middle East. In normal circumstances, his charm and communication skills would have made him an ideal conciliator, as he had been over Northern Ireland in 1998, but that was before Iraq.

Learning outcomes

In this section, you have looked at the ways in which Britain and its position in the world changed between 1990 and 2007. In 1990, Britain was coming to terms with the fall of Mrs Thatcher. Free market economics held sway; socialism was in retreat, both in Britain and in the world. You have seen how, by 2007, Britain had experienced life under a Labour government for ten years; and how many of the assumptions prevalent in 1990 had been proved wrong. You have seen how, by 2007, British society had changed and how Britain responded to the complicated post-Cold War world.

> ### Activity
> **Class debate**
>
> Working in groups, prepare the sub-headings for a brief speech supporting or opposing the view, 'Tony Blair's foreign policies gravely weakened Britain's position in the world'. When you have delivered your speeches in class, take a vote to ascertain the majority view.

Practice questions

(a) 'The mismanagement of Britain's foreign policies in the years 1990 to 2007 did lasting harm to Britain's position in the world'. Assess the validity of this view.   *(45 marks)*

> **Study tip**
> To answer this question, it is necessary to take an overview of British foreign policy from 1990 to 2007, covering the premierships of both John Major and Tony Blair. A relevant overall argument might involve completely agreeing with the key quotation; or rejecting it out of hand; or a more differentiated response that includes elements of both success and failure, or offers different assessments of Major and Blair. Answers cannot be comprehensive; it is essential to be concise and selective. On the other hand, the whole timescale needs to be addressed. It would not be enough here, for example, to focus in depth on Tony Blair and Iraq.

(b) 'Between 1964 and 2007, the Conservative Party ceased to be the natural party of government in Britain'. Assess the validity of this view.   *(45 marks)*

> **Study tip**
> Answers to synoptic essay questions covering most or all of the period studied need to have breadth but should also be concise and selective. A differentiated assessment of a few selected factors is better than an attempt to be comprehensive. You might start by considering exactly *what* the term 'natural party of government' actually means, in terms of its political significance. Then you might look at Conservative successes and failures between 1964 and 2007, always with a view to making an overall assessment of the extent to which the Conservative Party suffered a long-term decline (as the key quotation clearly implies) rather than just describing all the policies. A successful answer might include some differentiation; after all, the Conservatives were continuously in power for 18 years from 1979. Another form of differentiation could be deciding which factors mattered most, and which factors were also important but less than decisive.

Fig. 1 *The rebirth of the Conservatives? David Cameron winning support, 2007*

■ Britain in 2007

When trying to evaluate what happened to Britain between 1951 and 2007, it is a good idea to ask the questions all good historians ask about broad periods in history:

- ■ What was the situation in the beginning?
- ■ What was the situation at the end?
- ■ In between, what changed?
- ■ What stayed the same?

It is always important to balance change against continuity. Change, and the causes of change, often seem more obvious and easier to explain. But change is often a slower and more uneven process than it might appear.

Politics

During the years after 1951, there were several predictions that the two-party system would give way to a 'fundamental realignment of British politics'; and on more than one occasion it seemed that such predictions were on the edge of becoming reality. In the 1980s, the Labour Party came close to disintegration as the SDP and the Liberals ate into its traditional voting support. In the late 1990s, the Conservative Party seemed to be in danger of dying off as support grew for alternatives like the Referendum Party, UKIP and the BNP. The rise of support for nationalist parties in Wales, Scotland and Northern Ireland also undermined the foundations of Labour and the Conservatives; so did the rise of pressure groups and extra-parliamentary movements.

Seen from 2007, however, the sum total of all these changes appeared less than revolutionary. The two-party system showed remarkable tenacity. The Labour Party made a miraculous recovery from the depths of despair and disintegration in the early 1980s; twenty years later, the Conservatives survived a similar near-death experience and once more resembled a party of government. The Liberal revival produced a post-war high of 61 seats in the 2005 election but subsequently fell back in the opinion polls. The SNP had gained power in the Scottish Executive but outright independence for Scotland still seemed far away.

Outwardly, the nature of politics had changed enormously. It was no longer a part-time occupation, as in the 1950s. By 2007, most MPs had never had any career outside politics. The 24-hour news culture meant that it was necessary to respond every day and immediately, to events and issues as they happened. There was no time to mull things over before something hit the Sunday papers a few days ahead. Tony Blair's press secretary, Alastair Campbell, noted that from 1997 there was a daily government response to news stories; by the time Blair left office there was one in the morning, one at lunchtime and one in the evening.

At various times since 1951 it appeared that politics was reflecting social change in Britain. Harold Wilson and Edward Heath had been the first prime ministers educated at state secondary schools. Mrs Thatcher had changed the Conservative Party away from its old 'knights of the shires' image; Tony Blair had moved the Labour Party in the opposite direction, away from its old working class roots. By 2007, the Blair-Cameron style, all open-necked shirts and an informal, conversational way of talking, reflected their desire to be seen as classless and in tune with society. It might be said, however, that Anthony Charles Lynton Blair (Fettes College and Oxford) and the two most prominent Conservatives of 2007, David William Donald Cameron and Alexander Boris de Pfeffel Johnson (both Eton and Oxford, where they were members of the notorious Bullingdon drinking club) did not look much like the products of a social revolution.

The monarchy was another symbol of continuity and the strength of tradition. Queen Elizabeth II had reigned since 1952. In that time there had been royal scandals and an immense furore over the death of Princess Diana in 1997. None of this had done lasting damage to the monarchy; the Golden Jubilee in 2002 showed that respect for the Queen was as high as ever. Efforts to reform the House of Lords had amounted to not much more than tinkering; there were still 92 hereditary peers. The state opening of parliament and other ceremonials like trooping the colour looked just the same as they had done for generations before.

What happened between 1951 and the resignation of Tony Blair is already history; the Blair Era has ended. It is too early, however, to make any definitive judgements of Blair's 'place in history'; how Blair's legacy will be judged in the wisdom of hindsight, at some time still in the future. Much will depend on the successes or failures of the Labour government under his successor; but at the time of writing, in 2008, the fate of Gordon Brown is not yet history It can safely be left in the hands of journalists and other crystal-ball gazers.

Economy and society

There was vast economic change between 1951 and 2007. Whole areas of Britain were transformed by deindustrialisation. The central belt of Scotland no longer had the collieries, steel plants and car factories that had dominated the skyline until the 1980s. The great seaports were no longer labour-intensive hives of activity but marvels of mechanisation as computer-operated machinery sorted thousands of containers. Shopping had been taken over by new forms of retailing, such as supermarkets, out-of-town shopping centres and the internet. For most people, living standards were vastly higher than in 1961. Expectations were much higher, with most people treating as necessities things that would have been regarded as luxuries by their grandparents. The definitions of what constituted poverty had changed, too.

Even so, there was much continuity. Despite the hopes of governments, the pace of economic modernisation was almost always slow and uneven. The same old economic problems, under-investment, low productivity, worries about skills shortages, inflation and the balance of payments, seemed always to persist. The golden age after the war ended with the crisis and upheavals of the 1970s and 1980s; the sustained affluence from the early 1990s to 2007 tempted Gordon Brown to claim that his chancellorship had 'abolished boom and bust', but that was before Northern Rock hit the headlines in the summer of 2007, followed by the 'great crash' of 2008. The British economy was very different by 2008, with less emphasis on industry and huge emphasis on financial services, but it had not managed to escape from the past.

It is often claimed that Britain experienced a social revolution in this period. It is certainly true that there have been periods of accelerated social change as a result of the Second World War; in the 'sex-drugs-and-rock'n'roll' of the Sixties; in the 'Thatcher revolution'; and in the rise of the multicultural society since 1990. By 2008 large parts of Britain looked remarkably different from 1951. There is a cleaner environment, more urban development, more diversity in culture and ethnic background. As always, these changes need to be weighed against underlying continuities. Towns like Appleby in Cumbria, or Moffat in the Scottish borders, or cathedral cities like Ely and Lincoln, or villages in rural Gloucestershire, still looked much the same as they did fifty years before.

Even at the metropolitan centre, Britain was less changed than might have been expected in 1951. The BBC was still a national institution, funded by the licence fee. Large parts of the 'Establishment' were still intact. Oxford and Cambridge were still *the* elite universities, opening doors to the top. Independent schools, thought to be under threat in 1951 still provided 50 per cent of the Oxbridge intake. Even *Private Eye,* once the scourge of the Establishment had become part of the furniture. In his appearances on *Have I Got News For You,* the editor of *Private Eye,* Ian Hislop, seemed to be more a part of the Establishment himself than a fiery revolutionary.

Britain's position in the world

In 1951, Britain was still an empire, though the long process of decolonisation had already begun. Britain had an ambivalent relationship with Europe, encouraging integration from the sidelines but not willing to be fully engaged in it. Britain's foreign policy was dominated by the special relationship with the United States and by the pressures of the Cold War. By 2007, the international context was much changed. The long retreat from empire was finally over, symbolised by the sight of the royal yacht *Britannia* sailing out of Hong Kong harbour in 1997. The Cold War was over, too, symbolised by the cheering crowds celebrating on top of the Berlin Wall in 1989. Britain had been a member of the European Union since 1973.

All these changes were significant and real; but they did not represent complete transformation. The Empire was gone but the attitudes of empire still persisted. The Queen was still head of the Commonwealth. Britain was seen as having a special role in dealing with the problems of Africa, not least the collapse of Zimbabwe. Tony Blair's policy of 'liberal interventionism' seemed to show that the days of 'gunboat diplomacy' were not quite dead. Even sports commentators bemoaning the latest failures of England's football, rugby or cricket team, seemed incapable of forgetting that these games had been invented by Britain in an age when the Empire ruled the world.

Most of all perhaps, continuity showed through the special relationship with the United States. Maintaining this relationship had been a constant preoccupation of almost all governments (except perhaps Edward Heath's) since 1951. Alongside this was the British independent nuclear deterrent and Britain's place at the 'top table'. Nobody was more strongly committed to the special relationship than Tony Blair, right to the end of his premiership. Despite Iraq and the unpopularity of George W. Bush, nobody expected Gordon Brown's approach to the next American president to be much different from that of his predecessors.

So, as usual, assessing the development of post-war Britain – in politics, economy and society and foreign affairs – is open to many interpretations. For some, such as the right-wing columnist Peter Hitchens, the years from 1951 to 2007 were years of wrong turnings, of economic decline and the loss of 'the British way of life'. Others, such as the ever-optimistic Andrew Marr, see it very differently:

> In the course of this history, most political leaders have arrived eager and optimistic, found themselves in trouble of one kind or another, and left disappointed. Such indeed is the nature of life. But the rest of us need those optimistic politicians, the ones we'll laugh at and throw abuse at; and we need them more than ever. The threats facing the British are large ones. But in the years since 1945, having avoided nuclear devastation, tyranny and economic collapse, we British have no reason to despair, or to emigrate. In global terms, to be born British remains a wonderful stroke of luck.

1   *From Marr, A., A History of Modern Britain, 2007*

Glossary

A

Age of Affluence: the period of consumer prosperity and rising living standards from about 1950 to 1973, sometimes known as 'the long post-war boom'.

apartheid: term used in the Republic of South Africa before 1994 to define the policy of 'racial separation'.

B

balance of payments: the relationship between government expenditure and income, particularly in terms of exports and imports.

Big Bang: the deregulation of the London Stock Exchange on 27 October 1986.

BSE: Bovine spongiform encephalitis, an incurable disease in cattle that destroys the nervous system. An outbreak of BSE in the 1990s caused major disruption to British agriculture.

Butskellism: term invented by economists to describe 'consensus' centrist policies merging the ideas of Conservative moderates, symbolised by R. A. Butler, and Labour moderates, symbolised by Hugh Gaitskell.

C

clause four: the clause in the Labour Party constitution committing the party to nationalisation, i.e. state ownership of the 'commanding heights of the economy'

collectivist policies: policies based on the idea of government intervention in society and the economy.

competitiveness: term used by economists to measure the degree of economic efficiency in free competition with other economies.

D

decolonisation: the process by which colonial powers gave up control and granted national independence to former colonies.

deflationary pressures: usually caused by government policies to fight against the dangers of inflation, 'deflating' the economy by cutting spending and borrowing.

demographic change: changes in population, including birth and death rates, generational change and patterns of population movement.

deregulation: removing government controls and allowing greater competition. In the 1980s, there was deregulation of the financial markets; there was also deregulation in other areas, such as public transport.

détente: term used to define attempts to limit the dangers of the Cold War by reducing tensions and improving relations between the Soviet Bloc and the West.

devaluation: action to reduce the value of the pound sterling in relation to other currencies, such as the US dollar.

devolution: allowing a degree of self-government to Scotland, Northern Ireland and Wales. Devolution has also been proposed for regions within England.

E

EEC: European Economic Community, or Common Market, formed by the Treaty of Rome in 1957 created by 'The Six' – France, West Germany, Italy, Belgium, Netherlands and Luxembourg. The EEC became the EU in 1992.

EFTA: European Free Trade Area, formed in 1959. Member states were: Britain, Denmark, Norway, Sweden, Austria, Portugal and Switzerland.

EU: European Union, the name of the EEC after the Treaty of Maastricht in 1992.

Eurosceptic: people in Britain opposed to any steps towards further European integration or who demanded renegotiation of the terms of Britain's membership.

F

Falklands factor: the effect of victory in the 1982 Falklands War in boosting the popularity of the government.

first-past-the-post system: an electoral system in which seats are won by a simple majority, not by proportional representation.

flying pickets: mass pickets taken by bus to the scene of industrial disputes in order to add pressure on workers to join strikes.

G

Gross Domestic Product (GDP): a term for the measurement of the national wealth, by adding together the value of all economic production. The term Gross National Product is also used.

H

hard left: term used in the 1970s and 1980s to define extreme socialist movements within the Labour Party, such as the Militant Tendency.

I

infrastructure: term used to define the framework of a modern industrial economy, such as – roads, railways, telecommunications, power stations and public utilities.

L

long post-war boom: the period of prosperity and rising living standards in Britain and Europe after the Second World War, from about 1950 to 1973.

M

mass picketing: large groups of picketers (strikers who stand outside workplaces and try to persuade other workers to join the strike) organised to intimidate workers and to try to force workplaces to shut down by preventing access.

monetarism: monetarist ideas were particularly associated with the 'Chicago School' of economists, led by Milton Friedman. Monetarism proposed strict controls over the supply of money in order to combat inflation.

N

National Service: compulsory military service by young males for two years from the age of 18. National service was introduced in 1947 and abandoned in 1960.

NATO: the North Atlantic Treaty Organisation, a military alliance formed in 1949 under American leadership to defend the West against the threat of Soviet communism.

negative equity: term used when house prices fall and a homeowner is paying more for a mortgage than could be obtained by selling the property. This was a particular problem in the economic recession in Britain in the early 1990s.

New Commonwealth: countries, such as India, Pakistan, the West Indies and Bangladesh, were the (mostly non-white) countries who gained independence from Britain after 1945, as opposed to the 'old' white dominions, such as Australia, Canada and New Zealand.

Night of the Long Knives: name for Harold Macmillan's ruthless cabinet reshuffle in 1962 in which one-third of the cabinet was sacked.

O

OMOV: One Member One Vote: the change to the Labour Party constitution in 1993, giving the vote on party matters individual members of the party. This measure reduced the power of the trade unions because it ended the former system of block voting.

One Nation Tories: name first used in the 19th century by Conservatives wanting to promote centrist policies to appeal to broad sections of society, not just traditional supporters of Conservatism. The One Nation Group of Conservative MPs was formed in 1950.

P

post-war consensus: the idea that the main political parties in Britain were agreed about the key aims for British society after 1951, such as ensuring full employment, maintaining the welfare state and accepting government intervention in the economy.

prices and incomes policy: government policy to combat inflation by restricting wage rises and price increases through voluntary agreements between workers and employers.

privatisation: the policy of denationalisation, removing economic enterprises from state control and placing them under private ownership and management.

productivity: the measurement of production in relation to wage costs. High productivity leads to greater competitiveness; low productivity equates to inefficiency.

R

Referendum Party: a political party funded by James Goldsmith to fight the 1997 election on the specific issue of a referendum to decide whether Britain should leave the EU.

Right to Buy: the right of council tenants to buy the home they have been renting at a discounted price, introduced by the 1980 Housing Act.

run on the pound: A sudden fall in the value of the pound sterling on the international exchange markets.

S

stagflation: term invented by economists to describe periods when economic stagnation and rising inflation occur at the same time.

stop-go: name invented by economists to define the cycle of periods of growth and inflation, followed by periods of deflation and economic slowdown.

T

Third Way: a New Labour term for centrist policies that would avoid the right-wing and left-wing extremes and forge a new social and political consensus.

U

UKIP: United Kingdom Independence Party, supported mostly by former Conservatives who wished for Britain to immediately withdraw from the EU.

unilateralism: The idea of unilateral nuclear disarmament, abandoning Britain's nuclear weapons without waiting for international agreements.

W

weapons of mass destruction (WMD): the weapons that Saddam Hussein was believed to have developed in the 1990s, including biological, chemical and nuclear weapons.

welfare state: the name given to British society after 1945 when the National Health Service and schemes for social insurance were introduced, guaranteeing all citizens a 'safety net'.

wets: the nickname for moderate Conservatives who did not fully support the radical social and economic policies of Mrs Thatcher in the 1980s.

wildcat strike: a sudden, unofficial strike called out at local level, without reference to national trade union leaders.

working majority: the situation of a government when it has many more seats in parliament than all other parties combined and can pass legislation without needing to compromise.

Y

year of miracles: the events of 1989, when the Cold War ended and the states of East Central Europe suddenly and unexpectedly achieved freedom from Communist rule.

Bibliography

Britain, 1951–2007

Students

Black, J. (2000) *Modern British History Since 1900*, Longman

Cook, C. & Stevenson J. (1996) *Britain Since 1945*, Longman

Murphy, D. (ed.) (2000) *Britain 1914–2000*, Collins

Petheram, L. (2001) *Britain in the 20th Century*, Nelson Thornes

Teachers and extension

Childs, D. (1997) *Britain Since 1945*, Routledge

Clarke, P. (1996) *Hope and Glory: Britain 1900–1990*, Penguin

Davies, A. (1998) *British Politics and Europe*, Hodder & Stoughton

Fraser, T. G. (2000) *Ireland In Conflict 1922–1998*, Routledge

Hennessy, P. (2000) *The Prime Minister: The Office and its Holders Since 1945*, Penguin

Jefferys, K. (2000) *Finest and Darkest Hours*, Atlantic

Johnson, P. (ed.) (1994) *20th Century Britain: Economic, Social and Cultural Change*, Longman

Marr, A. (2007) *A History of Modern Britain*, Macmillan

Mayer, A. (2002) *Women in Britain 1900–2000*, Hodder

More, C. (2006) *Britain in the 20th Century*, Longman

Morgan, K. O. (1992) *The People's Peace: British History 1945–1990*, OUP

Ramsden, J. (1998) *An Appetite For Power: A History of the Conservative Party Since 1830*, HarperCollins

Tiratsoo, N. (ed.) (1999) *From Blitz to Blair*, Penguin

Winder, R. (2004) *Bloody Foreigners: The Story of Immigration to Britain*, Abacus

Websites

www.spartacus.schoolnet.co.uk

Lively in-depth accounts of important events can be found on the BBC 'On This Day' site:

www.news.bbc.co.uk/onthisday

Section 1 Britain, 1951–1964

Students

Roberts, M. (1999) *Britain 1858–1964*, Longman

Teachers and extension

Adelman, P. (1994) *Britain: Domestic Politics 1939–1964*, Hodder & Stoughton

Beckett, F. (2006) *Harold Macmillan*, Haus

Dutton, D. (2006) *Alec Douglas-Home*, Haus

Hennessy, P. (2007) *Having It So Good: Britain in the Fifties*, Macmillan

Wilby, P. (2006) *Anthony Eden*, Haus

Wrigley, C. (2006) *Winston Churchill*, Haus

DVD

Caton-Jones, M. (1989) *Scandal*

Crichton, C. (1951) *The Lavender Hill Mob*

Dearden, B. (1959) *Sapphire*

Leigh, M. (2004) *Vera Drake*

Marr, A. (2007) *The Land of Lost Content*, BBC

Reisz, K. (1961) *Saturday Night and Sunday Morning*

Section 2 Britain, 1964–1975

Students

Pearce, R. (1990) *Britain 1914–1979*, Longman

Teachers and extension

Conroy, H. (2006) *James Callaghan*, Haus

MacShane, D. (2006) *Edward Heath*, Haus

Routledge, P. (2006) *Harold Wilson*, Haus

Sandbrook, D. (2004) *White Heat: A Cultural History of Britain in the Sixties*, Collins

DVD

Greengrass, P. (2002) *Bloody Sunday*

Marr, A. (2006) *Harold, Ted and Jim: When the Modern Failed*, BBC

Narrazzano, S. (1966) *Georgy Girl*

O'Donell, D. (1999) *East Is East*

People's Century (1996) *1968: The Year of Youth*

Section 3 Britain, 1975–1990

Students

Lee, S. J. (1998) *Aspects of Modern British History 1914–1995*, Routledge

Teachers and extension

Beckett, C. (2006) *Thatcher*, Haus

Cole, J. (1992) *As It Seemed To Me At The Time*, Palgrave

Evans, E. (2004) *Thatcher and Thatcherism*, Routledge

Jenkins, S. (2007) *Thatcher and Sons: A Revolution in Three Acts*, Penguin

Pugh, A. & Flint, C. (1997) *Thatcher for Beginners*, Icon

Seldon, A. & Collings, J. (1999) *Britain Under Thatcher*, Longman

Seldon, A. & Hickson, K (2004) *New Labour, Old Labour: The Wilson and Callaghan Governments*, Routledge

Young, H. (1988) *One of Us: A Political Biography of Margaret Thatcher*, New Press

DVD

Deller, J. (2002) *The Battle of Orgreave*

Herman, M. (1996) *Brassed Off*

Marr, A. (2006) *The British Revolution*, BBC

Frears, S. (2003) *The Deal*

Section 4: Britain 1990–2007

Students

Rowe, C. (2004) *Britain 1929–1998*, Heinemann

Teachers and extension

Campbell, A. (2008) *The Blair Years: Extracts From The Alastair Campbell Diaries*, Arrow

Critchley, J. & Halcrow M. (1997) *Collapse of Stout Party: The Decline of the Tories*, Gollancz

Major, J. (2000) *John Major: The Autobiography*

Mallie, E. & McKittrick, D. (2001) *Endgame in Ireland*, Hodder & Stoughton

Naughtie, J. (1999) *The Rivals: The Intimate Story of a Political Marriage*, Fourth Estate

Rawnsley, A. (2000) *Servants of the People: The Inside Story of New Labour*, Penguin

Seldon, A. (2007) *Blair Unbound*, Pocket Books

Seldon, A. ed (2007) *Blair's Britain 1997–2007*, Cambridge UP

Taylor, R. (2006) *John Major*, Haus

Temple, M. (2006) *Tony Blair*, Haus

DVD

Boyle, D. (1996) *Trainspotting*

Chadha, G. (2002) *Bend It Like Beckham*

Frears, S. (2002) *Dirty Pretty Things*

Marr, A. (2007) *Nippy Metro People: Britain From 1990*, BBC

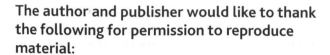

Acknowledgements

The author and publisher would like to thank the following for permission to reproduce material:

Source texts:

p8 Jay, D., *Change and Fortune: A Political Record*, 1980, published by Hutchinson, reprinted with permission of David Higham Associates Limited; pp9 (2), 57 Hennessy, P., *The Prime Minister: The Office and its Holders Since 1945*, 2000, (3) Lecture by Lawson, N., 'The Tide of Idea from Attlee to Thatcher', 1988, p12 in-text quote (Allen Lane The Penguin Press) © Peter Hennessy, 2000. Reprinted with permission of Penguin Books UK and Palgrave Macmillan; p10 (4) Coates, D., *The Labour Party and the Struggle for Socialism*, 1975, Cambridge University Press, 1975. Reprinted with permission of Cambridge University Press, (5) Barnett, C., *The Audit of War*, 1986, Macmillan. Reprinted with the permission of David Higham Associates Limited; p16 Macmillan, H., address to audience at Bedford football ground, 1957; p22 Thorneycroft, P., from a speech in parliament, 1958; pp27, 75, 106, 155, 177 Marr, A., *A History of Modern Britain*, Macmillan 2007. Reprinted with permission of Pan Macmillan; p32 Winder, R., *Bloody Foreigners*, 2004; p37 Booker, D., 'The Last Days of Emperor Macmillan', *Private Eye*, issue 34, p8 and 9, 5th April 1963. Reprinted with kind permission of Private Eye Magazine; p46 Heath, E., *The Course of My Life*, © Edward Heath 1998. Reproduced with permission of PFD (www.pfd.co.uk) on behalf of the Estate of Edward Heath; p50 Morgan, K. O., *The People's Peace: British History 1945–1990*, OUP 1990. Reprinted with permission of Oxford University Press; p55 Pimlott, B., *Harold Wilson*, © Ben Pimlott 1992. Reproduced with permission of Sheil Land Associates Ltd; p64 (2) Jefferys, K., *Finest and Darkest Hours*, Atlantic 2002. Reprinted with kind permission of Altantic Books, (3) Annan, N., *Our Age: The Generation that made Post-war Britain*, 1990, © Noel Annan. Reproduced with permission of the Estate of the author c/o Rogers, Coleridge and White Limited; p68 Morgan, K. O., *The Twentieth Century*, OUP 1984; p76 Hartnack, M., *40 years after UDI*, The Herald Online 2009; pp81 (5), 124 Walker, M., *The Cold War*, Fourth Estate 1993 © Martin Walker; p83 Cole, J., *As It Seemed To Me*, Weidenfeld and Nicholson 1995, © John Cole 1993 Reprinted with permission of The Orion Publishing Group Ltd and PFD (www.pfd.co.uk) on behalf of John Cole; p84 Young, H., *One Of Us: A Biography of Margaret Thatcher*, Macmillan 1989. Reprinted with permission of the Publisher; pp106, 130 Sergeant, J., *Maggie: Her Fatal Legacy*, Macmillan 2005. Reprinted with permission of Pan Macmillan and Lucas Alexander Whitley Ltd on behalf of the author;

p108 Davies, N., *Europe: A History*, 1996. Reprinted with permission of David Godwin Associates; p115 Wallis, S., *Revolution Destroyed?*, 2005, © Steve Wallis 2005. Reprinted with kind permssion of the author; p126 Critchley, J. and Halcrow, M., *Collapse of Stout Party*, Weidenfeld and Nicholson 1998. Reprinted with kind permission of David Higham Associates Ltd; p140 Seldon, A., *Major: A Political Life*, Weidenfeld and Nicholson 1997. Reprinted with permission of the Orion Publishing Group, London; p141 Rawnsley, A., *Servants of the People: The Inside Story of New Labour*, Hamish Hamilton 2000, © Andrew Rawnsley. Reprinted with permission of Penguin Group UK; p146 Seldon, A., *Blair Unbound*, Simon and Schuster 2007. Reprinted with permission of Simon and Schuster UK; p151 Sinclair, P., 'The Treasury and Economic Policy' in ed. Seldon, A., *Blair's Britain 1997–2007*, Cambridge University Press 2007. Reprinted with permission of Cambridge University Press; p160 MORI Poll August 2005, BBC *On This Day*; p172 Garton Ash, T., 'We friends of liberal international order face a new global disorder', in the *Guardian*, 11 September 2008, © Timothy Garton Ash. Reprinted with kind permission of the author

Some quoted texts are within the public domain

Some of the statistical diagrams and tables are adapted from material used in the *Longman Companion to Britain Since 1945* and from government statistics

Photographs:

Cover photograph: Times Newspapers / Rex Features

Anne Ronan Archive p55; Cartoon Museum / Solo Syndication pp25, 57, 97; Chris Rowe p4; Daily Express / Hulton Archive / Getty Images p109; Edimedia Archives pp123, 150; German Federal Government p165; Getty Images ppiv, 39, 44; Keystone / Getty Images p92; Getty Images / Evening Standard p49; Keystone / Hulton Archive / Getty Images p113; National Motor Museum / HIP / Topfoto p16; Public domain pp58, 87, 95, 128, 136, 141, 145, 168; The Advertising Archives p18; The Print Collector / HIP / Topfoto p78; Tom Stoddart / Getty Images p108; Topfoto pp1, 11, 13, 20, 27, 30, 31, 33, 36, 47, 52, 60, 62, 66, 68, 73, 75, 79, 83, 85, 88, 99, 100, 103, 105, 114, 115, 120, 126, 135, 140, 144, 155, 158, 160, 162, 163, 167, 173; World History Images p8, 41, 70, 116, 118, 172

The publisher would like to thank the following who assisted with, or supplied photographs which appear in this book: Topfoto, Ann Asquith and Jason Newman of Image Content Collections. Photo Research by Alexander Goldberg and Tara Roberts of Image Asset Management & uniquedimension.com

Index